AFTER the CAPE

Shadowline

image

AFTER THE CAPE VOLUME ONE (September, 2007) is published by Image Comics, Inc. 1942 University Avenue, Suite 305, Berkeley, CA 94704. Originally published as AFTER THE CAPE #1-3. Image and its logos are ® and © 2006 Image Comics, Inc. Shadowline and its logos are ® and © 2007 by Jim Valentino. AFTER THE CAPE and its logos are ™ and © HOWARD WONG, 2007. All rights reserved. The characters, events, and stories in this publication are entirely fictional. No portion of this book may be reporduced, save for purposes of review, without the express written consent of Mr. Wong. PRINTED IN CANDA.

ISBN: 978-1-58240-817-0

Created and Dialogued by

HOWARD WONG

Plotted by

JIM VALENTINO

Illustrated by

MARCO RUDY
MANNY TREMBLEY

Original Covers by

MARCO RUDY
JUAN FERREYRA
MANNY TREMBLEY

Lettering by

ED DUKESHIRE

Cover Colored by

FREDDY LOPEZ

Edited by

KRISTEN SIMON

Book Design and Graphics by

JIM VALENTINO

DEDICATION...

...To my wife and kids, whose love and support I
couldn't live without.
Thanks for loving a lug like me.
Howard Wong

I'd like to dedicate this to...hey you, reader, like
what you see? Then I dedicate this to you.

I dedicate it to moonlights, sunny days, jazz
and you (you know who you are).
Marco Rudy

Dedicated to Kris Simon, whose patience and
dedication brought this baby home.
Jim Valentino

CHAPTER ONE:
A LONG WAY DOWN

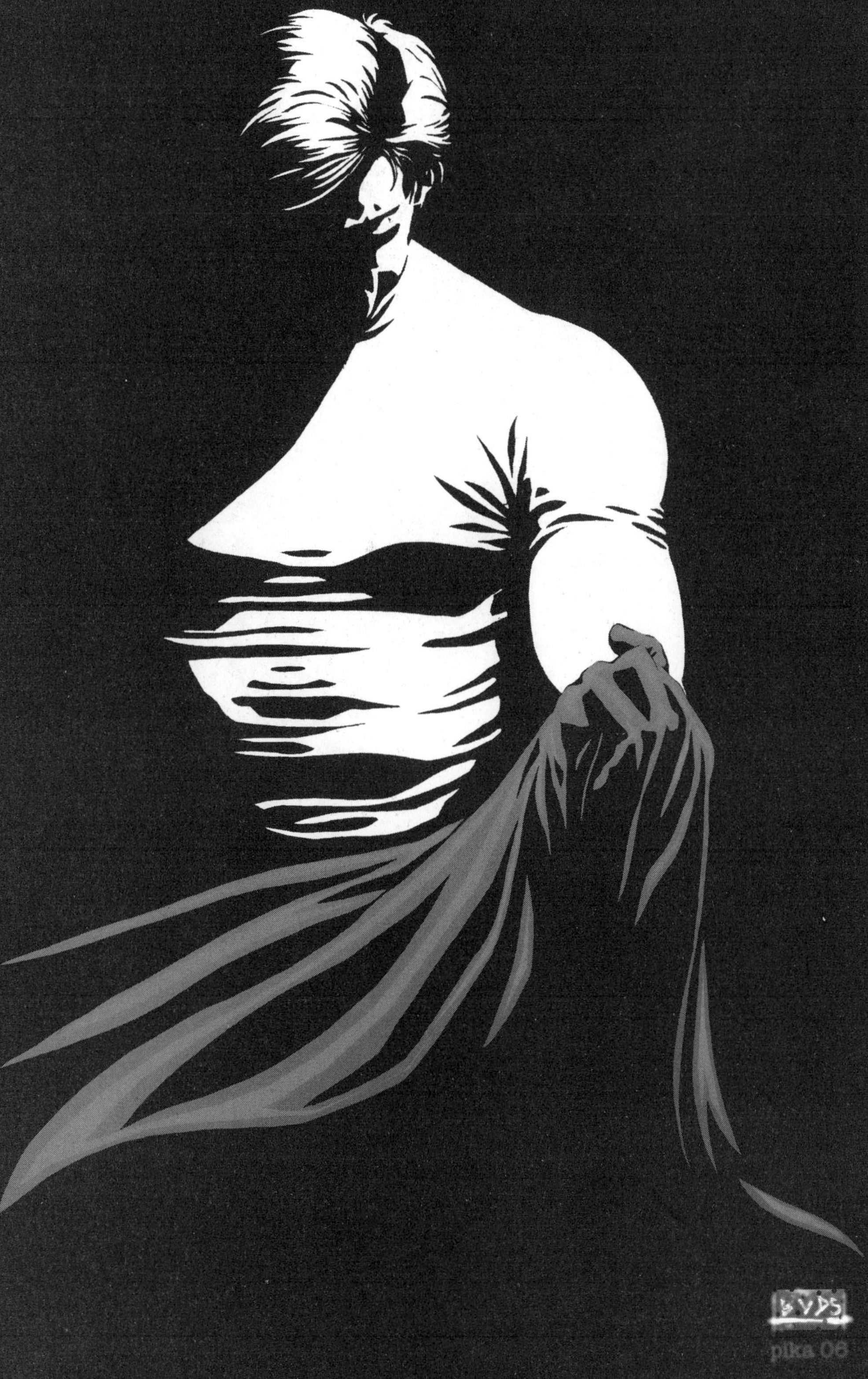

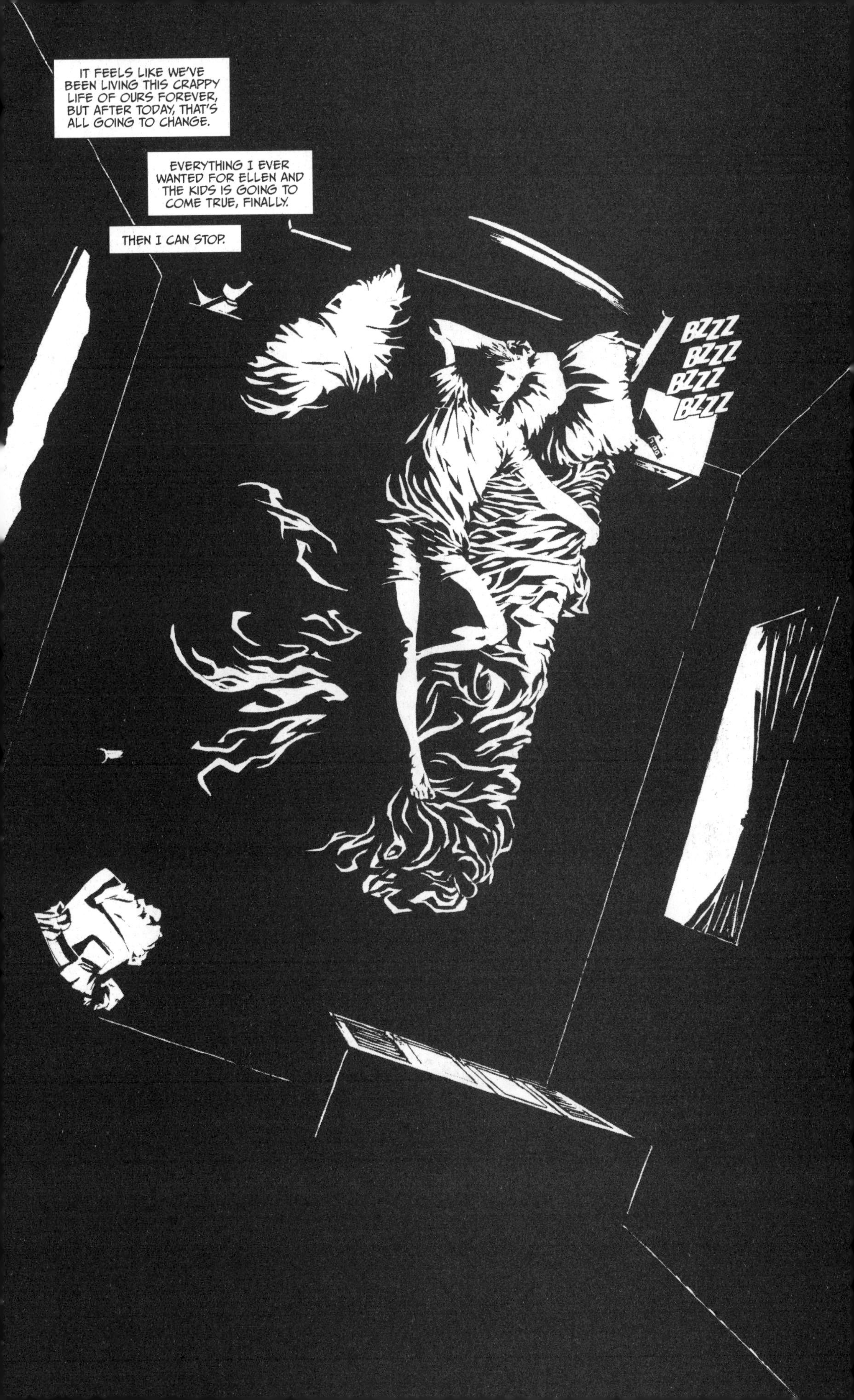
IT FEELS LIKE WE'VE BEEN LIVING THIS CRAPPY LIFE OF OURS FOREVER, BUT AFTER TODAY, THAT'S ALL GOING TO CHANGE.
EVERYTHING I EVER WANTED FOR ELLEN AND THE KIDS IS GOING TO COME TRUE, FINALLY.
THEN I CAN STOP.
BZZZ
BZZZ
BZZZ
BZZZ

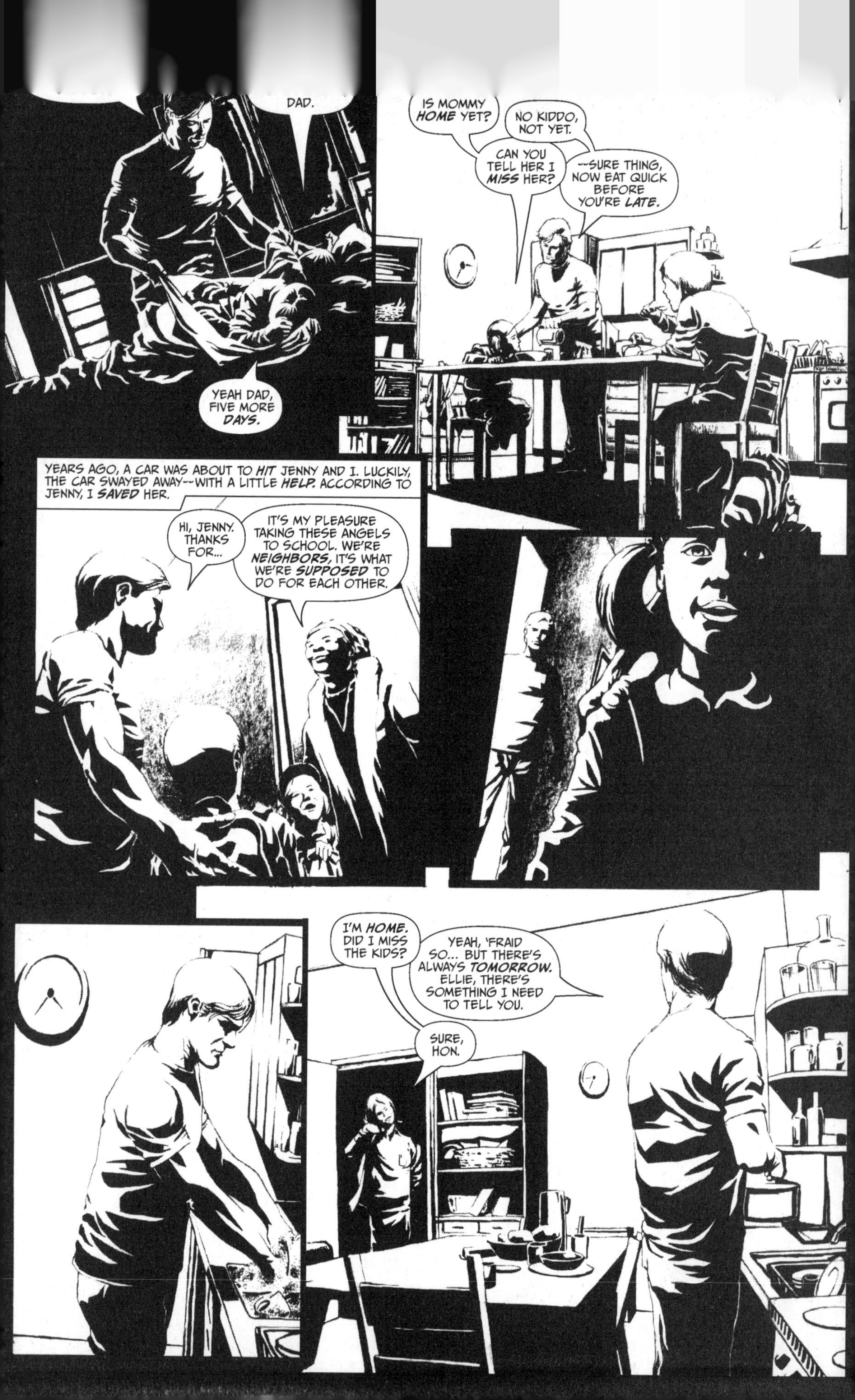
DAD.
YEAH DAD, FIVE MORE DAYS.
IS MOMMY HOME YET?
NO KIDDO, NOT YET.
CAN YOU TELL HER I MISS HER?
--SURE THING, NOW EAT QUICK BEFORE YOU'RE LATE.
YEARS AGO, A CAR WAS ABOUT TO HIT JENNY AND I. LUCKILY, THE CAR SWAYED AWAY--WITH A LITTLE HELP. ACCORDING TO JENNY, I SAVED HER.
HI, JENNY. THANKS FOR...
IT'S MY PLEASURE TAKING THESE ANGELS TO SCHOOL. WE'RE NEIGHBORS, IT'S WHAT WE'RE SUPPOSED TO DO FOR EACH OTHER.
I'M HOME. DID I MISS THE KIDS?
YEAH, 'FRAID SO... BUT THERE'S ALWAYS TOMORROW. ELLIE, THERE'S SOMETHING I NEED TO TELL YOU.
SURE, HON.

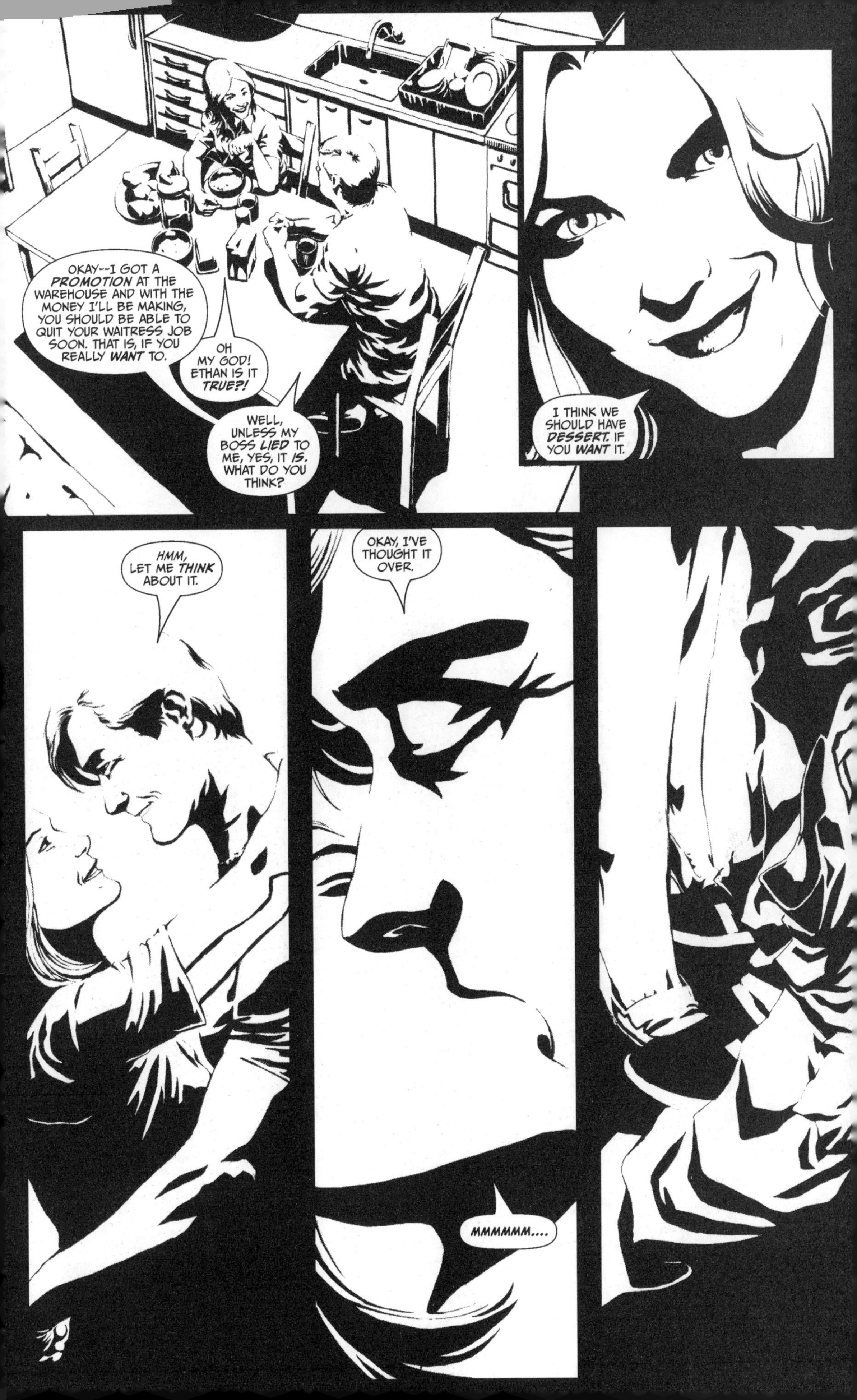
OKAY--I GOT A PROMOTION AT THE WAREHOUSE AND WITH THE MONEY I'LL BE MAKING, YOU SHOULD BE ABLE TO QUIT YOUR WAITRESS JOB SOON. THAT IS, IF YOU REALLY WANT TO.
OH MY GOD! ETHAN IS IT TRUE?!
WELL, UNLESS MY BOSS LIED TO ME, YES, IT IS. WHAT DO YOU THINK?
I THINK WE SHOULD HAVE DESSERT. IF YOU WANT IT.
HMM, LET ME THINK ABOUT IT.
OKAY, I'VE THOUGHT IT OVER.
MMMMMM....

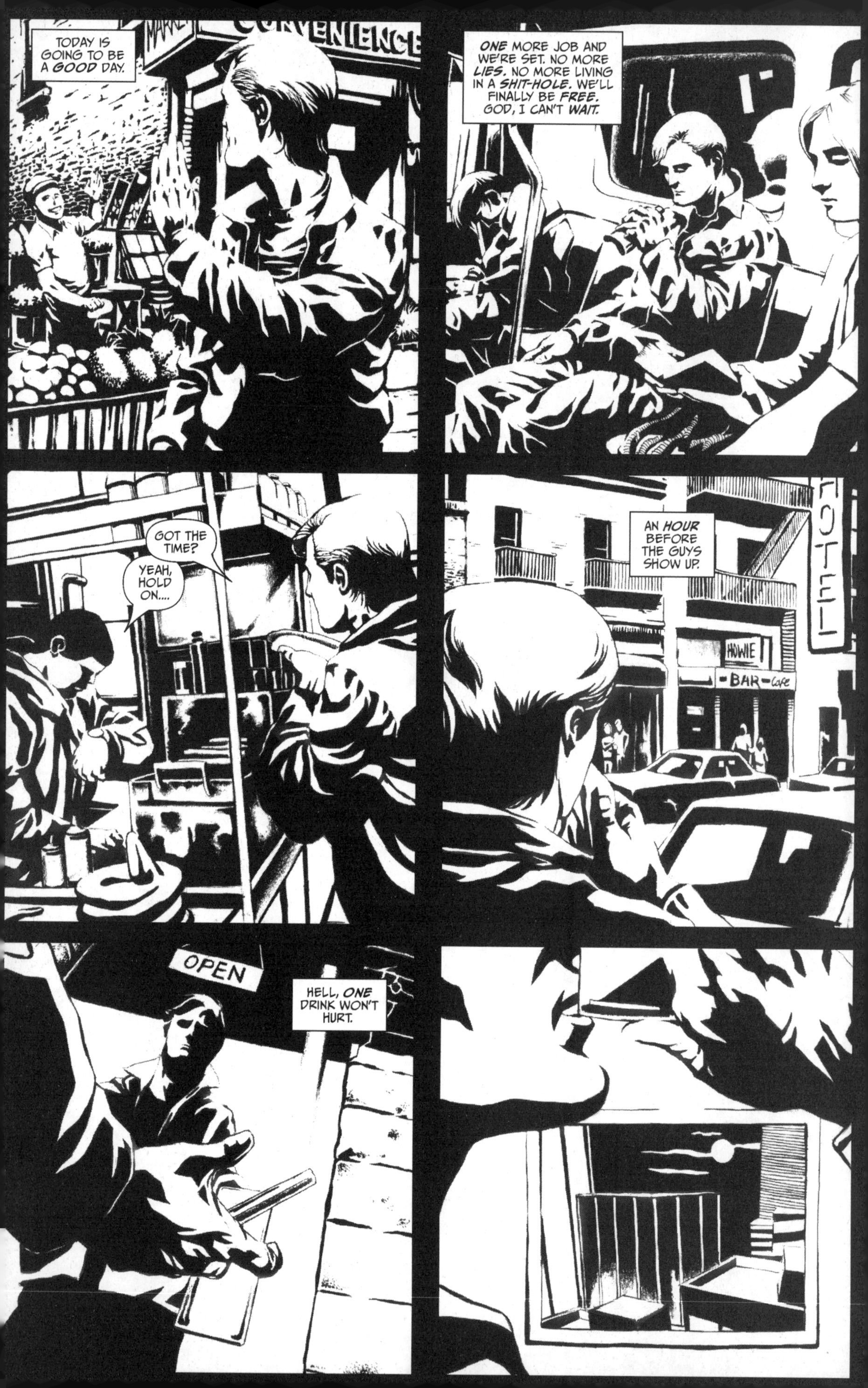
CONVENIENCE
TODAY IS GOING TO BE A GOOD DAY.
ONE MORE JOB AND WE'RE SET. NO MORE LIES. NO MORE LIVING IN A SHIT-HOLE. WE'LL FINALLY BE FREE. GOD, I CAN'T WAIT.
GOT THE TIME?
YEAH, HOLD ON....
HOTEL
AN HOUR BEFORE THE GUYS SHOW UP.
HOWIE
BAR
Cafe
OPEN
HELL, ONE DRINK WON'T HURT.

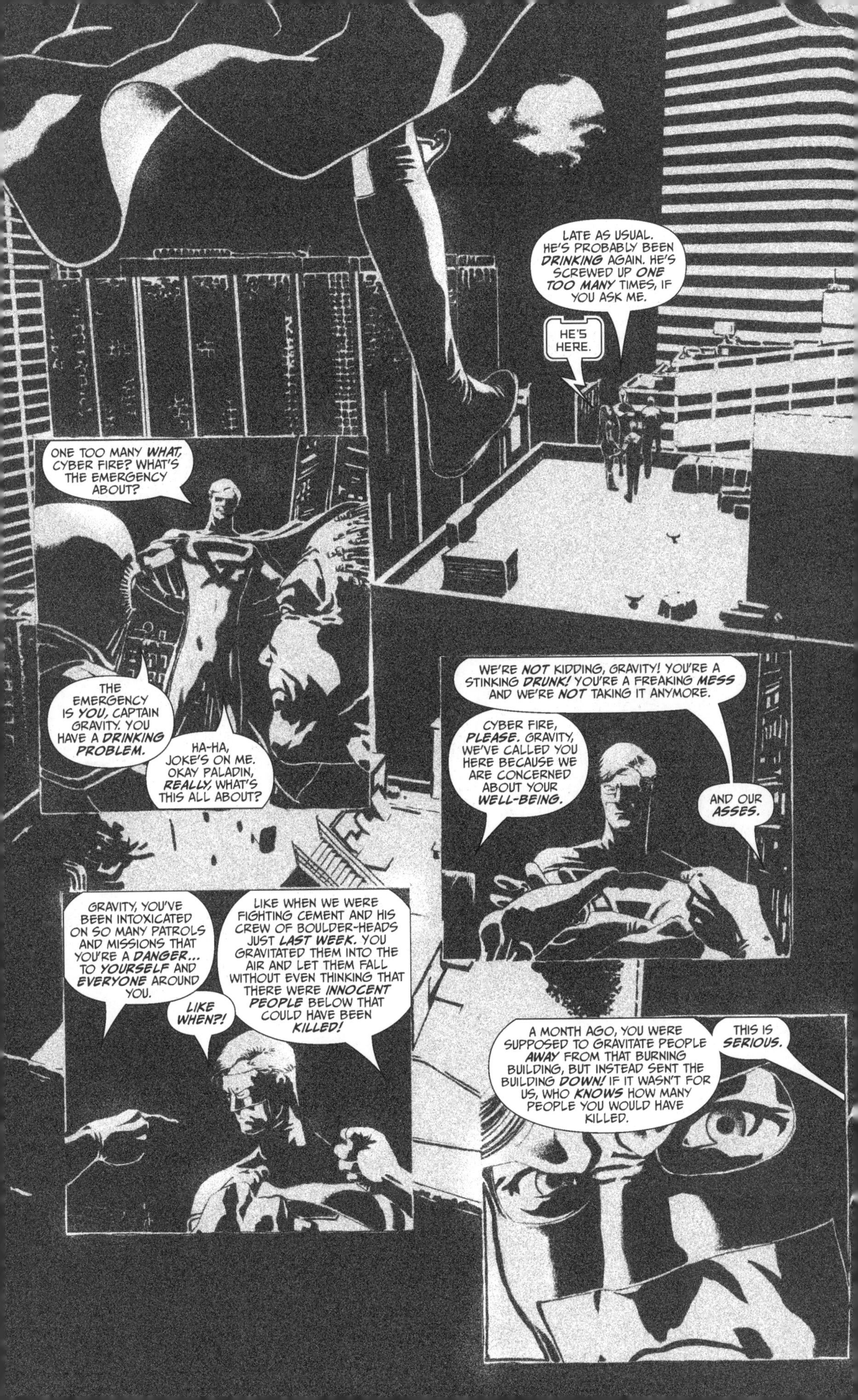
LATE AS USUAL. HE'S PROBABLY BEEN DRINKING AGAIN. HE'S SCREWED UP ONE TOO MANY TIMES, IF YOU ASK ME.
HE'S HERE.
ONE TOO MANY WHAT, CYBER FIRE? WHAT'S THE EMERGENCY ABOUT?
THE EMERGENCY IS YOU, CAPTAIN GRAVITY. YOU HAVE A DRINKING PROBLEM.
HA-HA, JOKE'S ON ME. OKAY PALADIN, REALLY, WHAT'S THIS ALL ABOUT?
WE'RE NOT KIDDING, GRAVITY! YOU'RE A STINKING DRUNK! YOU'RE A FREAKING MESS AND WE'RE NOT TAKING IT ANYMORE.
CYBER FIRE, PLEASE. GRAVITY, WE'VE CALLED YOU HERE BECAUSE WE ARE CONCERNED ABOUT YOUR WELL-BEING.
AND OUR ASSES.
GRAVITY, YOU'VE BEEN INTOXICATED ON SO MANY PATROLS AND MISSIONS THAT YOU'RE A DANGER... TO YOURSELF AND EVERYONE AROUND YOU.
LIKE WHEN?!
LIKE WHEN WE WERE FIGHTING CEMENT AND HIS CREW OF BOULDER-HEADS JUST LAST WEEK. YOU GRAVITATED THEM INTO THE AIR AND LET THEM FALL WITHOUT EVEN THINKING THAT THERE WERE INNOCENT PEOPLE BELOW THAT COULD HAVE BEEN KILLED!
A MONTH AGO, YOU WERE SUPPOSED TO GRAVITATE PEOPLE AWAY FROM THAT BURNING BUILDING, BUT INSTEAD SENT THE BUILDING DOWN! IF IT WASN'T FOR US, WHO KNOWS HOW MANY PEOPLE YOU WOULD HAVE KILLED.
THIS IS SERIOUS.

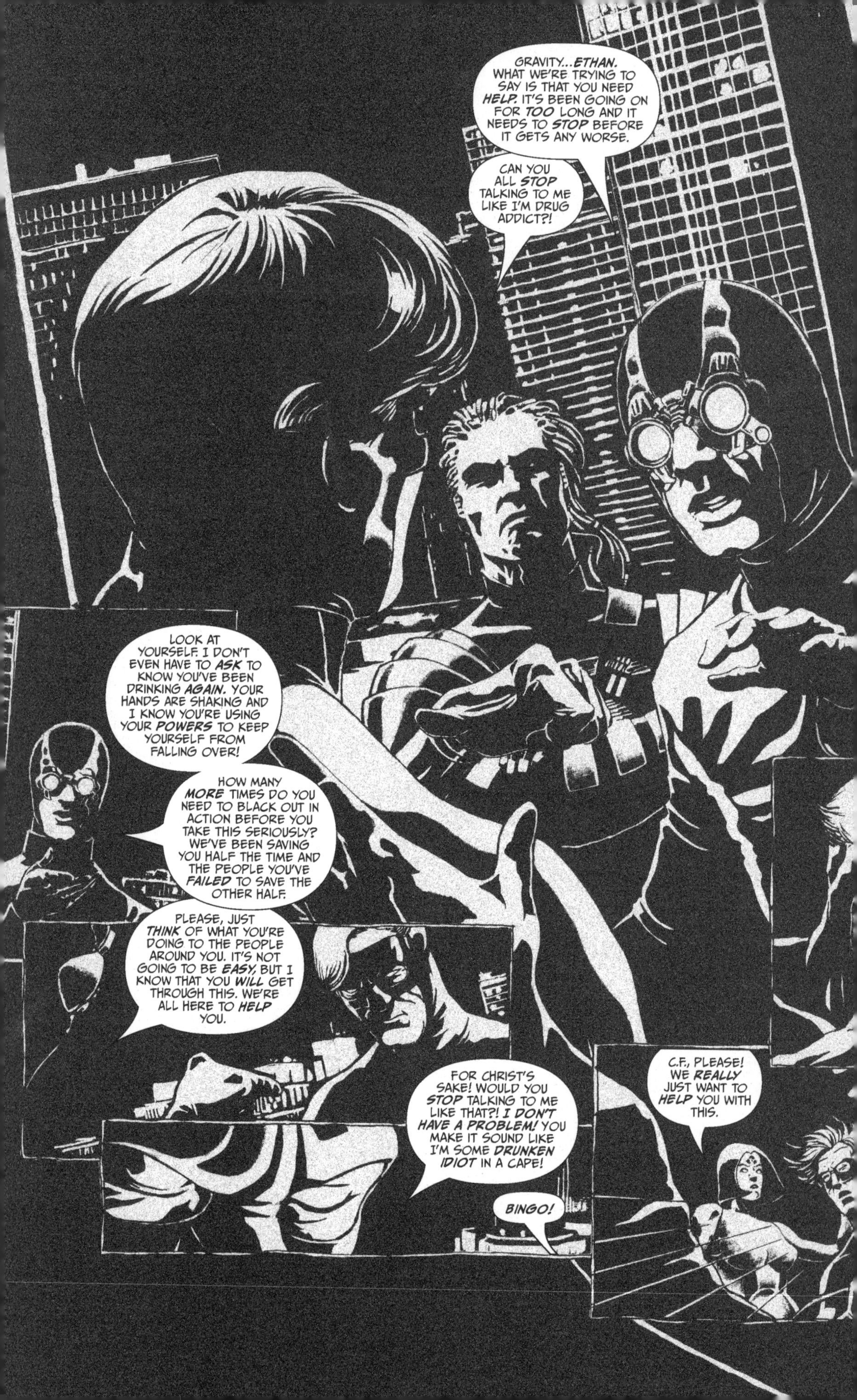
GRAVITY...ETHAN. WHAT WE'RE TRYING TO SAY IS THAT YOU NEED HELP. IT'S BEEN GOING ON FOR TOO LONG AND IT NEEDS TO STOP BEFORE IT GETS ANY WORSE.
CAN YOU ALL STOP TALKING TO ME LIKE I'M DRUG ADDICT?!
LOOK AT YOURSELF. I DON'T EVEN HAVE TO ASK TO KNOW YOU'VE BEEN DRINKING AGAIN. YOUR HANDS ARE SHAKING AND I KNOW YOU'RE USING YOUR POWERS TO KEEP YOURSELF FROM FALLING OVER!
HOW MANY MORE TIMES DO YOU NEED TO BLACK OUT IN ACTION BEFORE YOU TAKE THIS SERIOUSLY? WE'VE BEEN SAVING YOU HALF THE TIME AND THE PEOPLE YOU'VE FAILED TO SAVE THE OTHER HALF.
PLEASE, JUST THINK OF WHAT YOU'RE DOING TO THE PEOPLE AROUND YOU. IT'S NOT GOING TO BE EASY, BUT I KNOW THAT YOU WILL GET THROUGH THIS. WE'RE ALL HERE TO HELP YOU.
FOR CHRIST'S SAKE! WOULD YOU STOP TALKING TO ME LIKE THAT?! I DON'T HAVE A PROBLEM! YOU MAKE IT SOUND LIKE I'M SOME DRUNKEN IDIOT IN A CAPE!
BINGO!
C.F., PLEASE! WE REALLY JUST WANT TO HELP YOU WITH THIS.

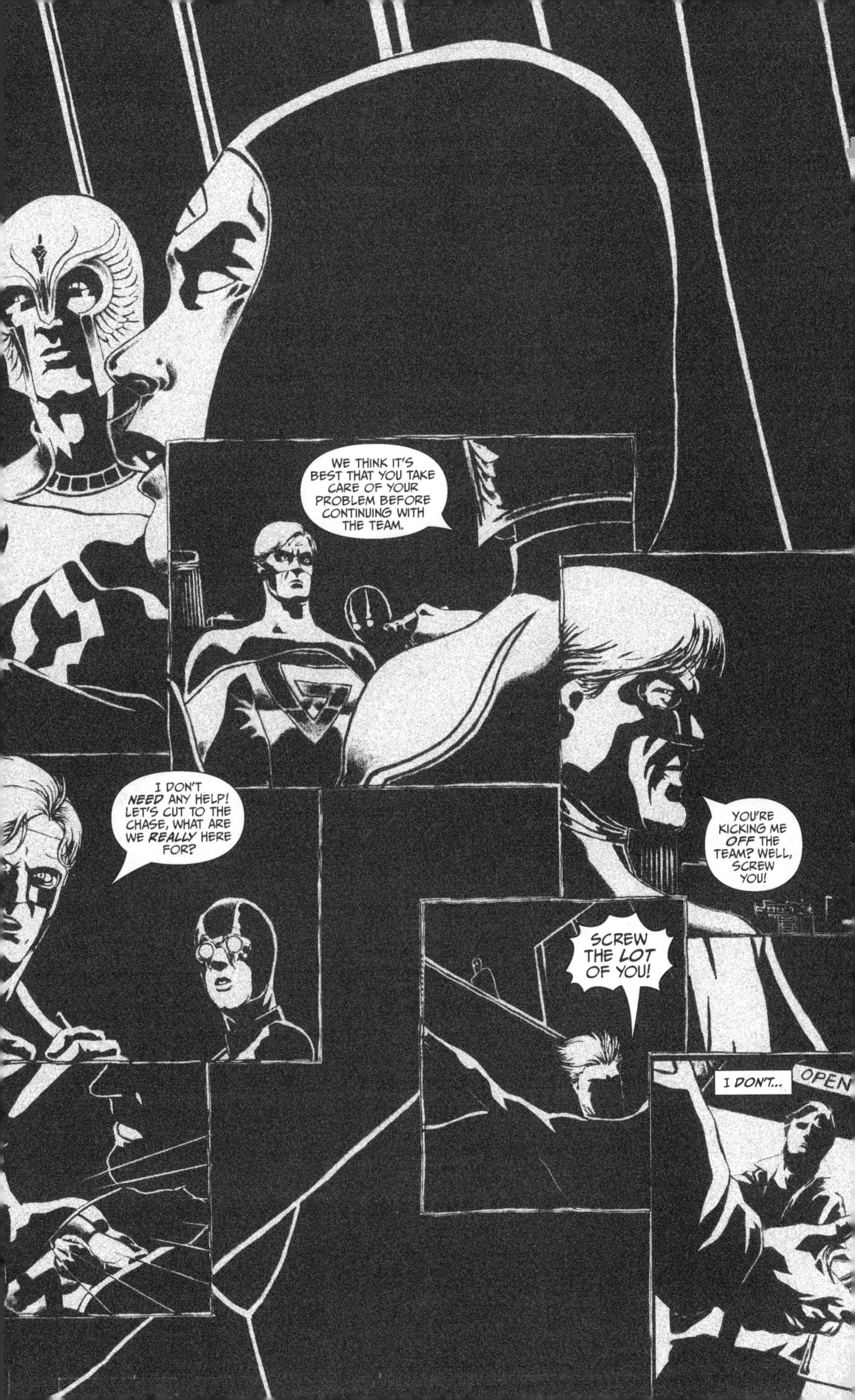
WE THINK IT'S BEST THAT YOU TAKE CARE OF YOUR PROBLEM BEFORE CONTINUING WITH THE TEAM.
YOU'RE KICKING ME *OFF* THE TEAM? WELL, SCREW YOU!
I DON'T *NEED* ANY HELP! LET'S CUT TO THE CHASE, WHAT ARE WE *REALLY* HERE FOR?
SCREW THE *LOT* OF YOU!
I *DON'T*...
OPEN

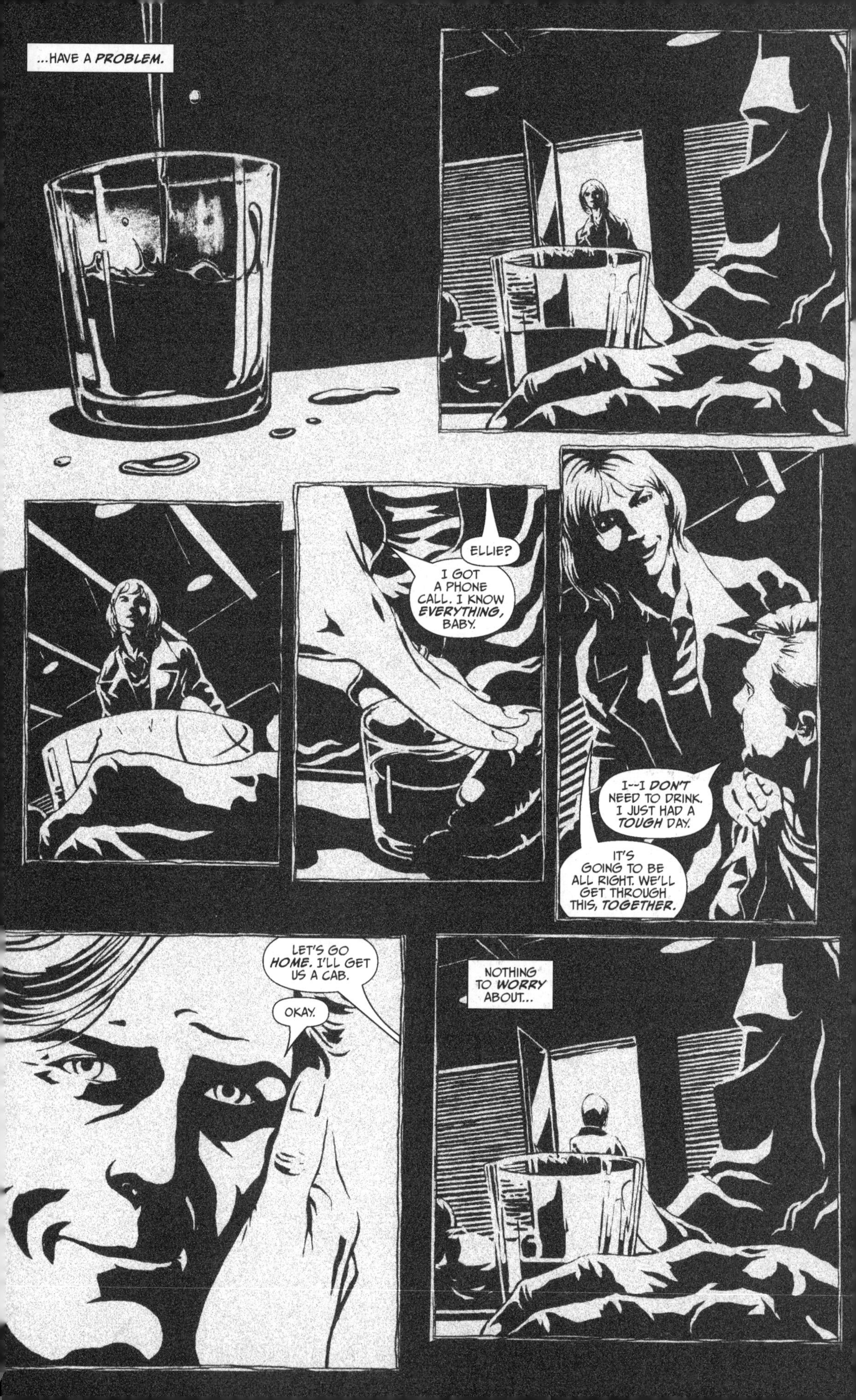

...HAVE A *PROBLEM.*
ELLIE?
I GOT A PHONE CALL. I KNOW *EVERYTHING,* BABY.
I--I *DON'T* NEED TO DRINK. I JUST HAD A *TOUGH* DAY.
IT'S GOING TO BE ALL RIGHT. WE'LL GET THROUGH THIS, *TOGETHER.*
LET'S GO *HOME.* I'LL GET US A CAB.
OKAY.
NOTHING TO *WORRY* ABOUT...

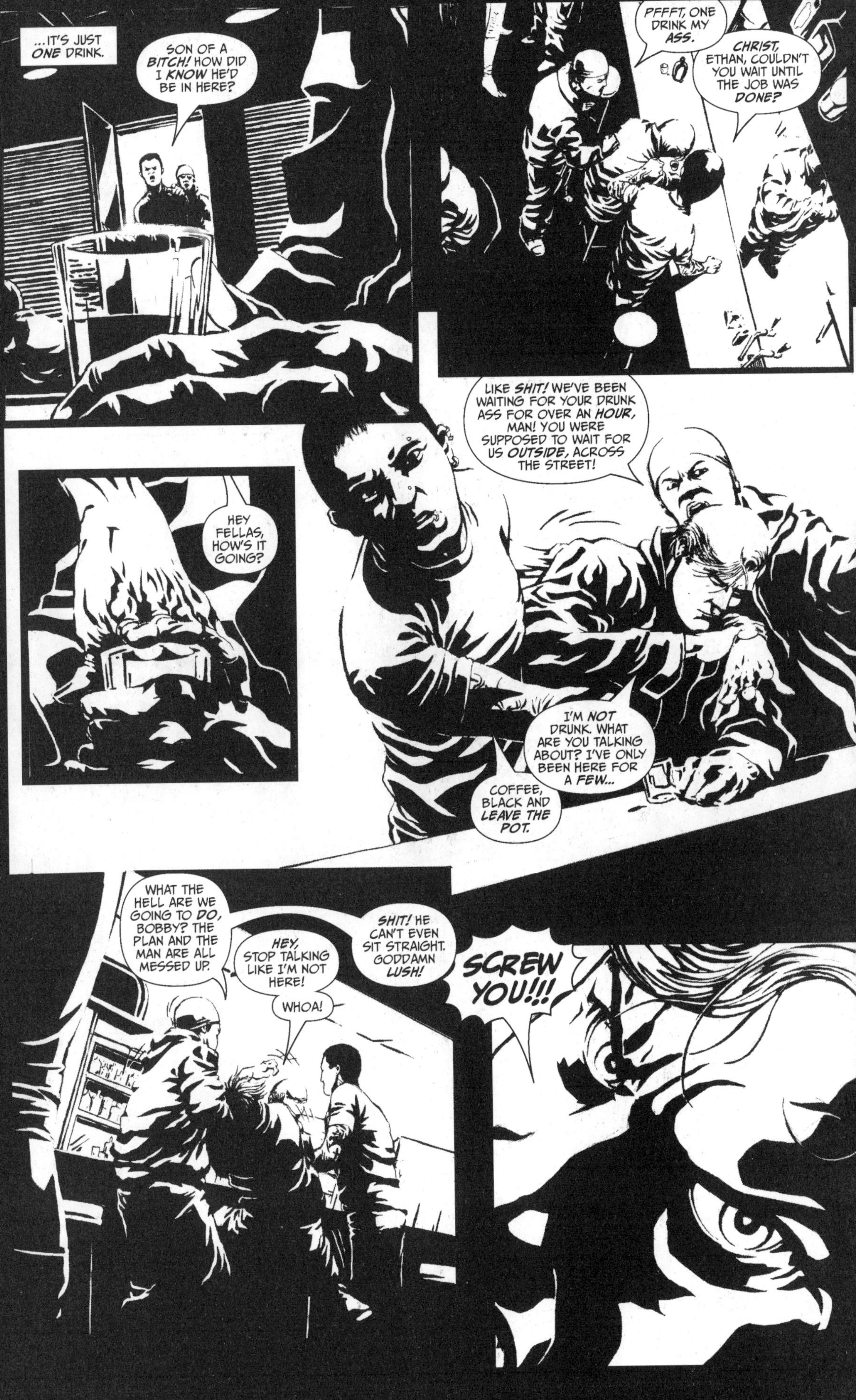
...IT'S JUST ONE DRINK.
SON OF A BITCH! HOW DID I KNOW HE'D BE IN HERE?
PFFFT, ONE DRINK MY ASS.
CHRIST, ETHAN, COULDN'T YOU WAIT UNTIL THE JOB WAS DONE?
HEY FELLAS, HOW'S IT GOING?
LIKE SHIT! WE'VE BEEN WAITING FOR YOUR DRUNK ASS FOR OVER AN HOUR, MAN! YOU WERE SUPPOSED TO WAIT FOR US OUTSIDE, ACROSS THE STREET!
I'M NOT DRUNK. WHAT ARE YOU TALKING ABOUT? I'VE ONLY BEEN HERE FOR A FEW...
COFFEE, BLACK AND LEAVE THE POT.
WHAT THE HELL ARE WE GOING TO DO, BOBBY? THE PLAN AND THE MAN ARE ALL MESSED UP.
HEY, STOP TALKING LIKE I'M NOT HERE!
SHIT! HE CAN'T EVEN SIT STRAIGHT. GODDAMN LUSH!
WHOA!
SCREW YOU!!!

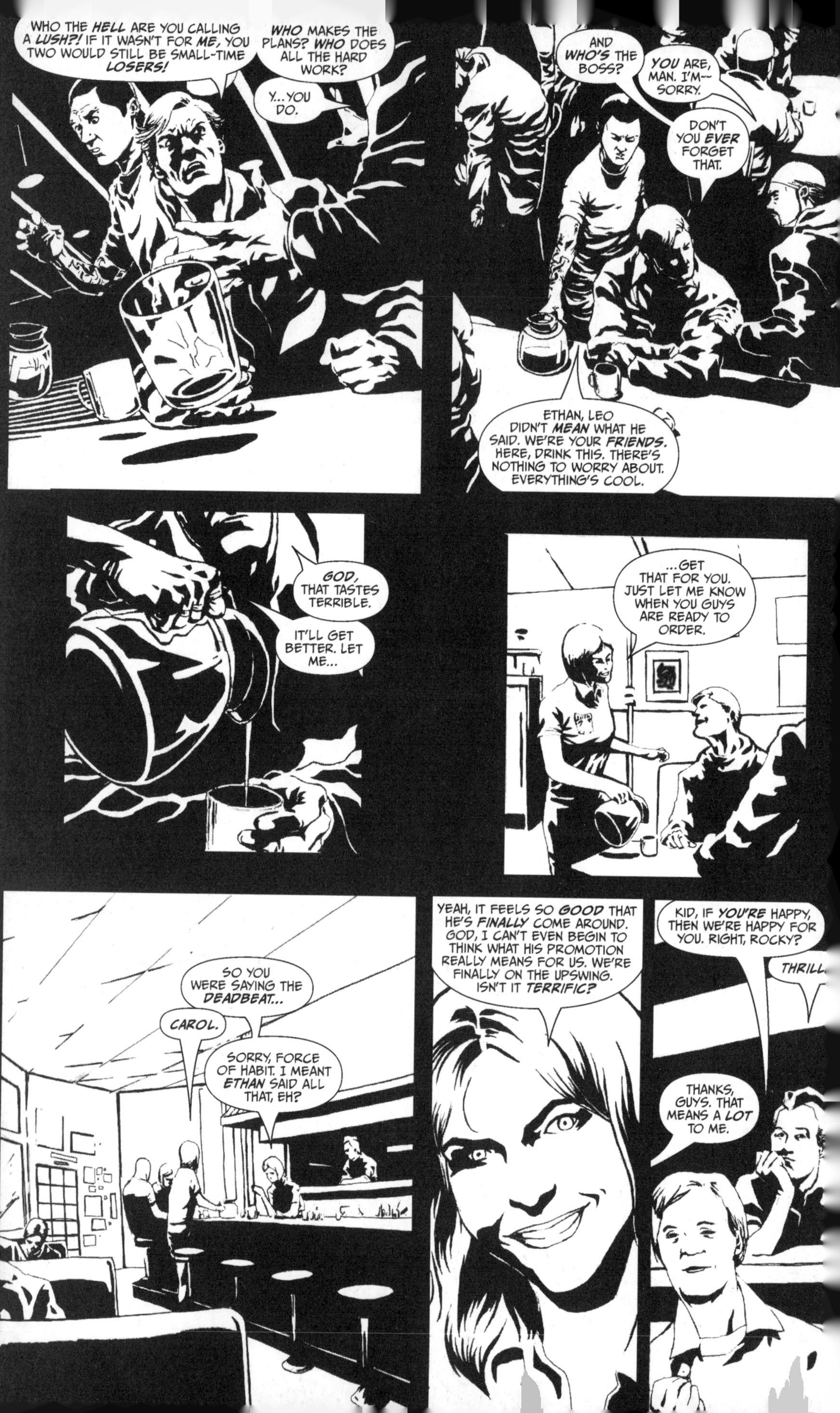
WHO THE HELL ARE YOU CALLING A LUSH?! IF IT WASN'T FOR ME, YOU TWO WOULD STILL BE SMALL-TIME LOSERS!
WHO MAKES THE PLANS? WHO DOES ALL THE HARD WORK?
Y...YOU DO.
AND WHO'S THE BOSS?
YOU ARE, MAN. I'M-- SORRY.
DON'T YOU EVER FORGET THAT.
ETHAN, LEO DIDN'T MEAN WHAT HE SAID. WE'RE YOUR FRIENDS. HERE, DRINK THIS. THERE'S NOTHING TO WORRY ABOUT. EVERYTHING'S COOL.
GOD, THAT TASTES TERRIBLE.
IT'LL GET BETTER. LET ME...
...GET THAT FOR YOU. JUST LET ME KNOW WHEN YOU GUYS ARE READY TO ORDER.
SO YOU WERE SAYING THE DEADBEAT...
CAROL.
SORRY, FORCE OF HABIT. I MEANT ETHAN SAID ALL THAT, EH?
YEAH, IT FEELS SO GOOD THAT HE'S FINALLY COME AROUND. GOD, I CAN'T EVEN BEGIN TO THINK WHAT HIS PROMOTION REALLY MEANS FOR US. WE'RE FINALLY ON THE UPSWING. ISN'T IT TERRIFIC?
KID, IF YOU'RE HAPPY, THEN WE'RE HAPPY FOR YOU. RIGHT, ROCKY?
THRILL
THANKS, GUYS. THAT MEANS A LOT TO ME.

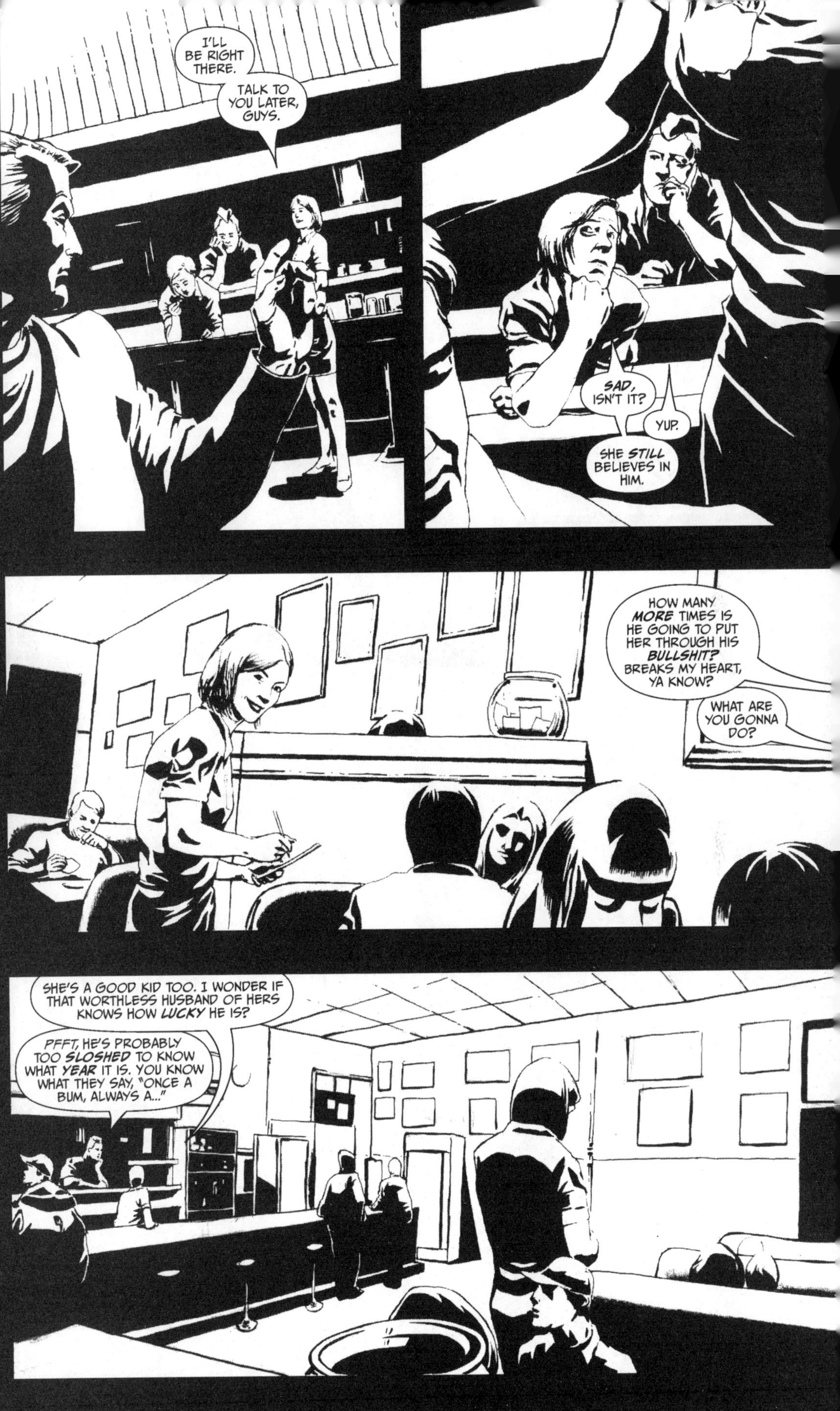
I'LL BE RIGHT THERE.
TALK TO YOU LATER, GUYS.
SAD, ISN'T IT?
YUP.
SHE STILL BELIEVES IN HIM.
HOW MANY MORE TIMES IS HE GOING TO PUT HER THROUGH HIS BULLSHIT? BREAKS MY HEART, YA KNOW?
WHAT ARE YOU GONNA DO?
SHE'S A GOOD KID TOO. I WONDER IF THAT WORTHLESS HUSBAND OF HERS KNOWS HOW LUCKY HE IS?
PFFT, HE'S PROBABLY TOO SLOSHED TO KNOW WHAT YEAR IT IS. YOU KNOW WHAT THEY SAY, "ONCE A BUM, ALWAYS A..."

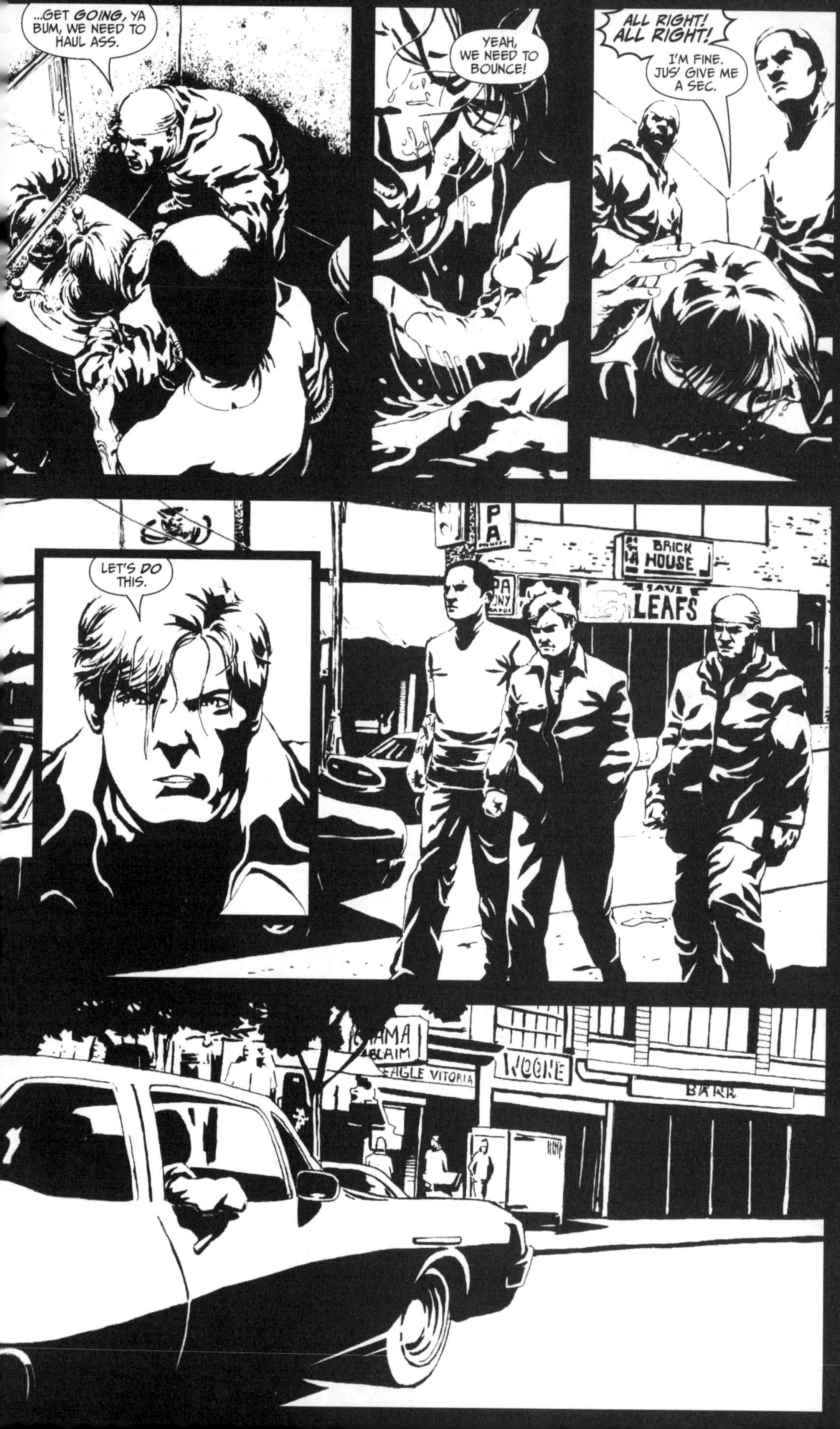
...GET *GOING*, YA BUM, WE NEED TO HAUL ASS.
YEAH, WE NEED TO BOUNCE!
ALL RIGHT! ALL RIGHT!
I'M FINE. JUS' GIVE ME A SEC.
LET'S *DO* THIS.
BRICK HOUSE
LEAFS
EAGLE VITORIA
BANK

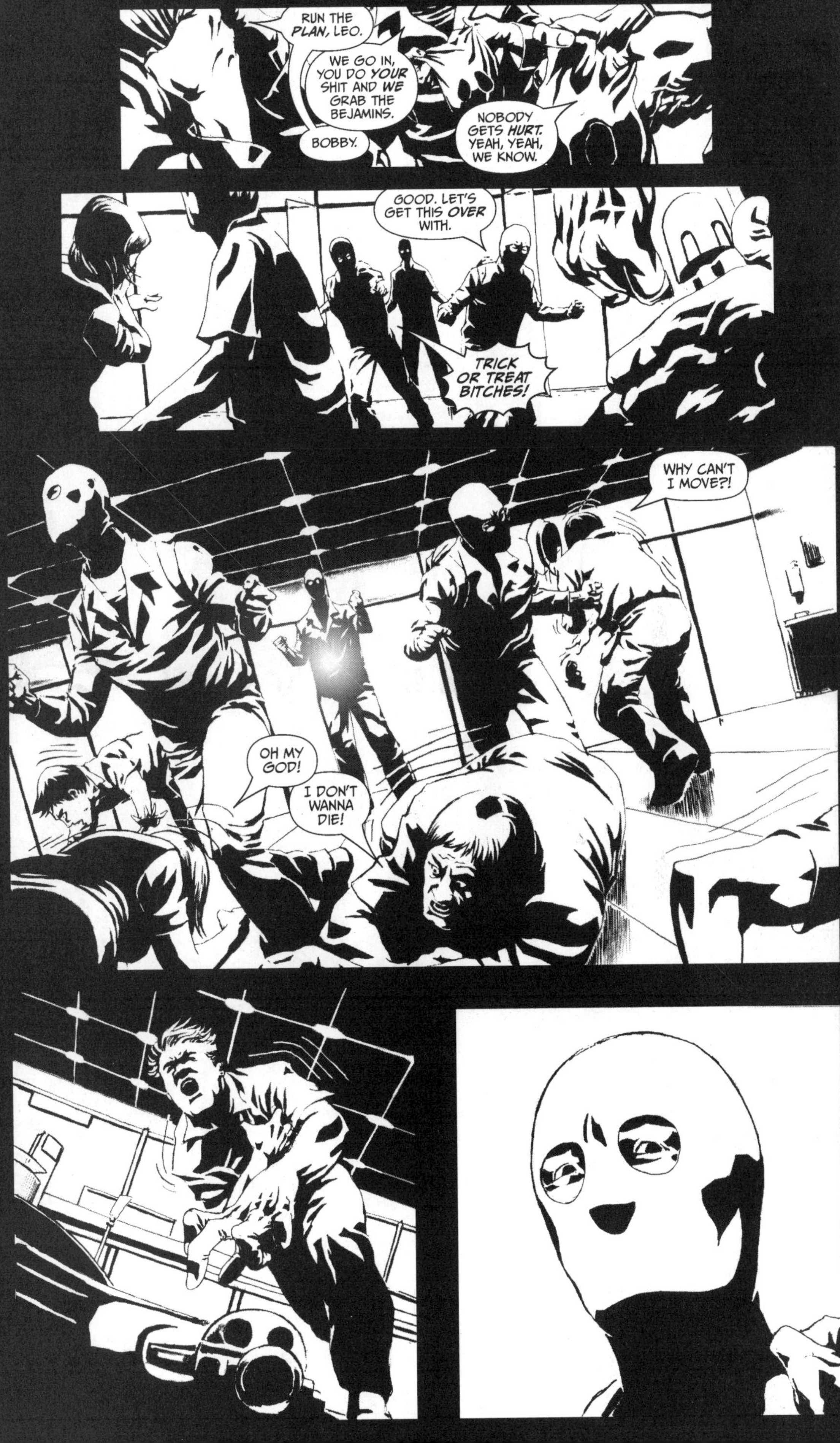
RUN THE PLAN, LEO.
WE GO IN, YOU DO YOUR SHIT AND WE GRAB THE BEJAMINS.
BOBBY.
NOBODY GETS HURT. YEAH, YEAH, WE KNOW.
GOOD. LET'S GET THIS OVER WITH.
TRICK OR TREAT BITCHES!
WHY CAN'T I MOVE?!
OH MY GOD!
I DON'T WANNA DIE!

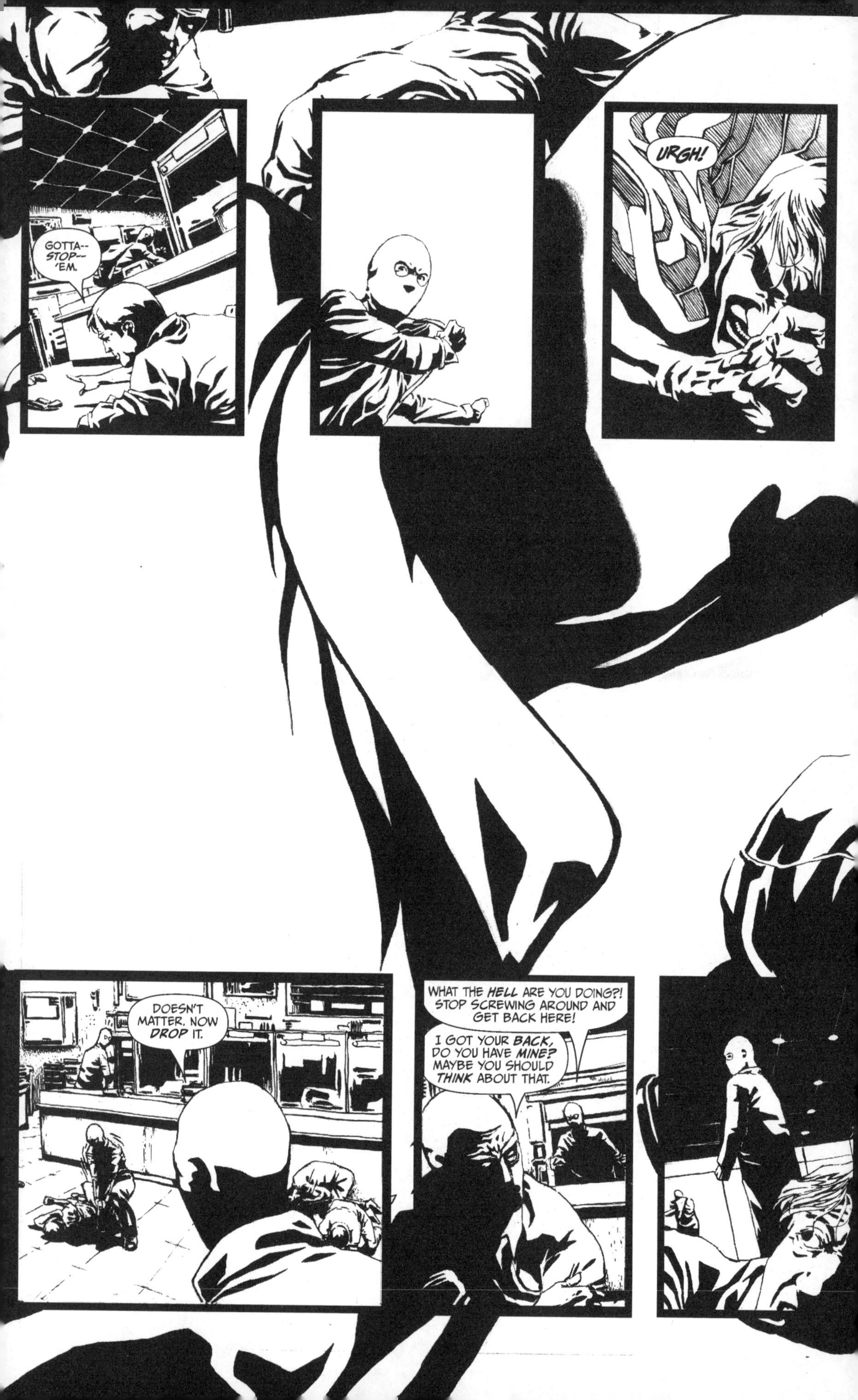
GOTTA-- STOP-- 'EM.
URGH!
DOESN'T MATTER. NOW DROP IT.
WHAT THE HELL ARE YOU DOING?! STOP SCREWING AROUND AND GET BACK HERE!
I GOT YOUR BACK, DO YOU HAVE MINE? MAYBE YOU SHOULD THINK ABOUT THAT.

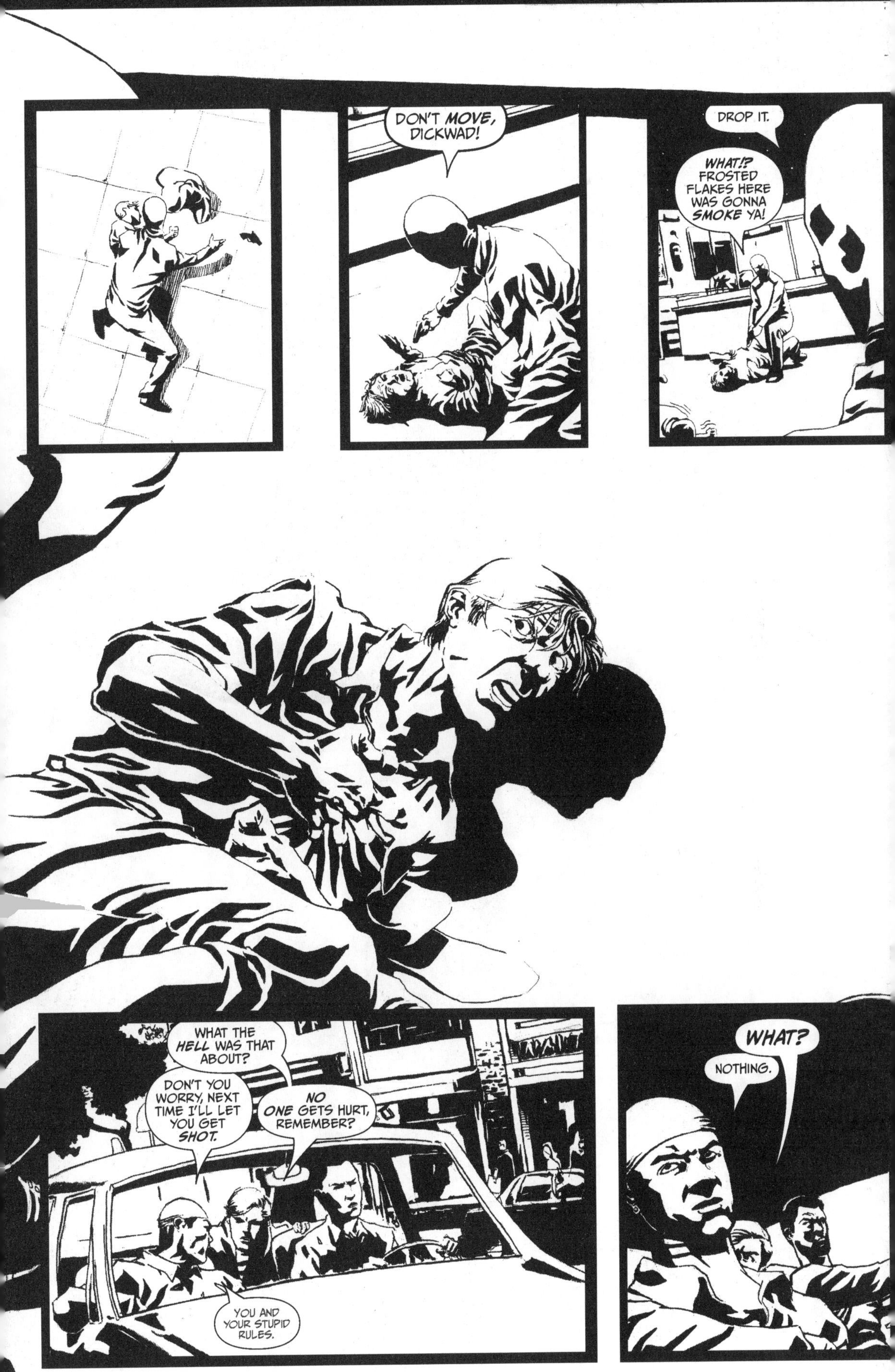
DON'T MOVE, DICKWAD!
DROP IT.
WHAT!? FROSTED FLAKES HERE WAS GONNA SMOKE YA!
WHAT THE HELL WAS THAT ABOUT?
DON'T YOU WORRY, NEXT TIME I'LL LET YOU GET SHOT.
NO ONE GETS HURT, REMEMBER?
YOU AND YOUR STUPID RULES.
WHAT?
NOTHING.

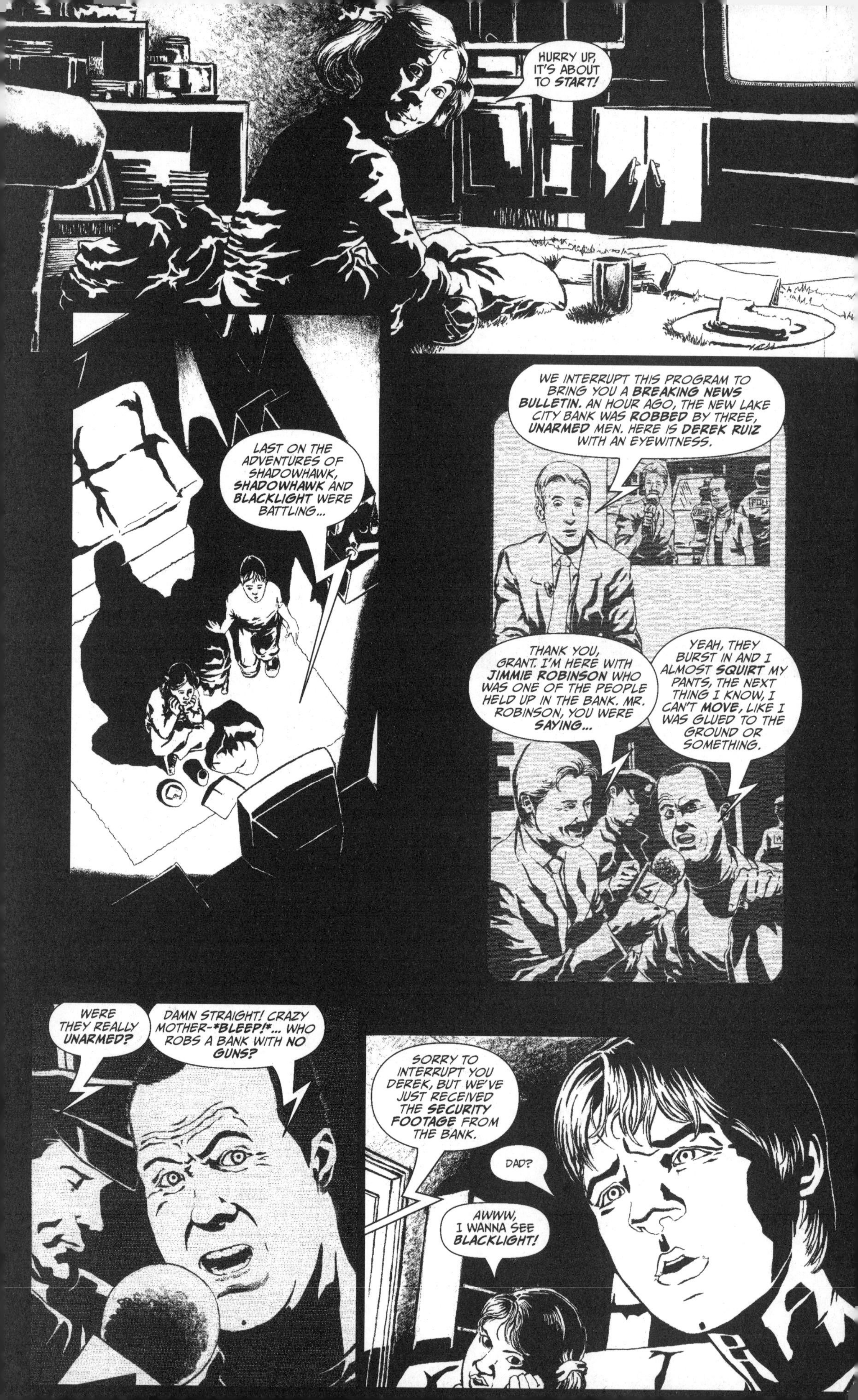
HURRY UP, IT'S ABOUT TO START!
LAST ON THE ADVENTURES OF SHADOWHAWK, SHADOWHAWK AND BLACKLIGHT WERE BATTLING...
WE INTERRUPT THIS PROGRAM TO BRING YOU A BREAKING NEWS BULLETIN. AN HOUR AGO, THE NEW LAKE CITY BANK WAS ROBBED BY THREE, UNARMED MEN. HERE IS DEREK RUIZ WITH AN EYEWITNESS.
THANK YOU, GRANT. I'M HERE WITH JIMMIE ROBINSON WHO WAS ONE OF THE PEOPLE HELD UP IN THE BANK. MR. ROBINSON, YOU WERE SAYING...
YEAH, THEY BURST IN AND I ALMOST SQUIRT MY PANTS, THE NEXT THING I KNOW, I CAN'T MOVE, LIKE I WAS GLUED TO THE GROUND OR SOMETHING.
WERE THEY REALLY UNARMED?
DAMN STRAIGHT! CRAZY MOTHER-*BLEEP!*... WHO ROBS A BANK WITH NO GUNS?
SORRY TO INTERRUPT YOU DEREK, BUT WE'VE JUST RECEIVED THE SECURITY FOOTAGE FROM THE BANK.
DAD?
AWWW, I WANNA SEE BLACKLIGHT!

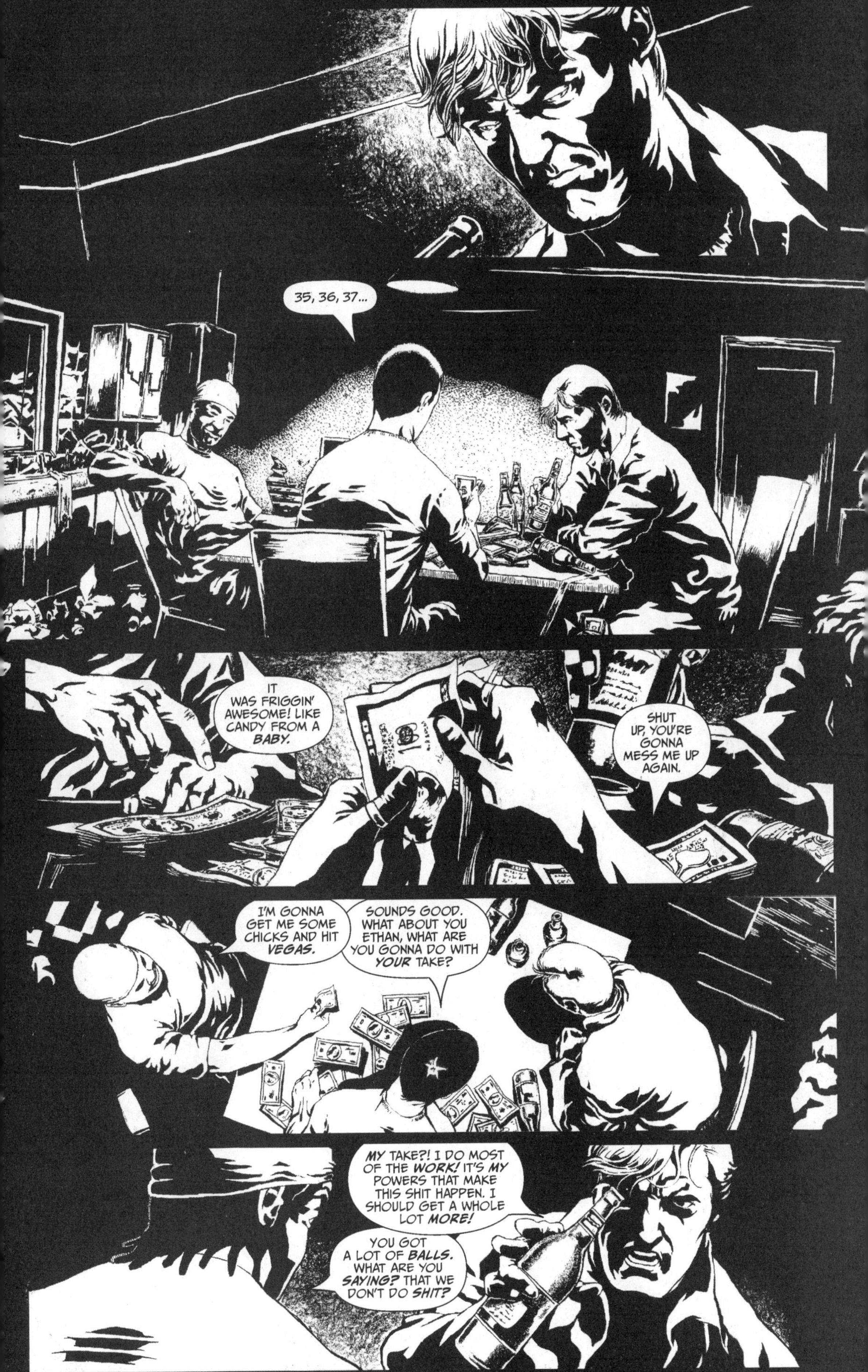
35, 36, 37...
IT WAS FRIGGIN' AWESOME! LIKE CANDY FROM A BABY.
SHUT UP, YOU'RE GONNA MESS ME UP AGAIN.
I'M GONNA GET ME SOME CHICKS AND HIT VEGAS.
SOUNDS GOOD. WHAT ABOUT YOU ETHAN, WHAT ARE YOU GONNA DO WITH YOUR TAKE?
MY TAKE?! I DO MOST OF THE WORK! IT'S MY POWERS THAT MAKE THIS SHIT HAPPEN. I SHOULD GET A WHOLE LOT MORE!
YOU GOT A LOT OF BALLS. WHAT ARE YOU SAYING? THAT WE DON'T DO SHIT?

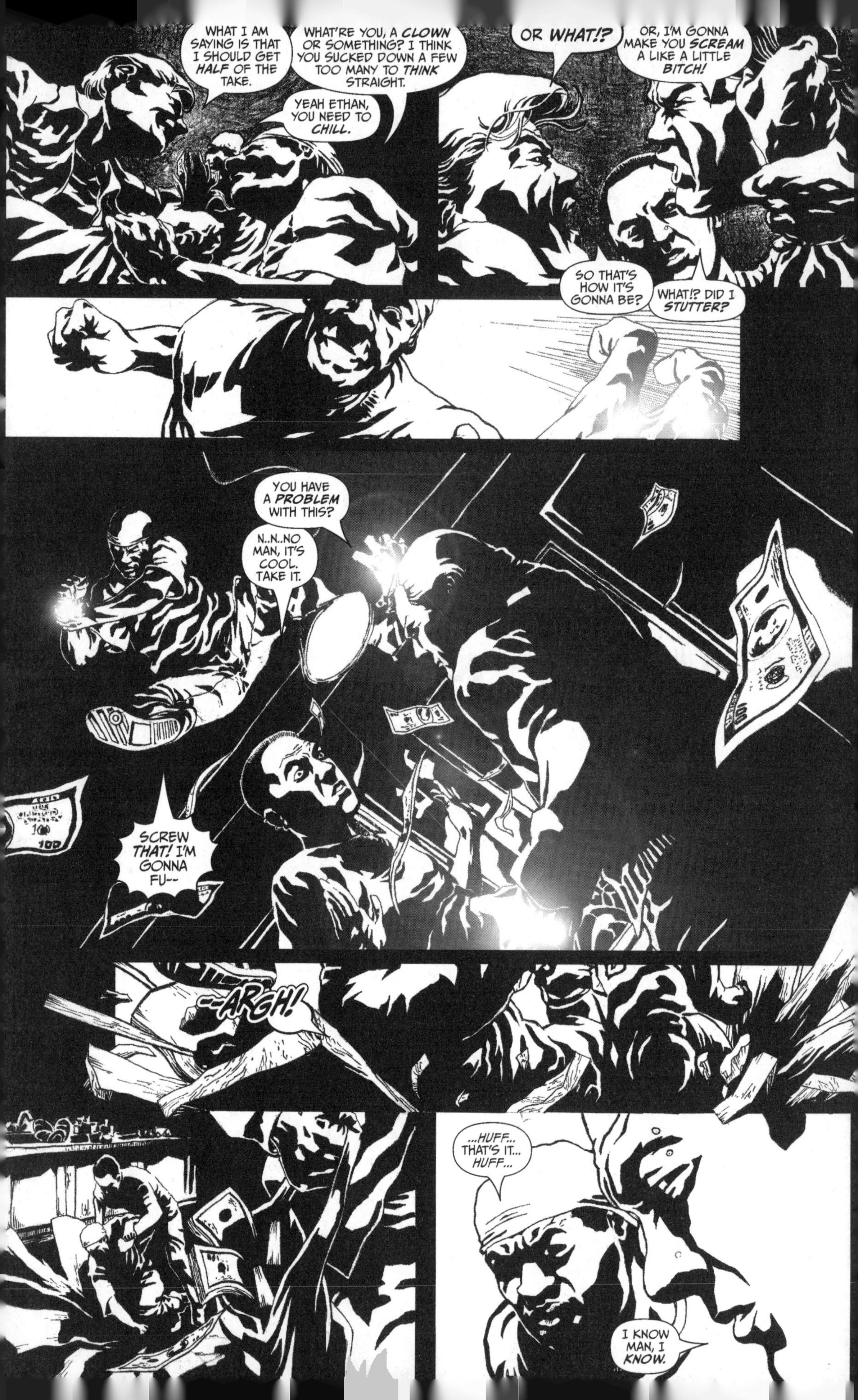

WHAT I AM SAYING IS THAT I SHOULD GET HALF OF THE TAKE.
WHAT'RE YOU, A CLOWN OR SOMETHING? I THINK YOU SUCKED DOWN A FEW TOO MANY TO THINK STRAIGHT.
YEAH ETHAN, YOU NEED TO CHILL.
OR WHAT!?
OR, I'M GONNA MAKE YOU SCREAM A LIKE A LITTLE BITCH!
SO THAT'S HOW IT'S GONNA BE?
WHAT!? DID I STUTTER?
YOU HAVE A PROBLEM WITH THIS?
N..N..NO MAN, IT'S COOL. TAKE IT.
SCREW THAT! I'M GONNA FU--
--ARGH!
...HUFF... THAT'S IT... HUFF...
I KNOW MAN, I KNOW.

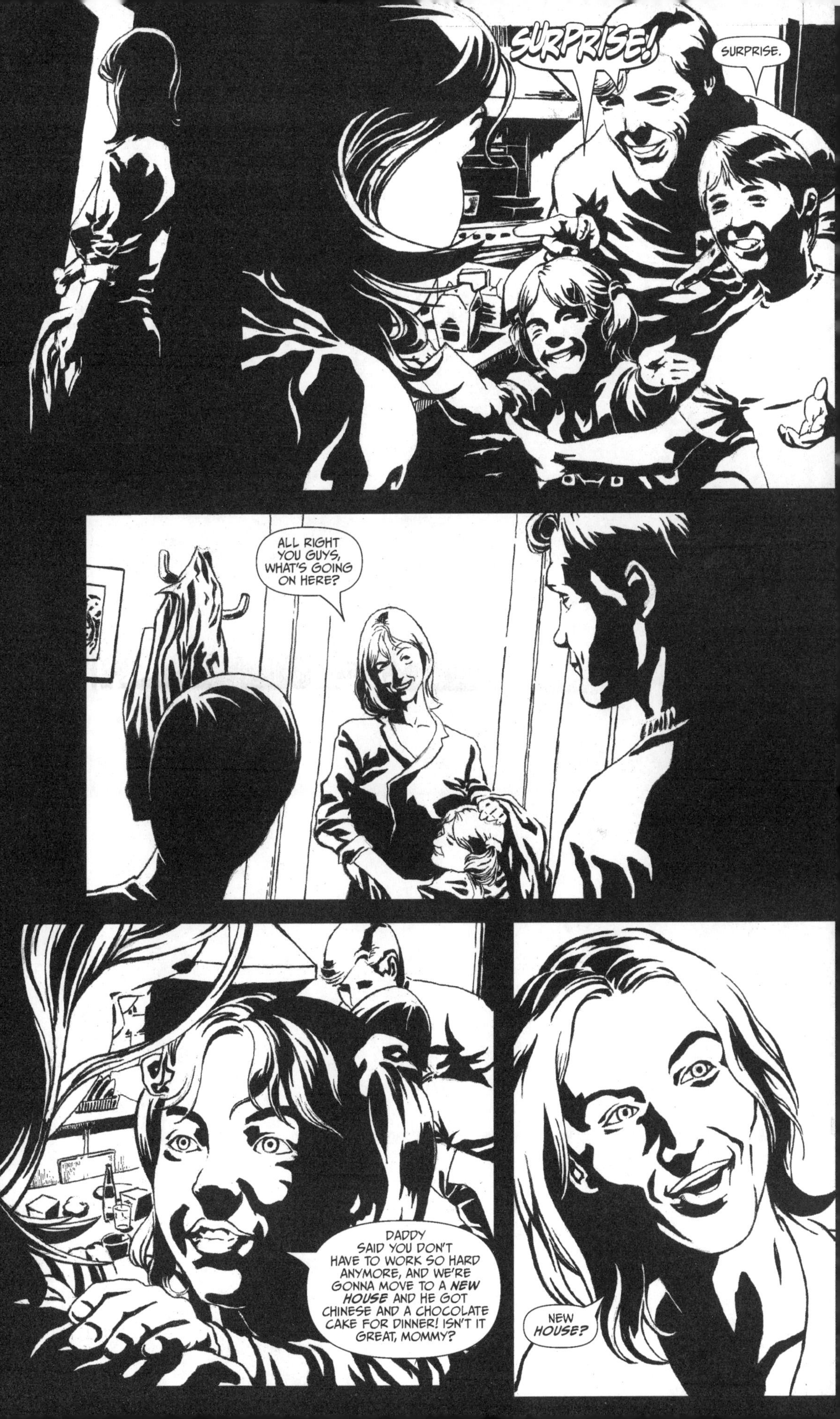
SURPRISE!
SURPRISE.
ALL RIGHT YOU GUYS, WHAT'S GOING ON HERE?
DADDY SAID YOU DON'T HAVE TO WORK SO HARD ANYMORE, AND WE'RE GONNA MOVE TO A NEW HOUSE AND HE GOT CHINESE AND A CHOCOLATE CAKE FOR DINNER! ISN'T IT GREAT, MOMMY?
NEW HOUSE?

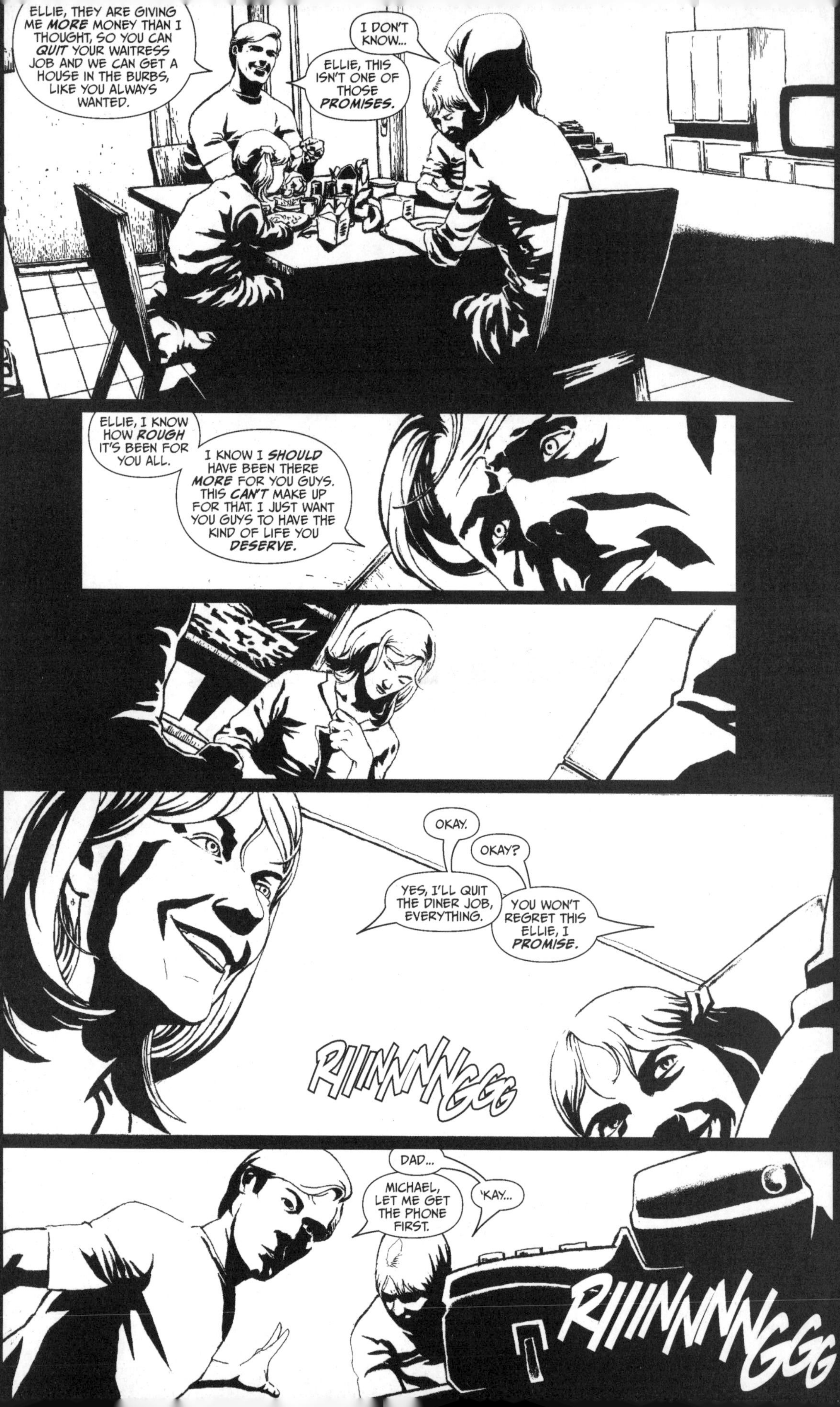

ELLIE, THEY ARE GIVING ME MORE MONEY THAN I THOUGHT, SO YOU CAN QUIT YOUR WAITRESS JOB AND WE CAN GET A HOUSE IN THE BURBS, LIKE YOU ALWAYS WANTED.
I DON'T KNOW...
ELLIE, THIS ISN'T ONE OF THOSE PROMISES.
ELLIE, I KNOW HOW ROUGH IT'S BEEN FOR YOU ALL.
I KNOW I SHOULD HAVE BEEN THERE MORE FOR YOU GUYS. THIS CAN'T MAKE UP FOR THAT. I JUST WANT YOU GUYS TO HAVE THE KIND OF LIFE YOU DESERVE.
OKAY.
OKAY?
YES, I'LL QUIT THE DINER JOB, EVERYTHING.
YOU WON'T REGRET THIS ELLIE, I PROMISE.
RIIINNNNGGG
DAD...
MICHAEL, LET ME GET THE PHONE FIRST.
'KAY...
RIIINNNNNGGG

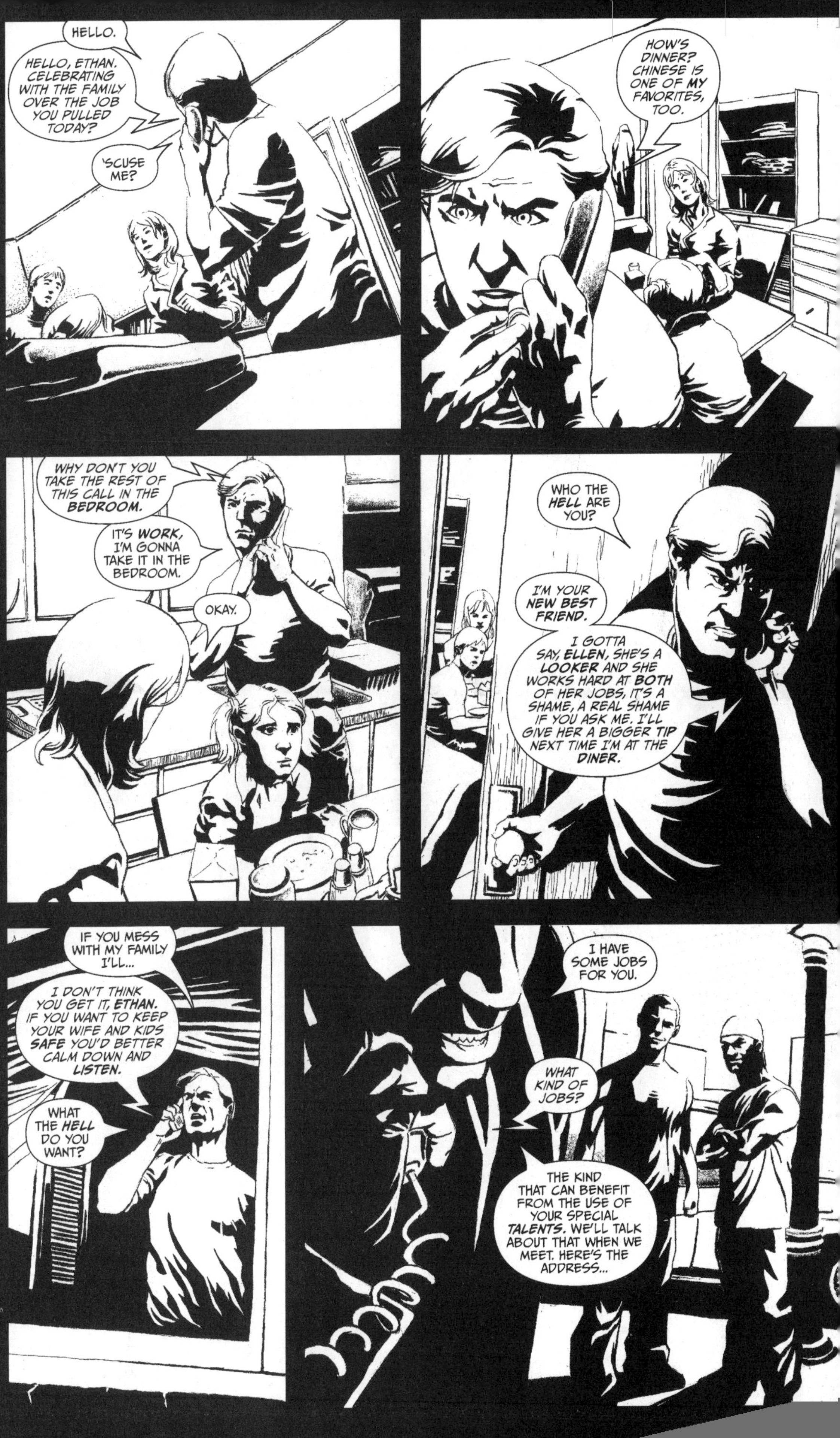
HELLO.
HELLO, ETHAN. CELEBRATING WITH THE FAMILY OVER THE JOB YOU PULLED TODAY?
'SCUSE ME?
HOW'S DINNER? CHINESE IS ONE OF MY FAVORITES, TOO.
WHY DON'T YOU TAKE THE REST OF THIS CALL IN THE BEDROOM.
IT'S WORK, I'M GONNA TAKE IT IN THE BEDROOM.
OKAY.
WHO THE HELL ARE YOU?
I'M YOUR NEW BEST FRIEND.
I GOTTA SAY, ELLEN, SHE'S A LOOKER AND SHE WORKS HARD AT BOTH OF HER JOBS, IT'S A SHAME, A REAL SHAME IF YOU ASK ME. I'LL GIVE HER A BIGGER TIP NEXT TIME I'M AT THE DINER.
IF YOU MESS WITH MY FAMILY I'LL...
I DON'T THINK YOU GET IT, ETHAN. IF YOU WANT TO KEEP YOUR WIFE AND KIDS SAFE YOU'D BETTER CALM DOWN AND LISTEN.
WHAT THE HELL DO YOU WANT?
I HAVE SOME JOBS FOR YOU.
WHAT KIND OF JOBS?
THE KIND THAT CAN BENEFIT FROM THE USE OF YOUR SPECIAL TALENTS. WE'LL TALK ABOUT THAT WHEN WE MEET. HERE'S THE ADDRESS...

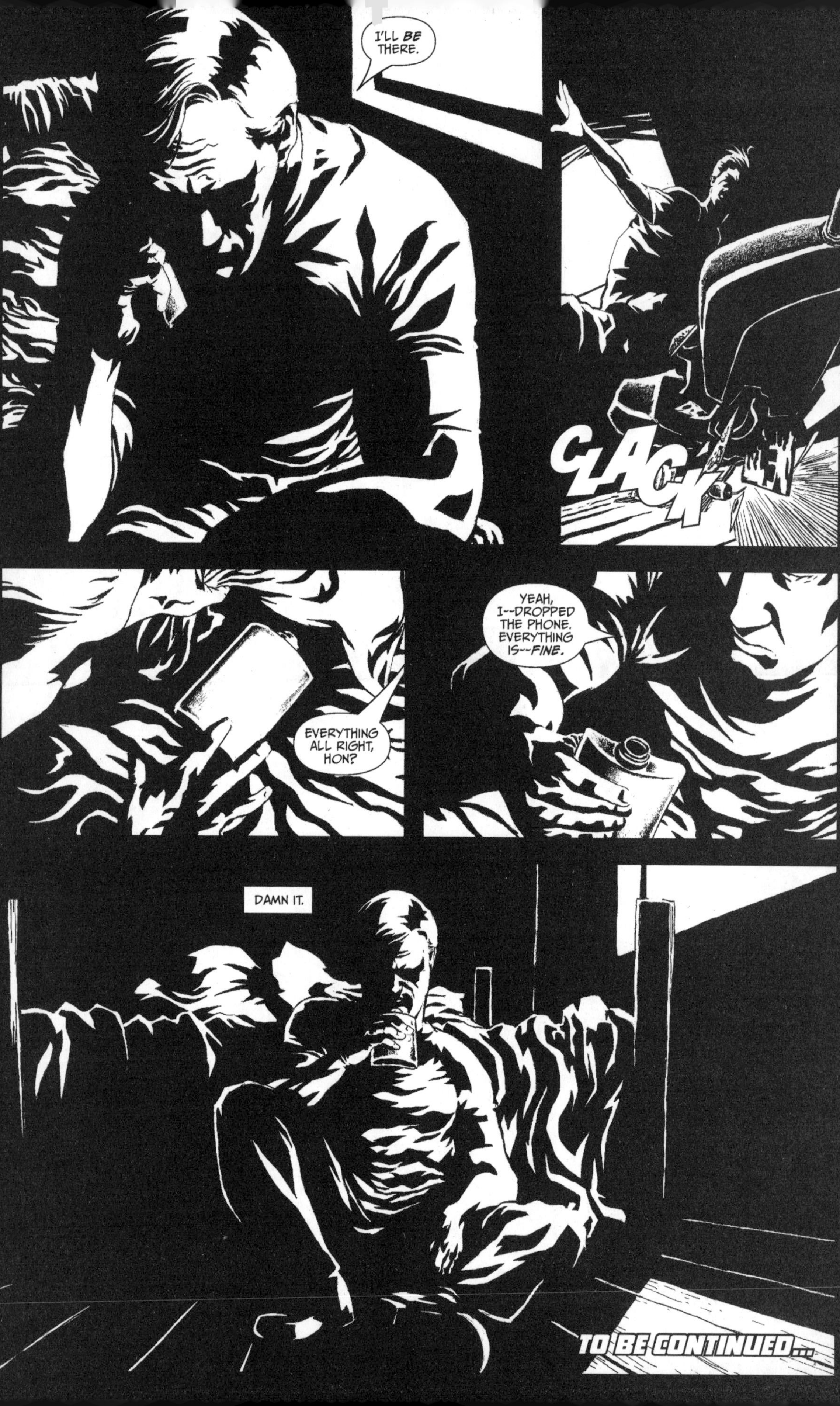
I'LL BE THERE.
CLACK
EVERYTHING ALL RIGHT, HON?
YEAH, I--DROPPED THE PHONE. EVERYTHING IS--FINE.
DAMN IT.
TO BE CONTINUED...

CHAPTER TWO: NO WAY OUT

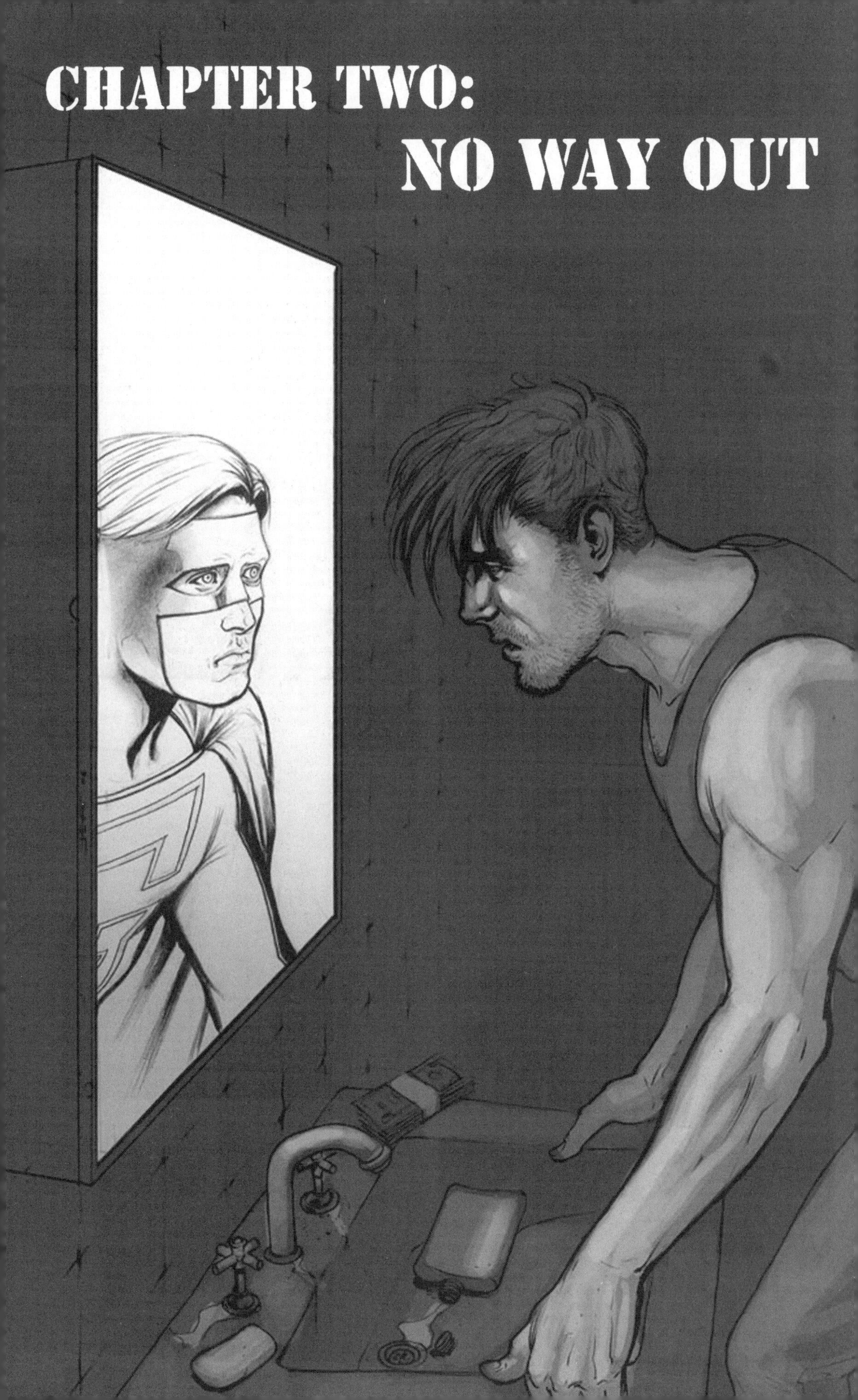

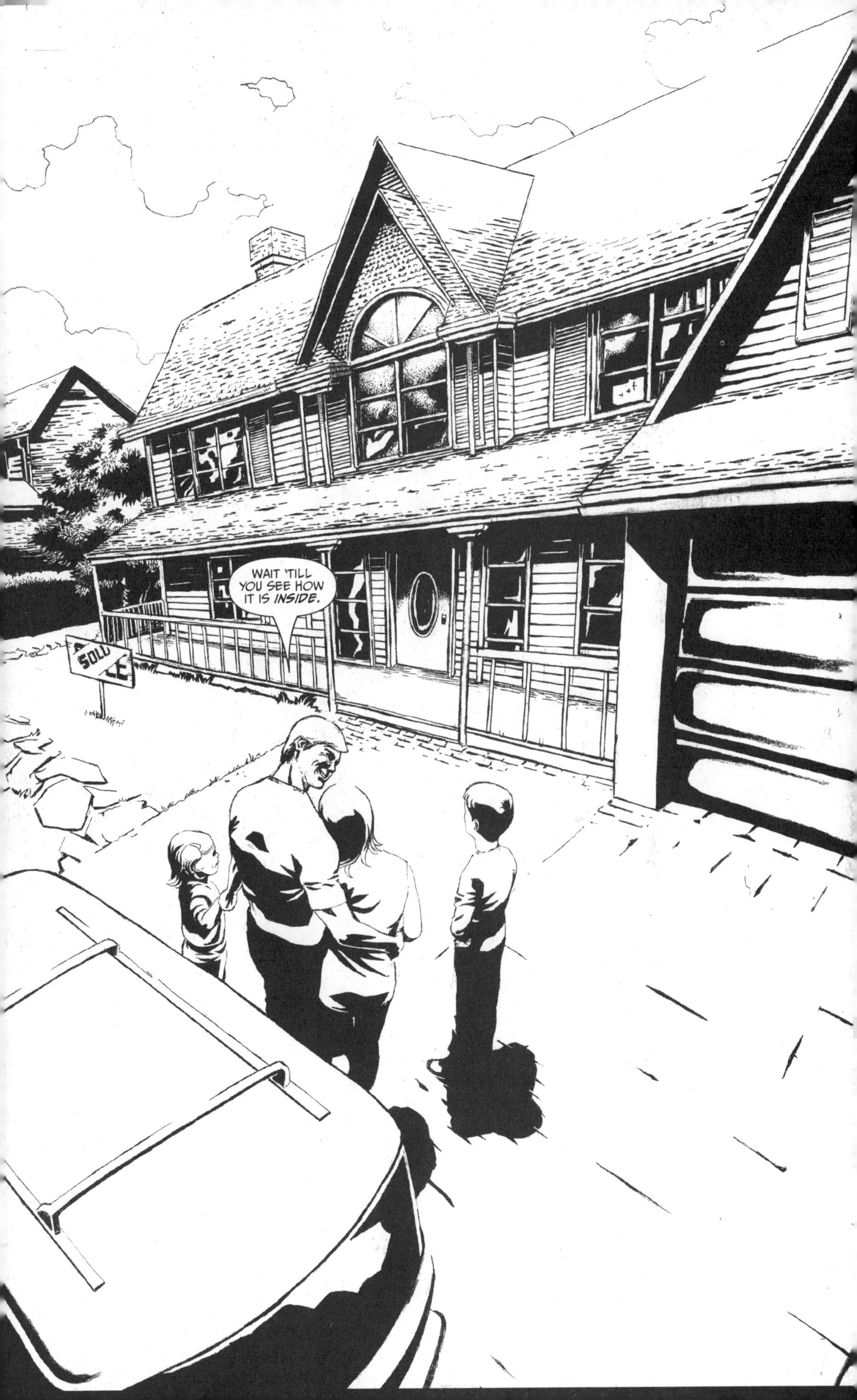
WAIT 'TILL YOU SEE HOW IT IS INSIDE.
SOLD

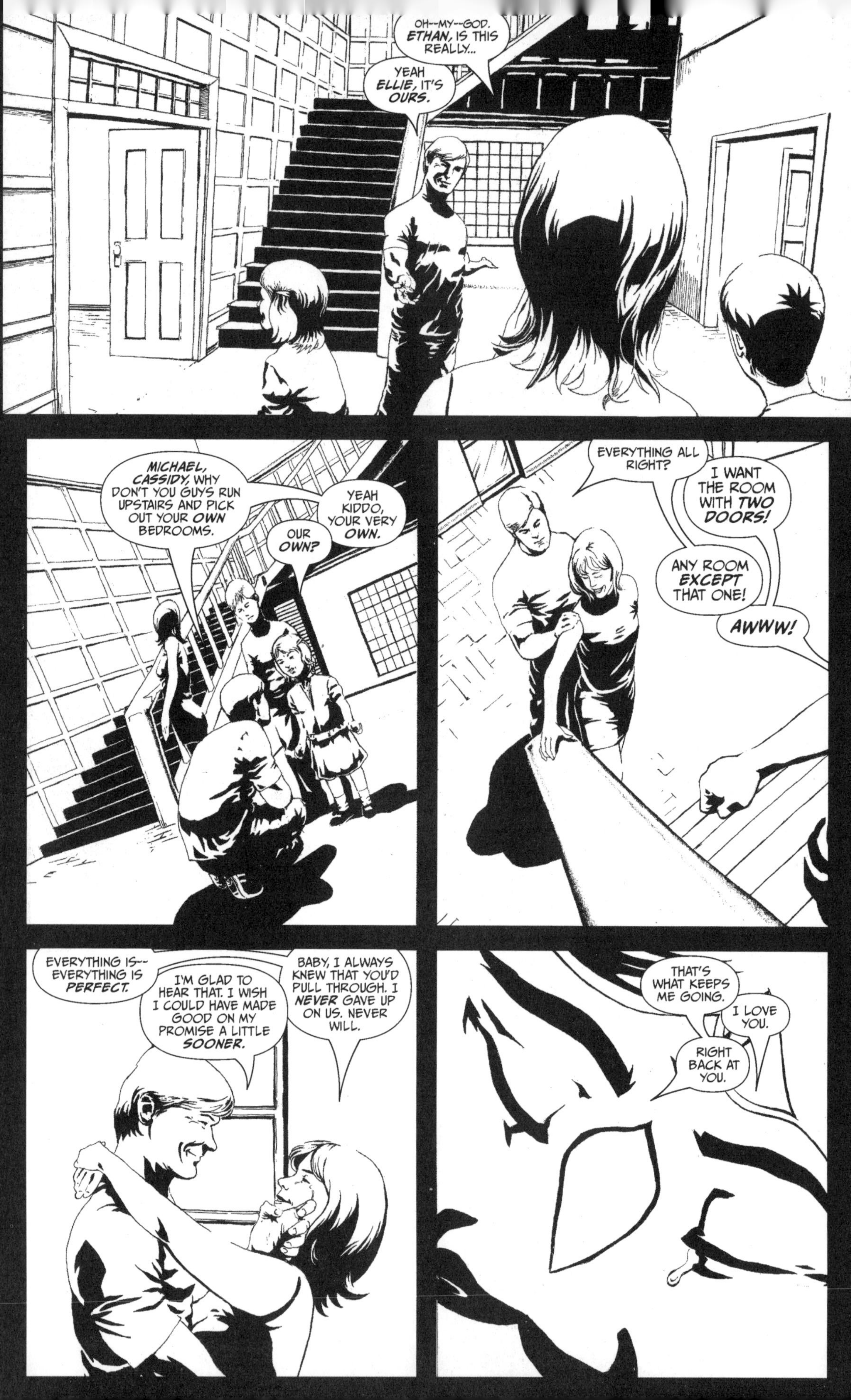
OH--MY--GOD. ETHAN, IS THIS REALLY...
YEAH ELLIE, IT'S OURS.
MICHAEL, CASSIDY, WHY DON'T YOU GUYS RUN UPSTAIRS AND PICK OUT YOUR OWN BEDROOMS.
OUR OWN?
YEAH KIDDO, YOUR VERY OWN.
EVERYTHING ALL RIGHT?
I WANT THE ROOM WITH TWO DOORS!
ANY ROOM EXCEPT THAT ONE!
AWWW!
EVERYTHING IS-- EVERYTHING IS PERFECT.
I'M GLAD TO HEAR THAT. I WISH I COULD HAVE MADE GOOD ON MY PROMISE A LITTLE SOONER.
BABY, I ALWAYS KNEW THAT YOU'D PULL THROUGH. I NEVER GAVE UP ON US. NEVER WILL.
THAT'S WHAT KEEPS ME GOING.
I LOVE YOU.
RIGHT BACK AT YOU.

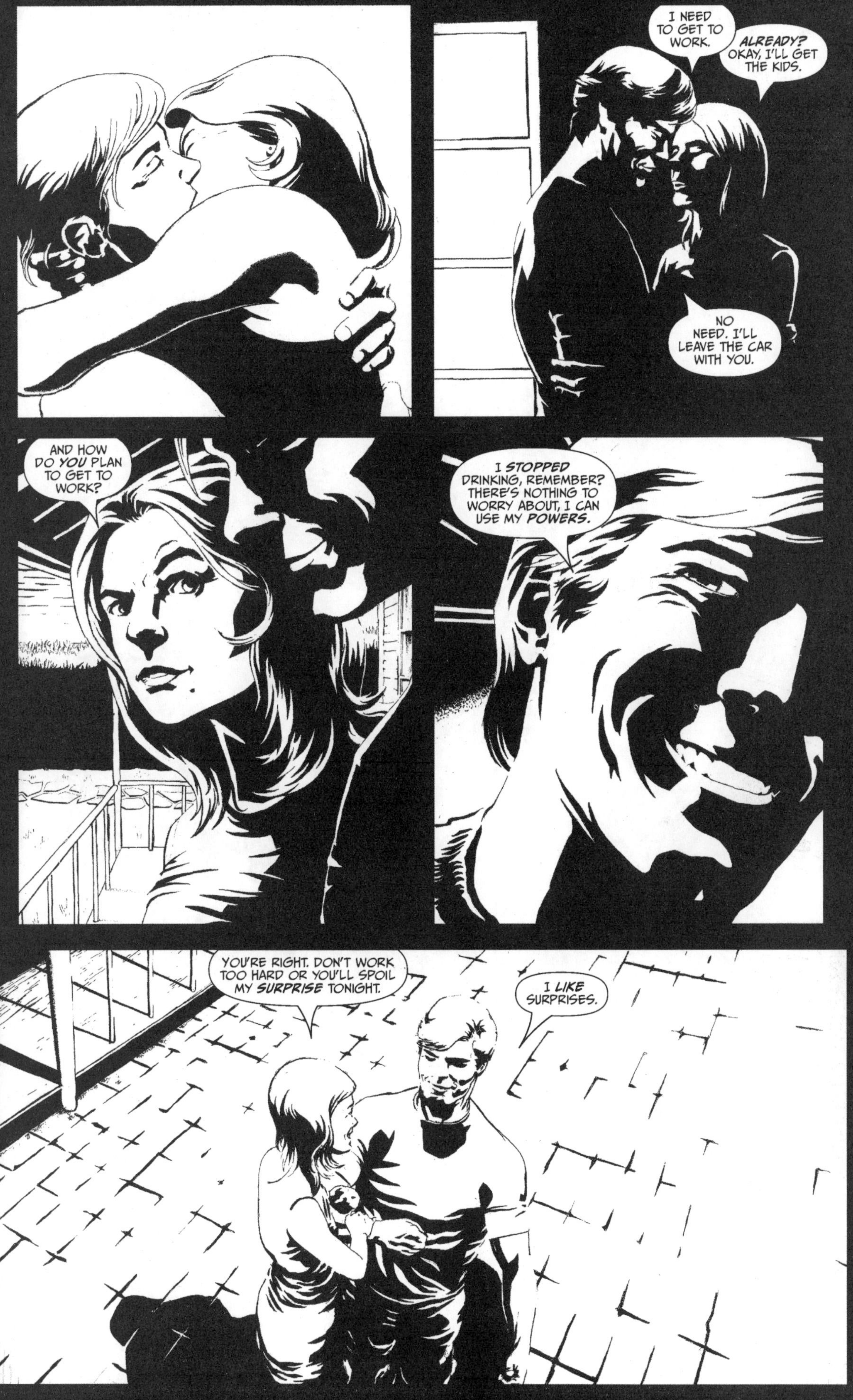
I NEED TO GET TO WORK.
ALREADY? OKAY, I'LL GET THE KIDS.
NO NEED. I'LL LEAVE THE CAR WITH YOU.
AND HOW DO YOU PLAN TO GET TO WORK?
I STOPPED DRINKING, REMEMBER? THERE'S NOTHING TO WORRY ABOUT, I CAN USE MY POWERS.
YOU'RE RIGHT. DON'T WORK TOO HARD OR YOU'LL SPOIL MY SURPRISE TONIGHT.
I LIKE SURPRISES.

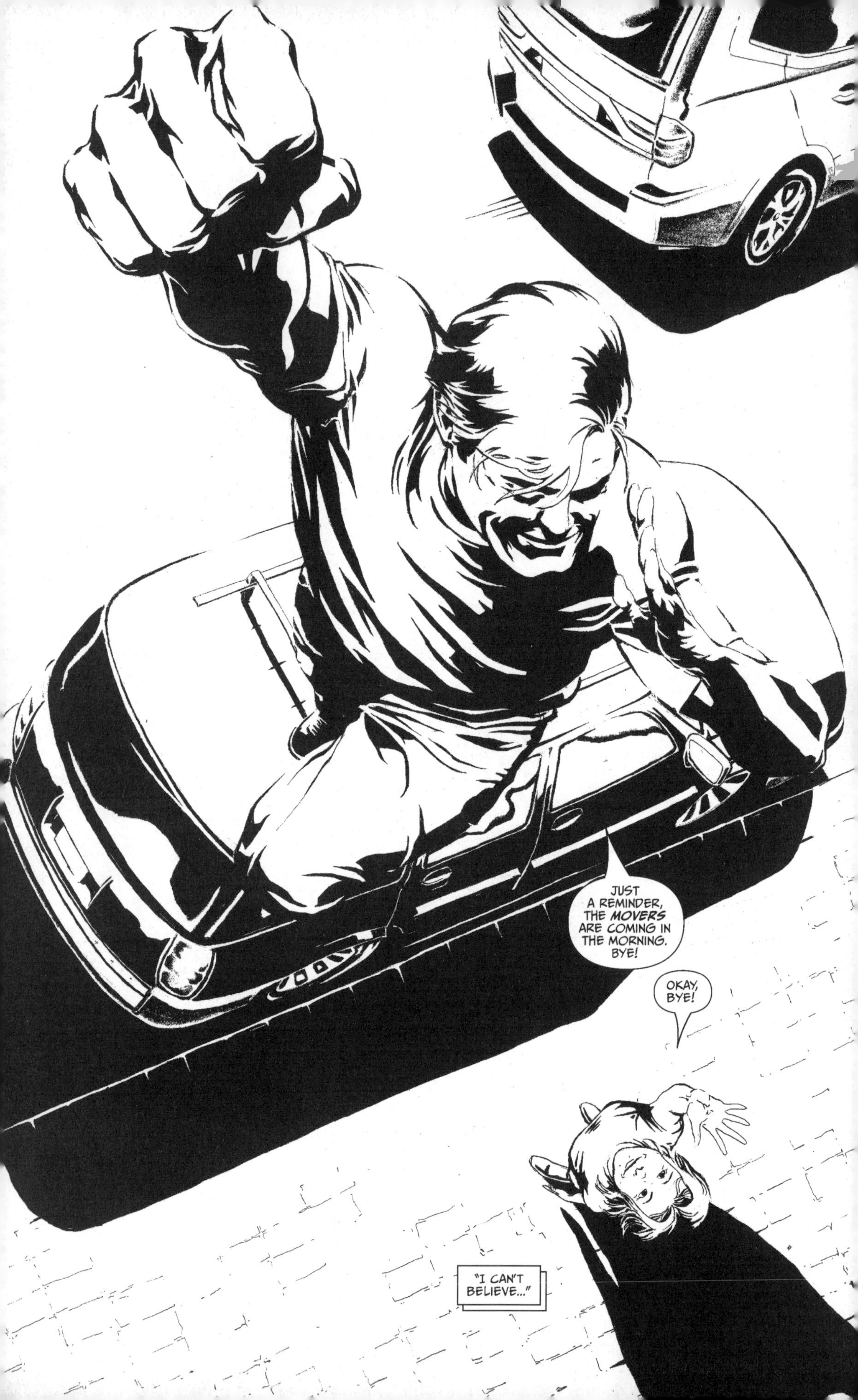
JUST A REMINDER, THE *MOVERS* ARE COMING IN THE MORNING. BYE!
OKAY, BYE!
"I CAN'T BELIEVE..."

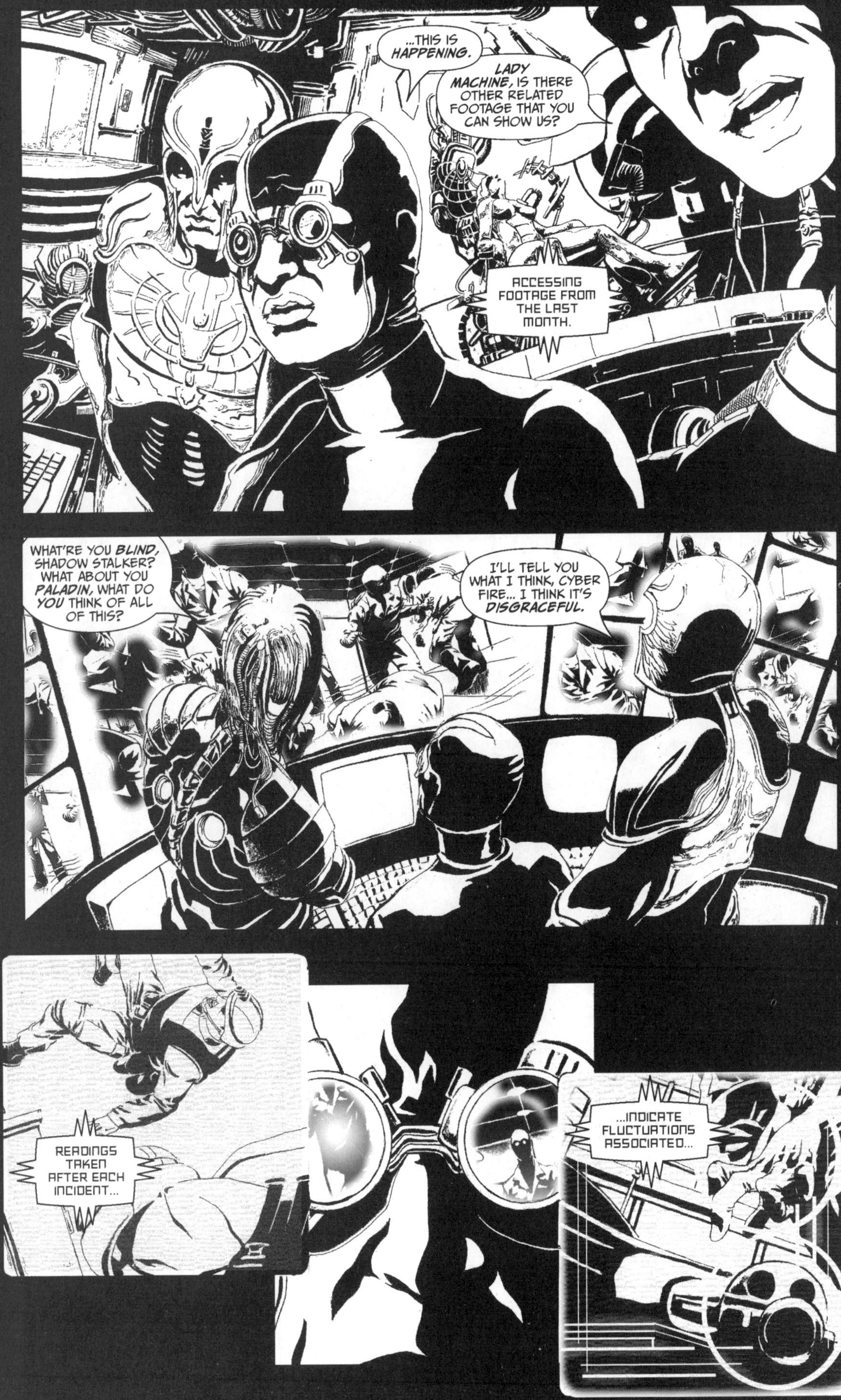
...THIS IS HAPPENING.
LADY MACHINE, IS THERE OTHER RELATED FOOTAGE THAT YOU CAN SHOW US?
ACCESSING FOOTAGE FROM THE LAST MONTH.
WHAT'RE YOU BLIND, SHADOW STALKER? WHAT ABOUT YOU PALADIN, WHAT DO YOU THINK OF ALL OF THIS?
I'LL TELL YOU WHAT I THINK, CYBER FIRE... I THINK IT'S DISGRACEFUL.
READINGS TAKEN AFTER EACH INCIDENT...
...INDICATE FLUCTUATIONS ASSOCIATED...

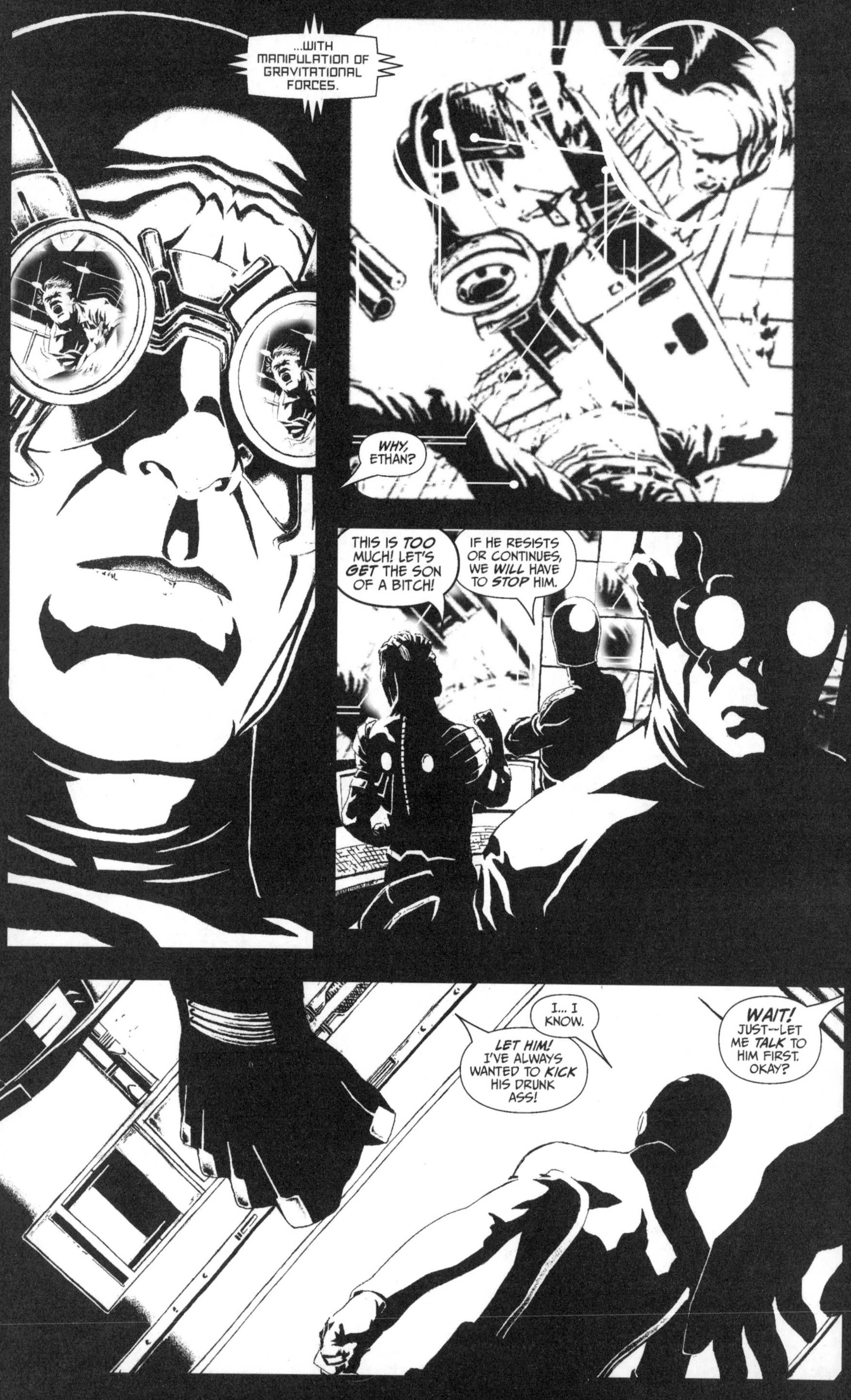
...WITH MANIPULATION OF GRAVITATIONAL FORCES.
WHY, ETHAN?
THIS IS TOO MUCH! LET'S GET THE SON OF A BITCH!
IF HE RESISTS OR CONTINUES, WE WILL HAVE TO STOP HIM.
I... I KNOW.
LET HIM! I'VE ALWAYS WANTED TO KICK HIS DRUNK ASS!
WAIT! JUST--LET ME TALK TO HIM FIRST. OKAY?

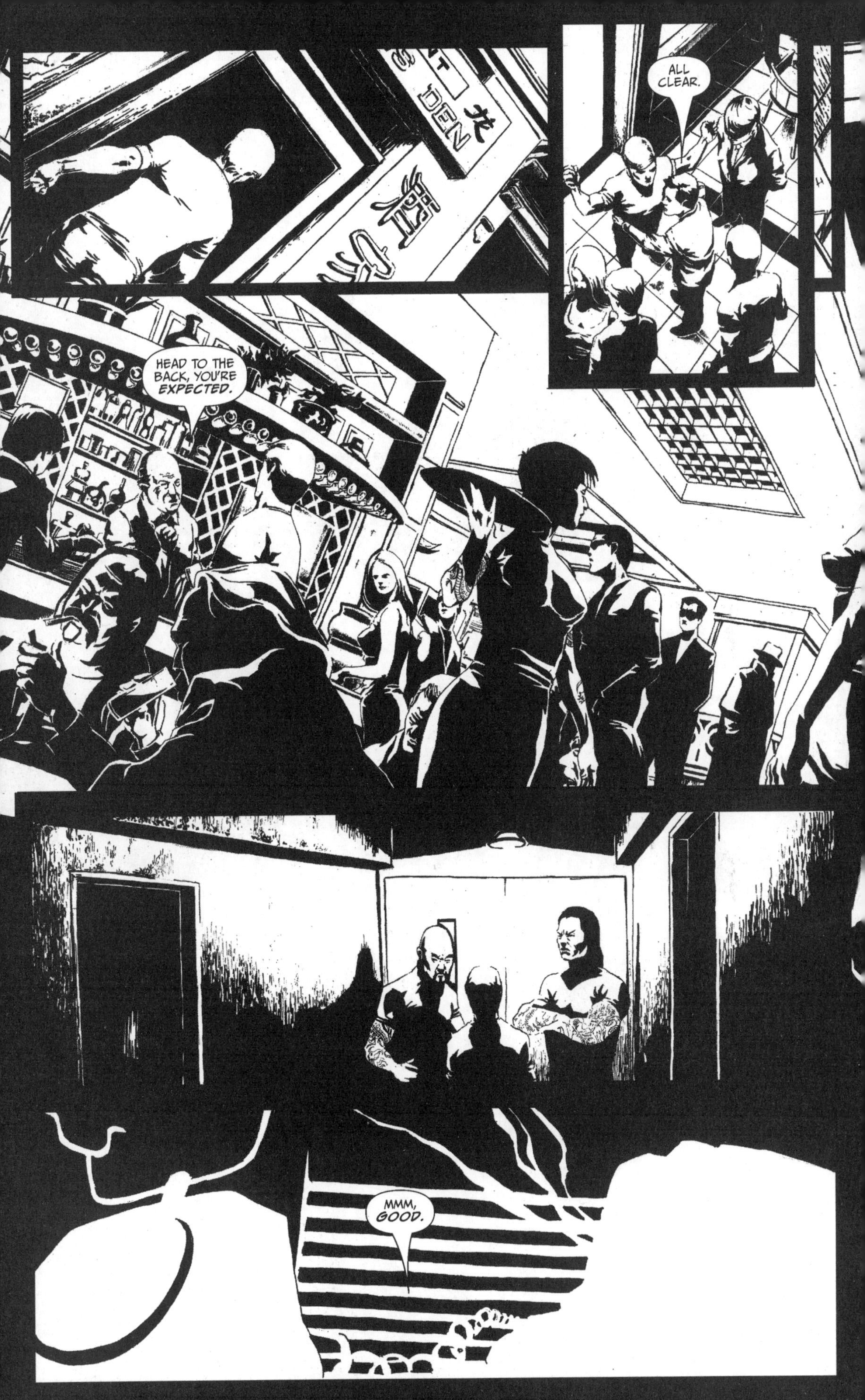
ALL CLEAR.
HEAD TO THE BACK, YOU'RE *EXPECTED*.
MMM, *GOOD*.

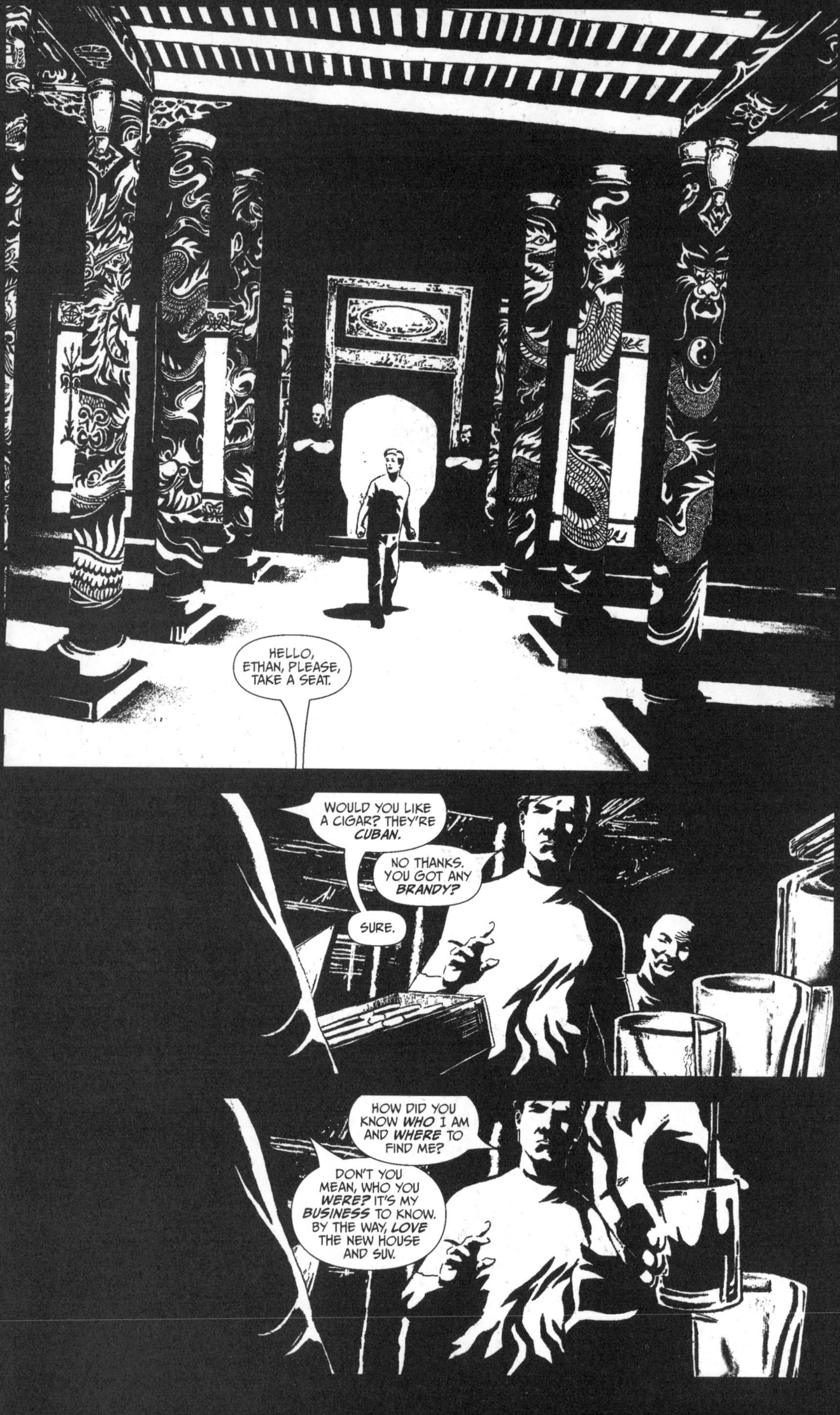
HELLO, ETHAN, PLEASE, TAKE A SEAT.
WOULD YOU LIKE A CIGAR? THEY'RE *CUBAN.*
NO THANKS. YOU GOT ANY *BRANDY?*
SURE.
HOW DID YOU KNOW *WHO* I AM AND *WHERE* TO FIND ME?
DON'T YOU MEAN, WHO YOU *WERE?* IT'S MY *BUSINESS* TO KNOW. BY THE WAY, *LOVE* THE NEW HOUSE AND SUV.

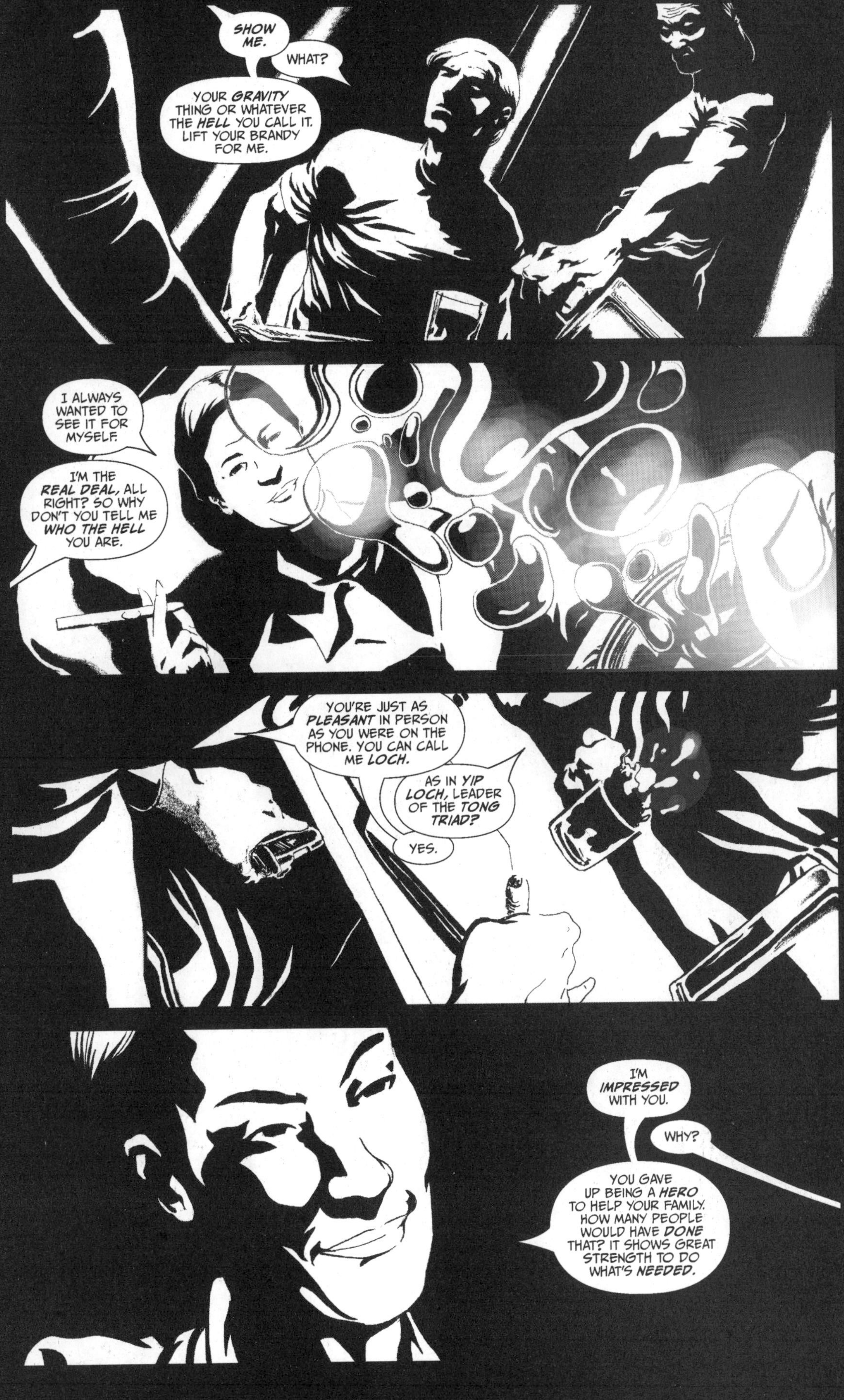
SHOW ME.
WHAT?
YOUR GRAVITY THING OR WHATEVER THE HELL YOU CALL IT. LIFT YOUR BRANDY FOR ME.
I ALWAYS WANTED TO SEE IT FOR MYSELF.
I'M THE REAL DEAL, ALL RIGHT? SO WHY DON'T YOU TELL ME WHO THE HELL YOU ARE.
YOU'RE JUST AS PLEASANT IN PERSON AS YOU WERE ON THE PHONE. YOU CAN CALL ME LOCH.
AS IN YIP LOCH, LEADER OF THE TONG TRIAD?
YES.
I'M IMPRESSED WITH YOU.
WHY?
YOU GAVE UP BEING A HERO TO HELP YOUR FAMILY. HOW MANY PEOPLE WOULD HAVE DONE THAT? IT SHOWS GREAT STRENGTH TO DO WHAT'S NEEDED.

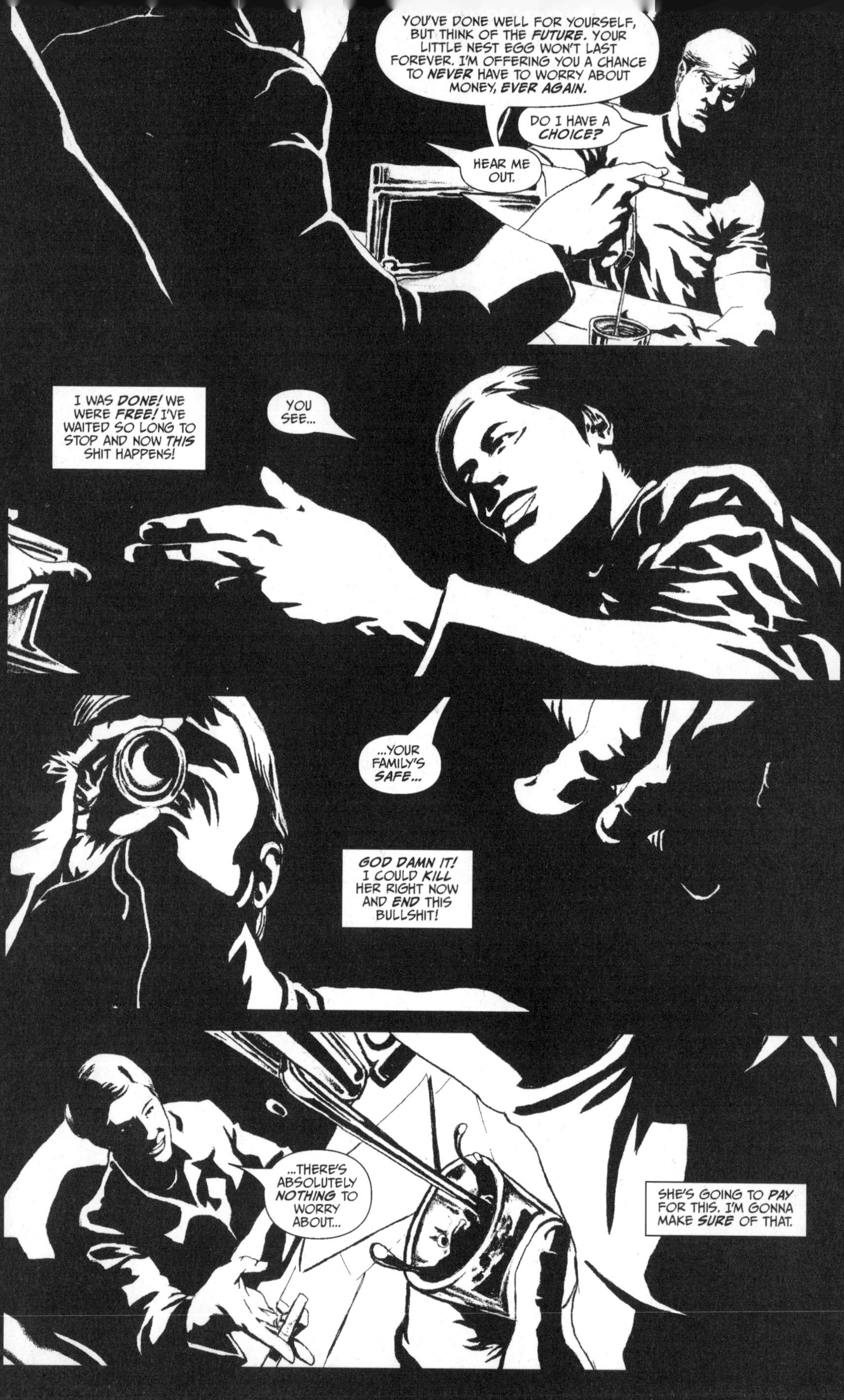
YOU'VE DONE WELL FOR YOURSELF, BUT THINK OF THE FUTURE. YOUR LITTLE NEST EGG WON'T LAST FOREVER. I'M OFFERING YOU A CHANCE TO NEVER HAVE TO WORRY ABOUT MONEY, EVER AGAIN.
DO I HAVE A CHOICE?
HEAR ME OUT.
I WAS DONE! WE WERE FREE! I'VE WAITED SO LONG TO STOP AND NOW THIS SHIT HAPPENS!
YOU SEE...
...YOUR FAMILY'S SAFE...
GOD DAMN IT! I COULD KILL HER RIGHT NOW AND END THIS BULLSHIT!
...THERE'S ABSOLUTELY NOTHING TO WORRY ABOUT...
SHE'S GOING TO PAY FOR THIS. I'M GONNA MAKE SURE OF THAT.

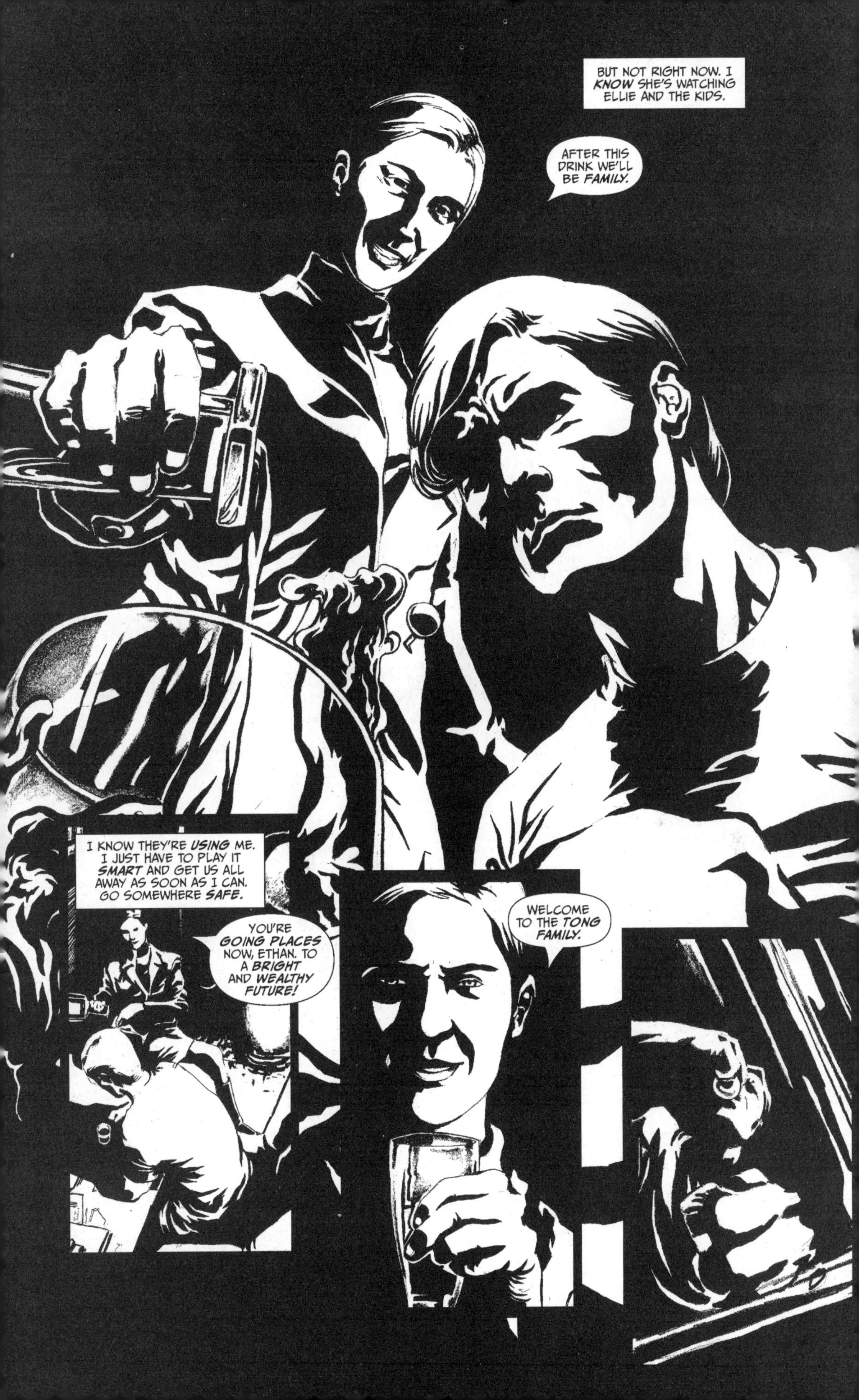
BUT NOT RIGHT NOW. I KNOW SHE'S WATCHING ELLIE AND THE KIDS.
AFTER THIS DRINK WE'LL BE FAMILY.
I KNOW THEY'RE USING ME. I JUST HAVE TO PLAY IT SMART AND GET US ALL AWAY AS SOON AS I CAN. GO SOMEWHERE SAFE.
YOU'RE GOING PLACES NOW, ETHAN. TO A BRIGHT AND WEALTHY FUTURE!
WELCOME TO THE TONG FAMILY.

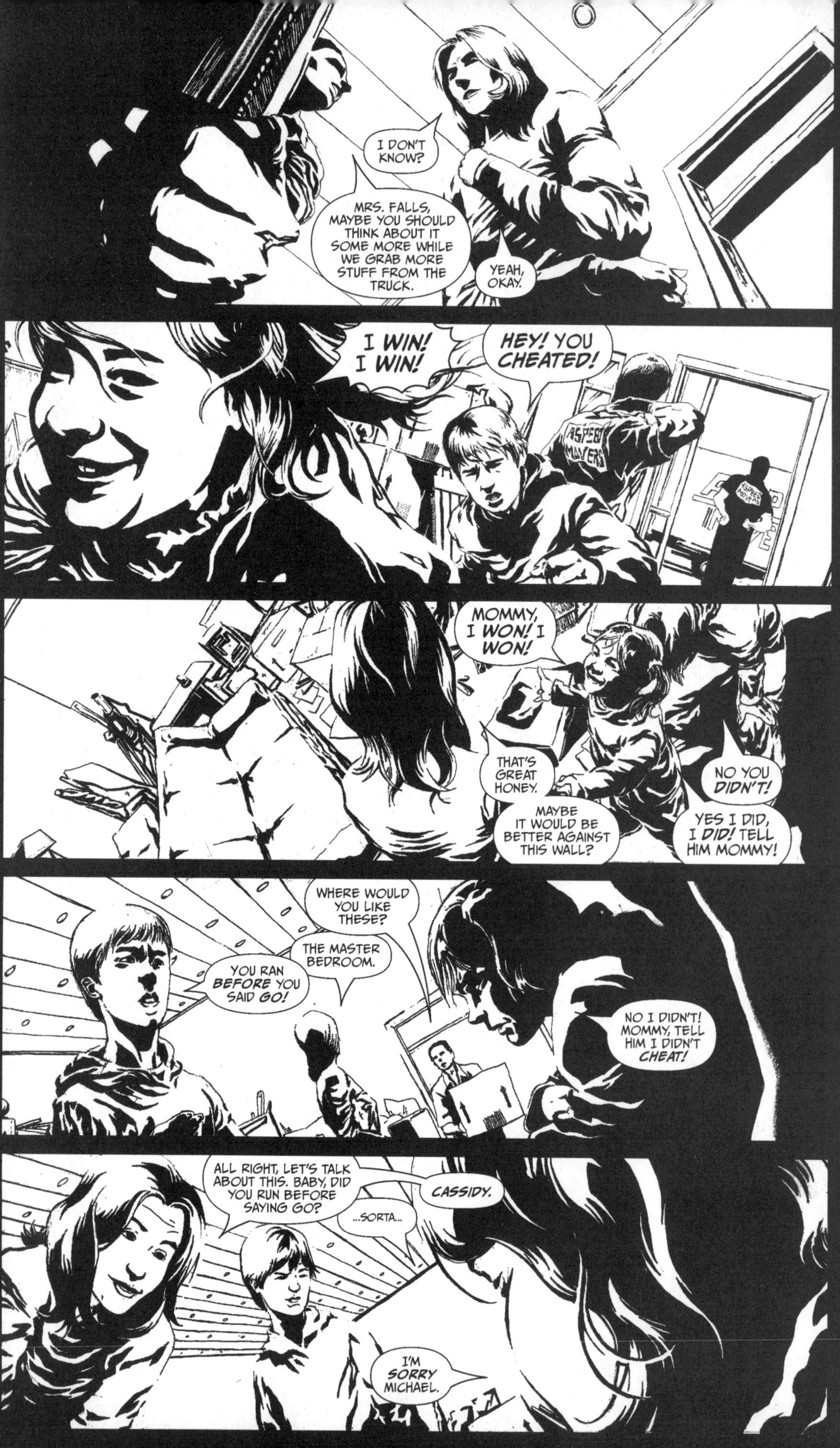

I DON'T KNOW?
MRS. FALLS, MAYBE YOU SHOULD THINK ABOUT IT SOME MORE WHILE WE GRAB MORE STUFF FROM THE TRUCK.
YEAH, OKAY.
I WIN! I WIN!
HEY! YOU CHEATED!
ASPEN MOVERS
MOMMY, I WON! I WON!
THAT'S GREAT HONEY.
MAYBE IT WOULD BE BETTER AGAINST THIS WALL?
NO YOU DIDN'T!
YES I DID, I DID! TELL HIM MOMMY!
WHERE WOULD YOU LIKE THESE?
THE MASTER BEDROOM.
YOU RAN BEFORE YOU SAID GO!
NO I DIDN'T! MOMMY, TELL HIM I DIDN'T CHEAT!
ALL RIGHT, LET'S TALK ABOUT THIS. BABY, DID YOU RUN BEFORE SAYING GO?
CASSIDY.
...SORTA...
I'M SORRY MICHAEL.

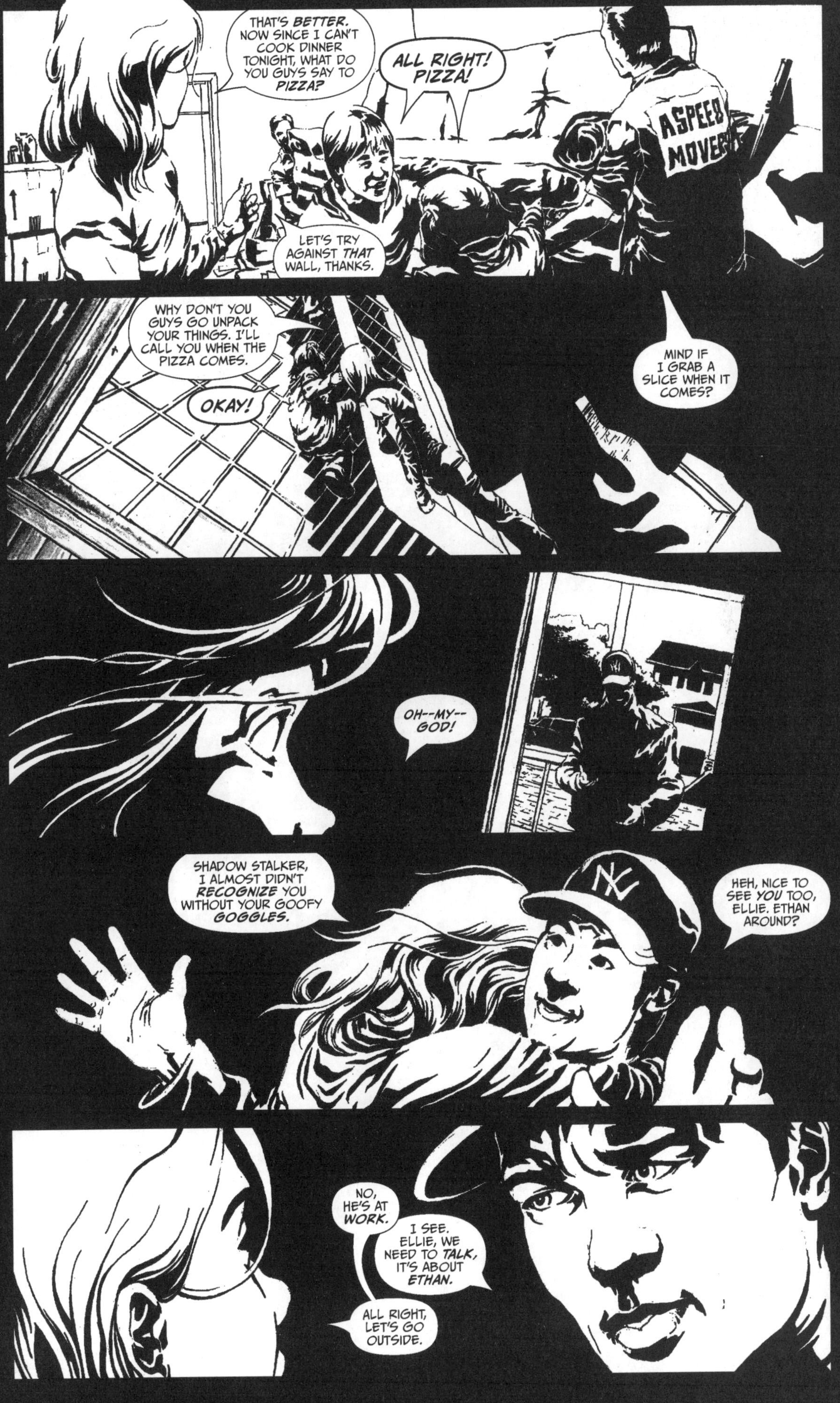
THAT'S BETTER. NOW SINCE I CAN'T COOK DINNER TONIGHT, WHAT DO YOU GUYS SAY TO PIZZA?
ALL RIGHT! PIZZA!
ASPEED MOVERS
LET'S TRY AGAINST THAT WALL, THANKS.
WHY DON'T YOU GUYS GO UNPACK YOUR THINGS. I'LL CALL YOU WHEN THE PIZZA COMES.
OKAY!
MIND IF I GRAB A SLICE WHEN IT COMES?
OH--MY--GOD!
SHADOW STALKER, I ALMOST DIDN'T RECOGNIZE YOU WITHOUT YOUR GOOFY GOGGLES.
HEH, NICE TO SEE YOU TOO, ELLIE. ETHAN AROUND?
NO, HE'S AT WORK.
I SEE. ELLIE, WE NEED TO TALK, IT'S ABOUT ETHAN.
ALL RIGHT, LET'S GO OUTSIDE.

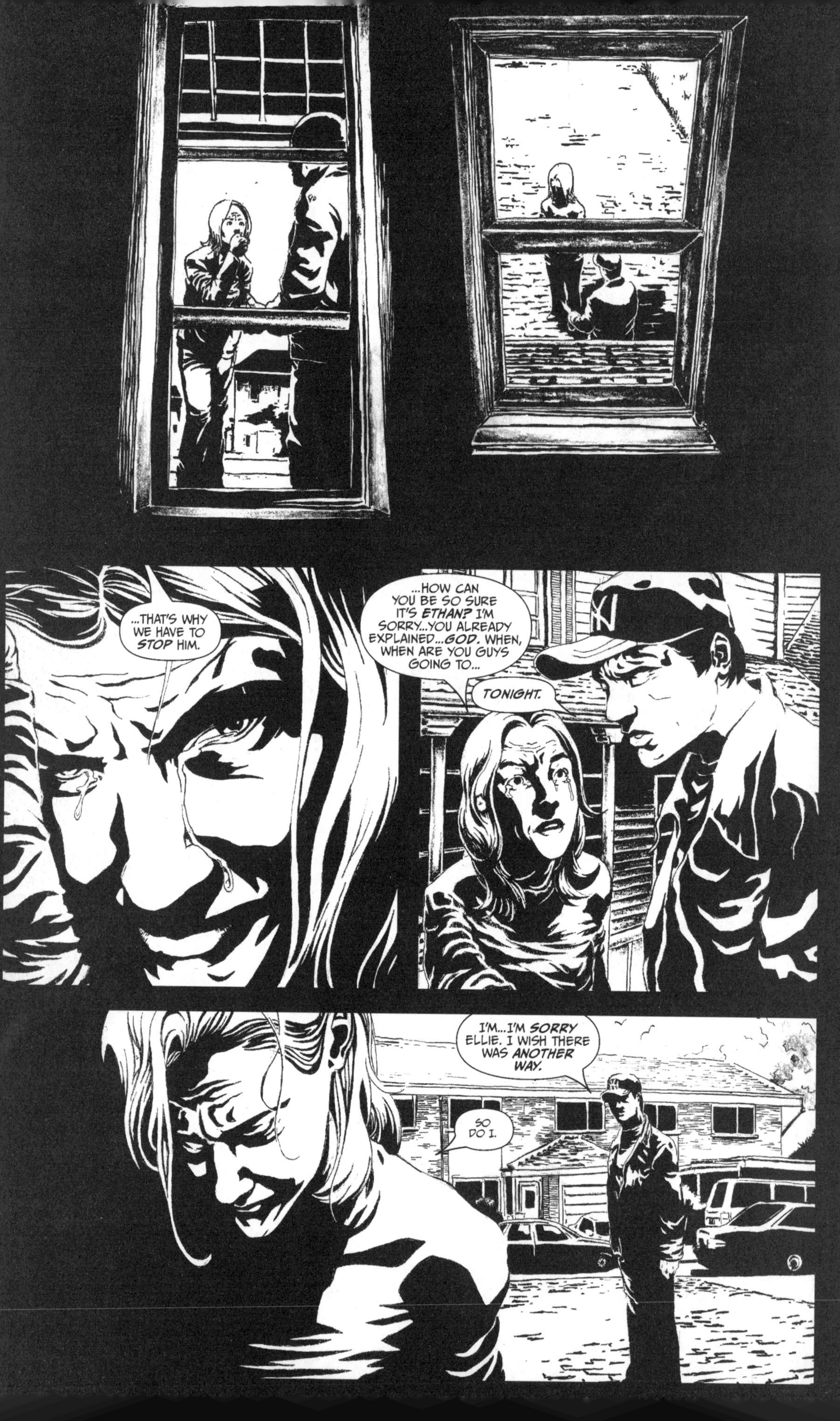
...THAT'S WHY WE HAVE TO *STOP* HIM.
...HOW CAN YOU BE SO SURE IT'S *ETHAN?* I'M SORRY...YOU ALREADY EXPLAINED...*GOD.* WHEN, WHEN ARE YOU GUYS GOING TO...
TONIGHT.
I'M...I'M *SORRY* ELLIE. I WISH THERE WAS *ANOTHER WAY.*
SO DO I.

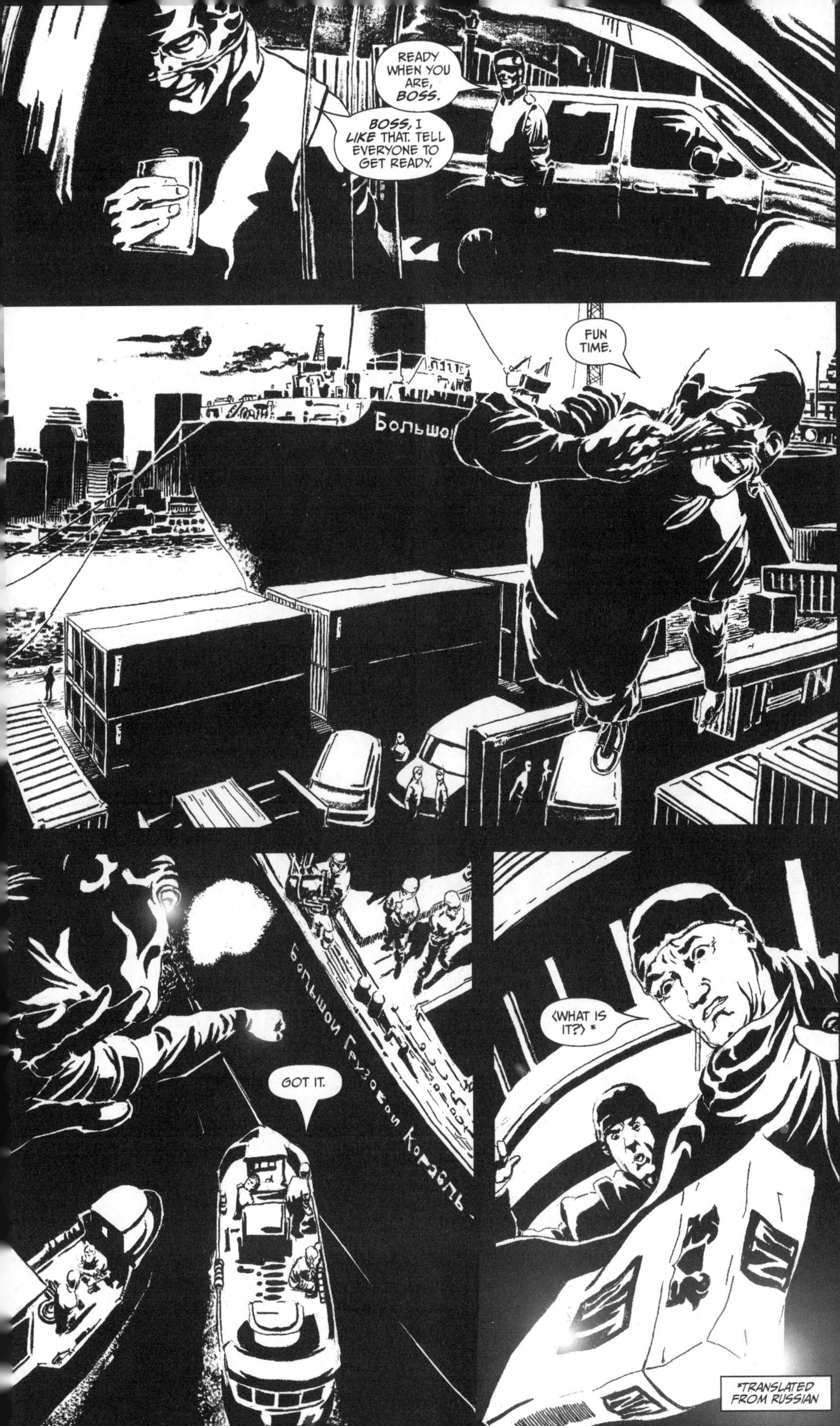

READY WHEN YOU ARE, **BOSS.**
BOSS, I **LIKE** THAT. TELL EVERYONE TO GET READY.
FUN TIME.
Большой Грузовой Корабль
GOT IT.
<WHAT IS IT?> *
*TRANSLATED FROM RUSSIAN

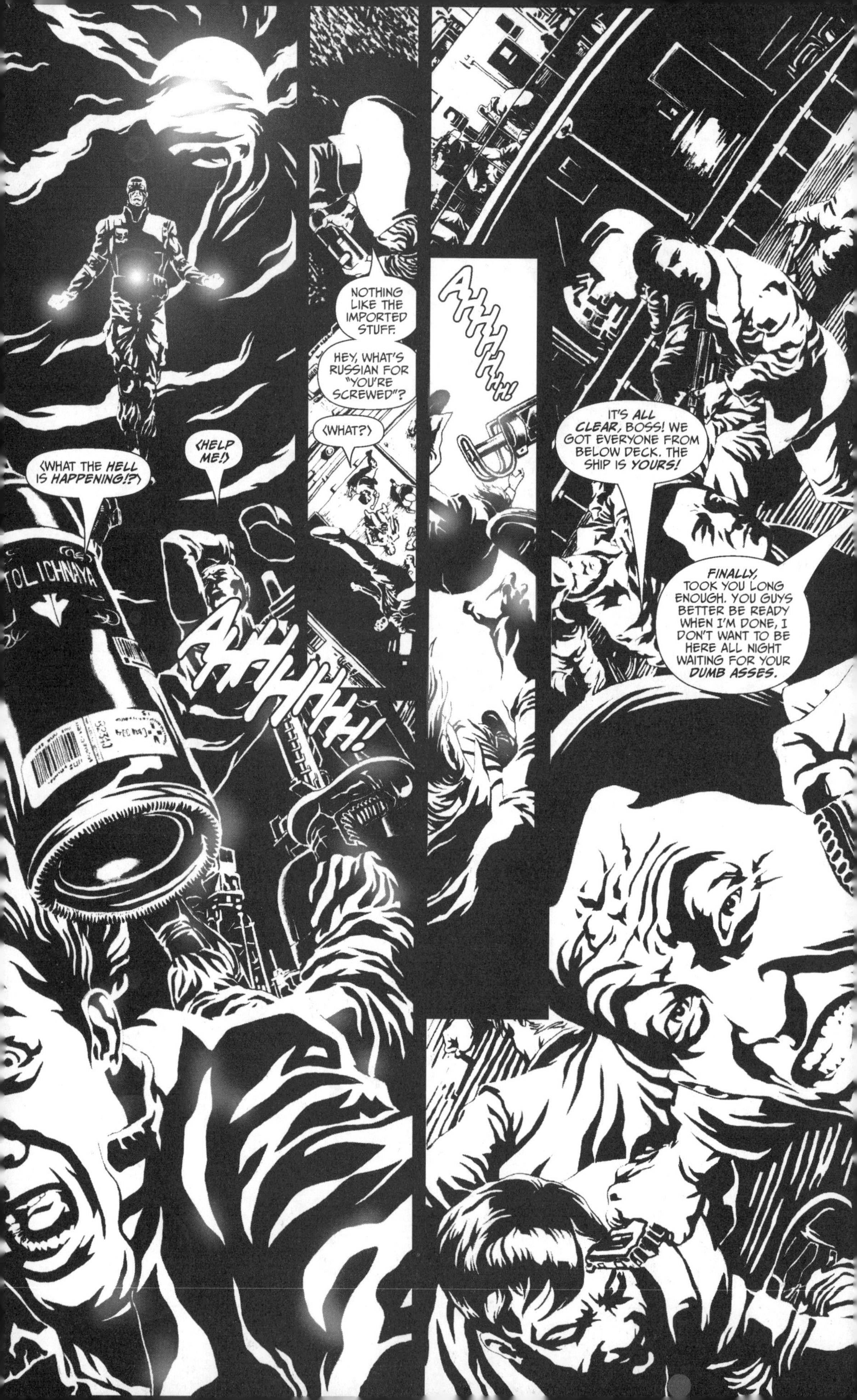

‹WHAT THE HELL IS HAPPENING!?›
‹HELP ME!›
STOLICHNAYA
AHHHHHH!
NOTHING LIKE THE IMPORTED STUFF.
HEY, WHAT'S RUSSIAN FOR "YOU'RE SCREWED"?
‹WHAT?›
AHHHHHH!
IT'S ALL CLEAR, BOSS! WE GOT EVERYONE FROM BELOW DECK. THE SHIP IS YOURS!
FINALLY, TOOK YOU LONG ENOUGH. YOU GUYS BETTER BE READY WHEN I'M DONE, I DON'T WANT TO BE HERE ALL NIGHT WAITING FOR YOUR DUMB ASSES.

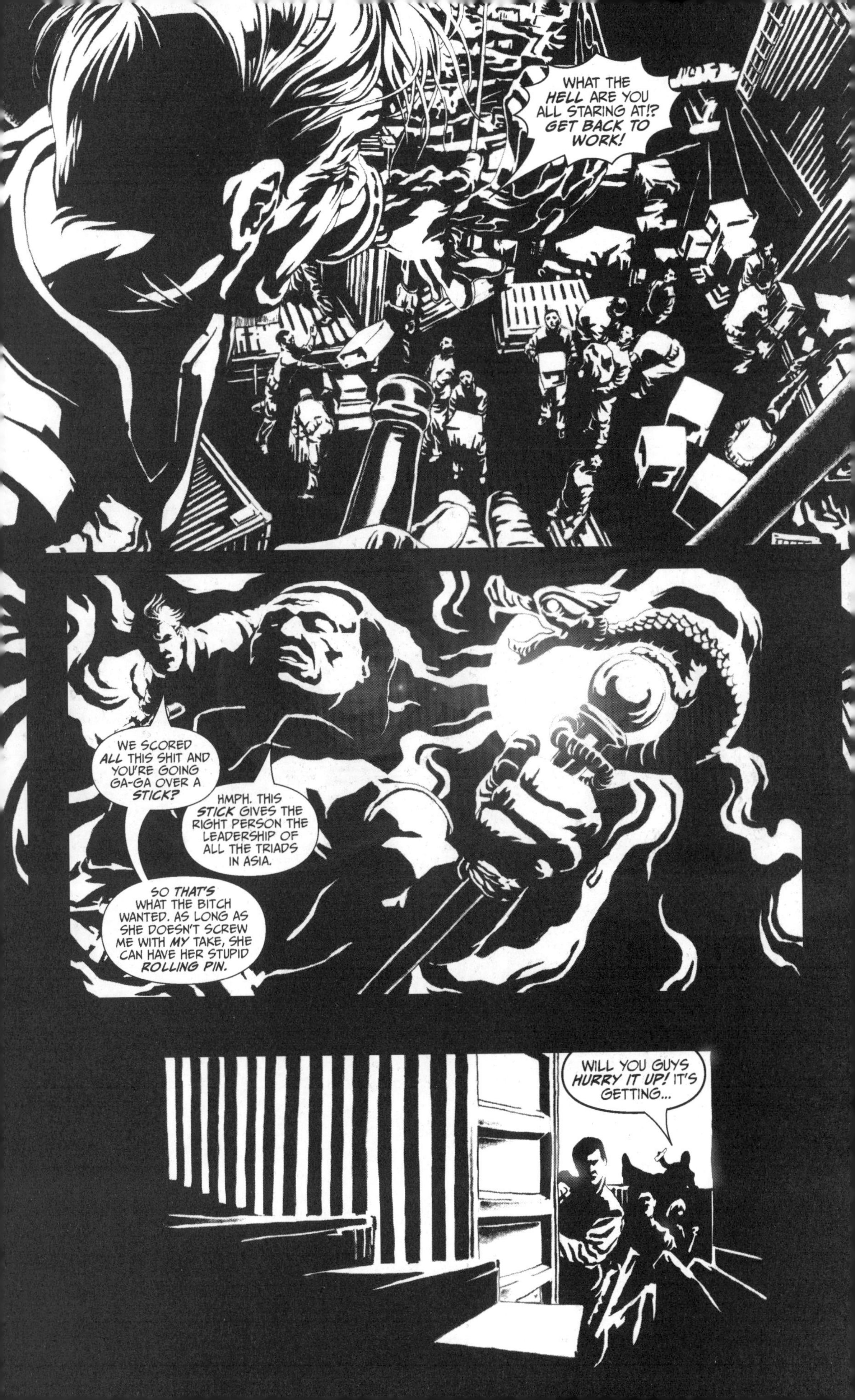
WHAT THE HELL ARE YOU ALL STARING AT!? GET BACK TO WORK!
WE SCORED ALL THIS SHIT AND YOU'RE GOING GA-GA OVER A STICK?
HMPH. THIS STICK GIVES THE RIGHT PERSON THE LEADERSHIP OF ALL THE TRIADS IN ASIA.
SO THAT'S WHAT THE BITCH WANTED. AS LONG AS SHE DOESN'T SCREW ME WITH MY TAKE, SHE CAN HAVE HER STUPID ROLLING PIN.
WILL YOU GUYS HURRY IT UP! IT'S GETTING...

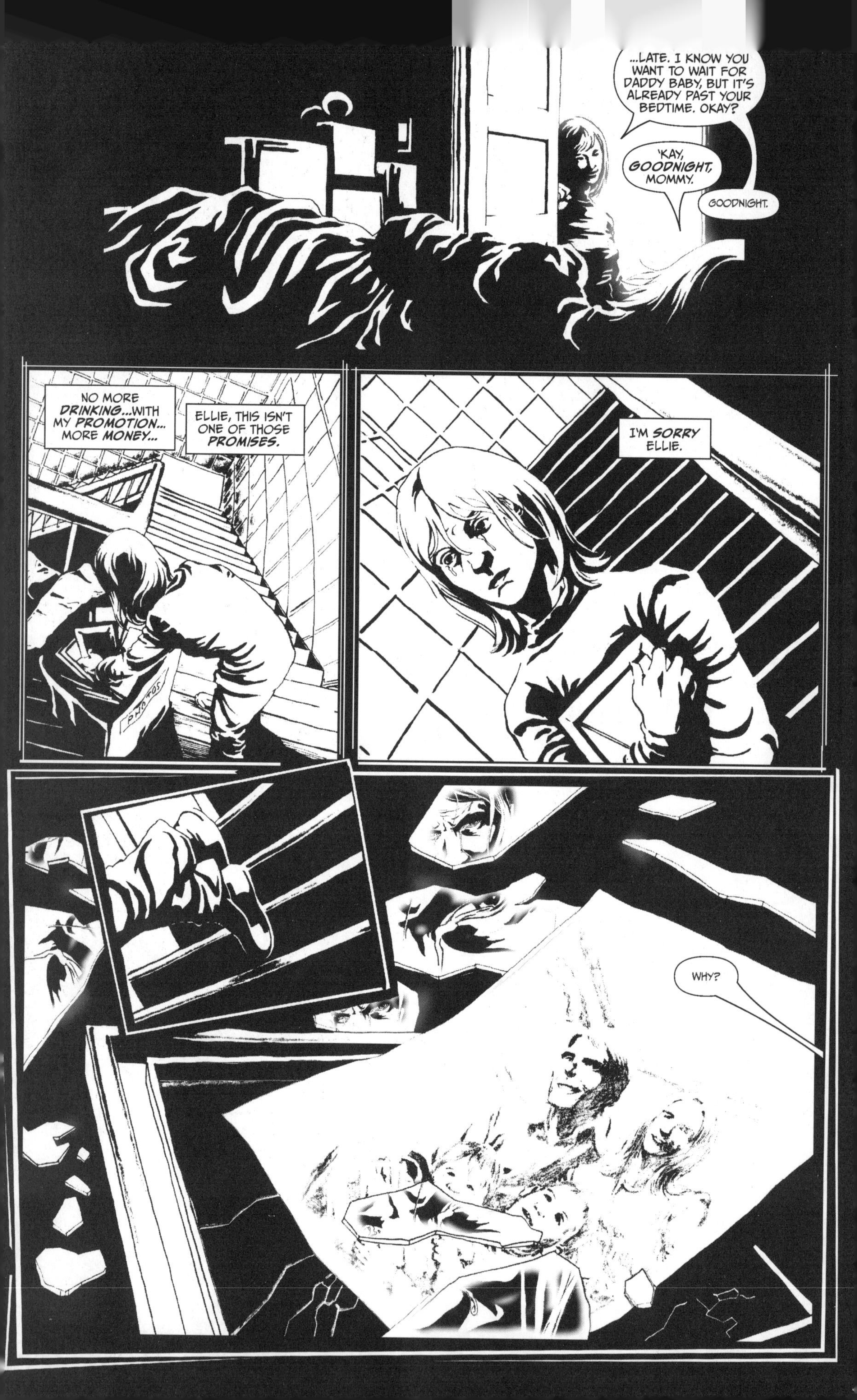
...LATE. I KNOW YOU WANT TO WAIT FOR DADDY BABY, BUT IT'S ALREADY PAST YOUR BEDTIME. OKAY?
'KAY, GOODNIGHT, MOMMY.
GOODNIGHT.
NO MORE DRINKING...WITH MY PROMOTION... MORE MONEY...
ELLIE, THIS ISN'T ONE OF THOSE PROMISES.
PHOTOS
I'M SORRY ELLIE.
WHY?

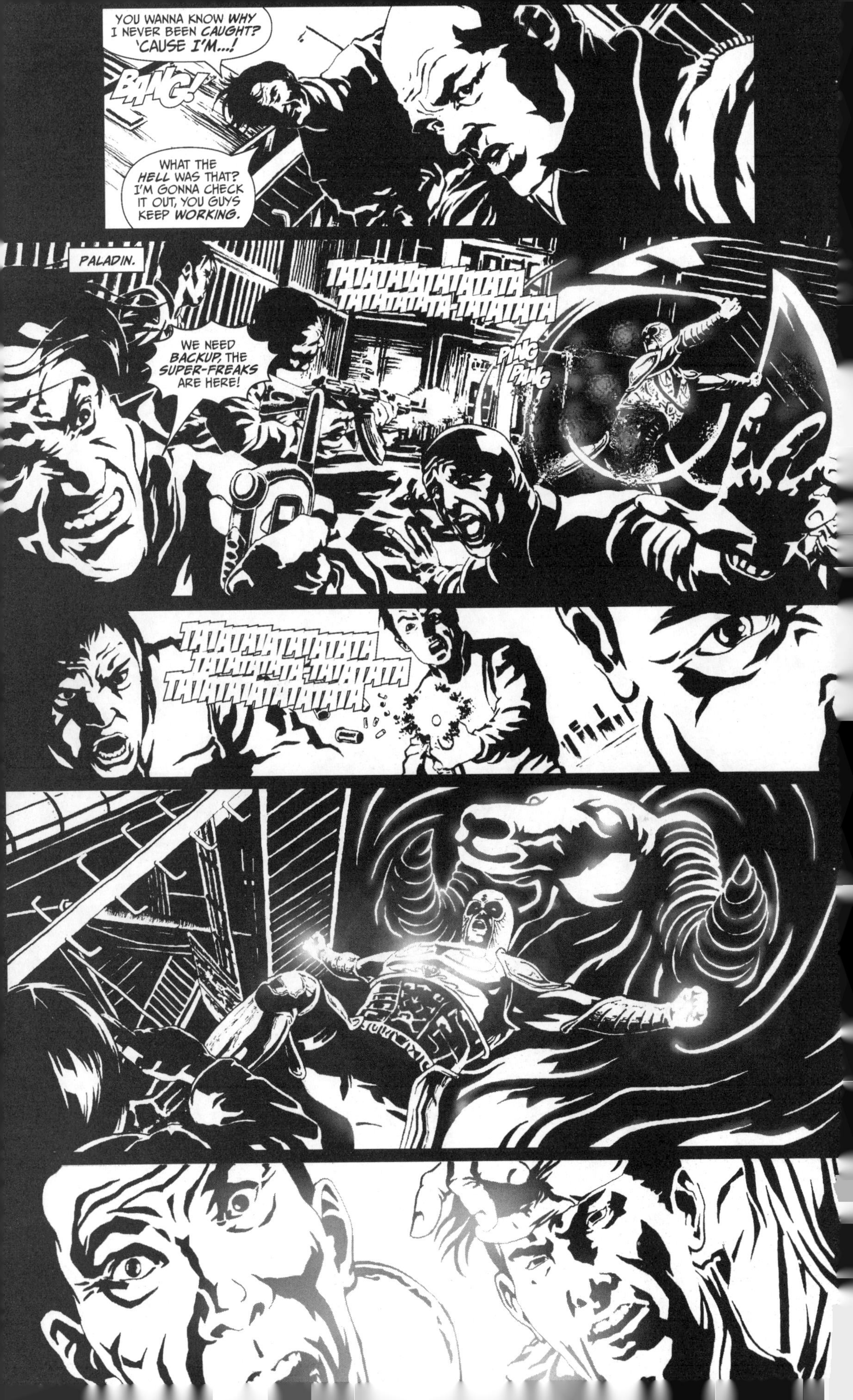

YOU WANNA KNOW WHY I NEVER BEEN CAUGHT? 'CAUSE I'M...!
BANG!
WHAT THE HELL WAS THAT? I'M GONNA CHECK IT OUT, YOU GUYS KEEP WORKING.
PALADIN.
TATATATATATATATATA TATATATATA-TATATATA
WE NEED BACKUP, THE SUPER-FREAKS ARE HERE!
PING PANG
TATATATATATATATATA TATATATATA-TATATATA TATATATATATATATATA

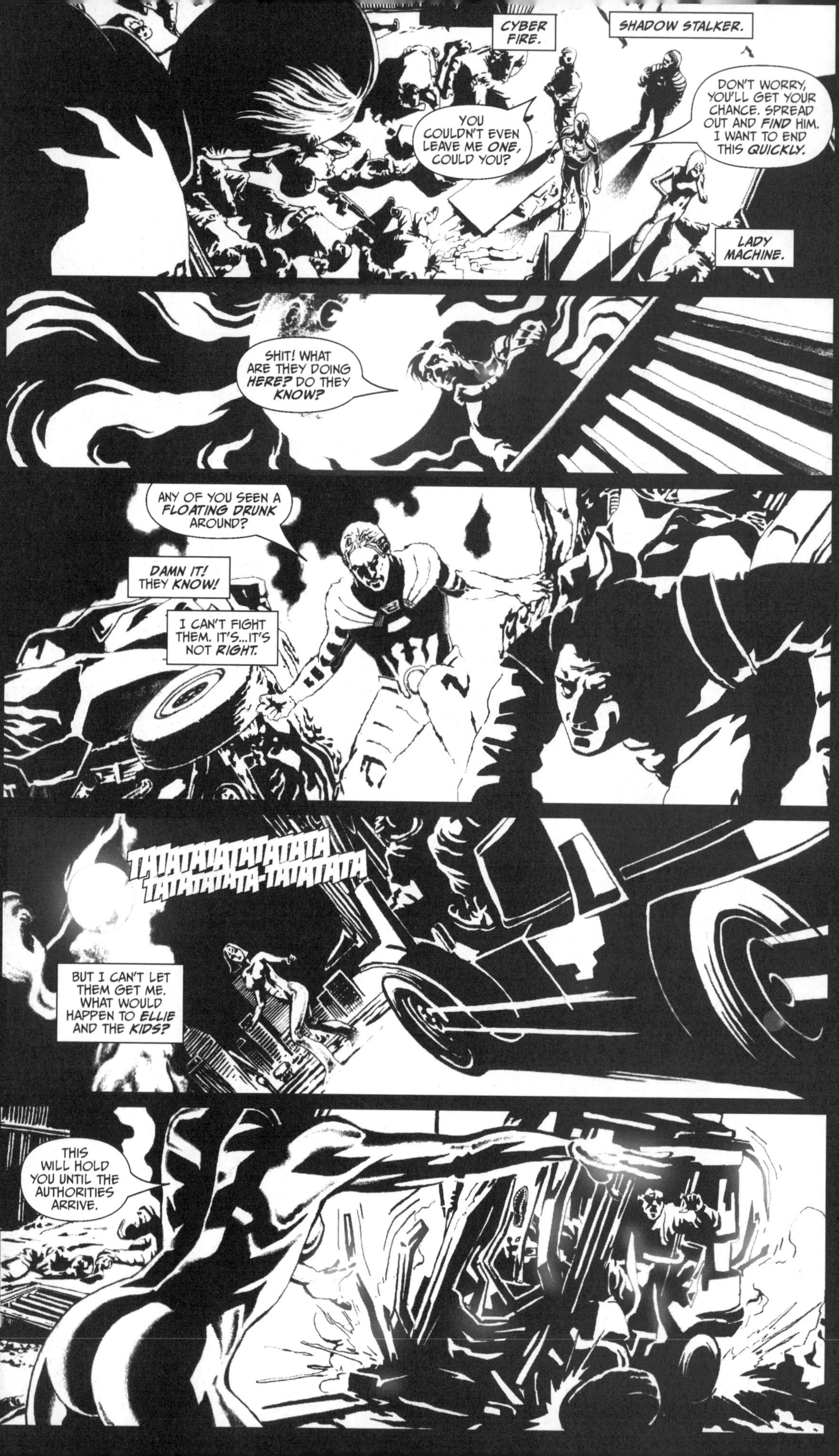
CYBER FIRE.
SHADOW STALKER.
YOU COULDN'T EVEN LEAVE ME ONE, COULD YOU?
DON'T WORRY, YOU'LL GET YOUR CHANCE. SPREAD OUT AND FIND HIM. I WANT TO END THIS QUICKLY.
LADY MACHINE.
SHIT! WHAT ARE THEY DOING HERE? DO THEY KNOW?
ANY OF YOU SEEN A FLOATING DRUNK AROUND?
DAMN IT! THEY KNOW!
I CAN'T FIGHT THEM. IT'S...IT'S NOT RIGHT.
TATATATATATATATATA TATATATATA-TATATATA
BUT I CAN'T LET THEM GET ME. WHAT WOULD HAPPEN TO ELLIE AND THE KIDS?
THIS WILL HOLD YOU UNTIL THE AUTHORITIES ARRIVE.

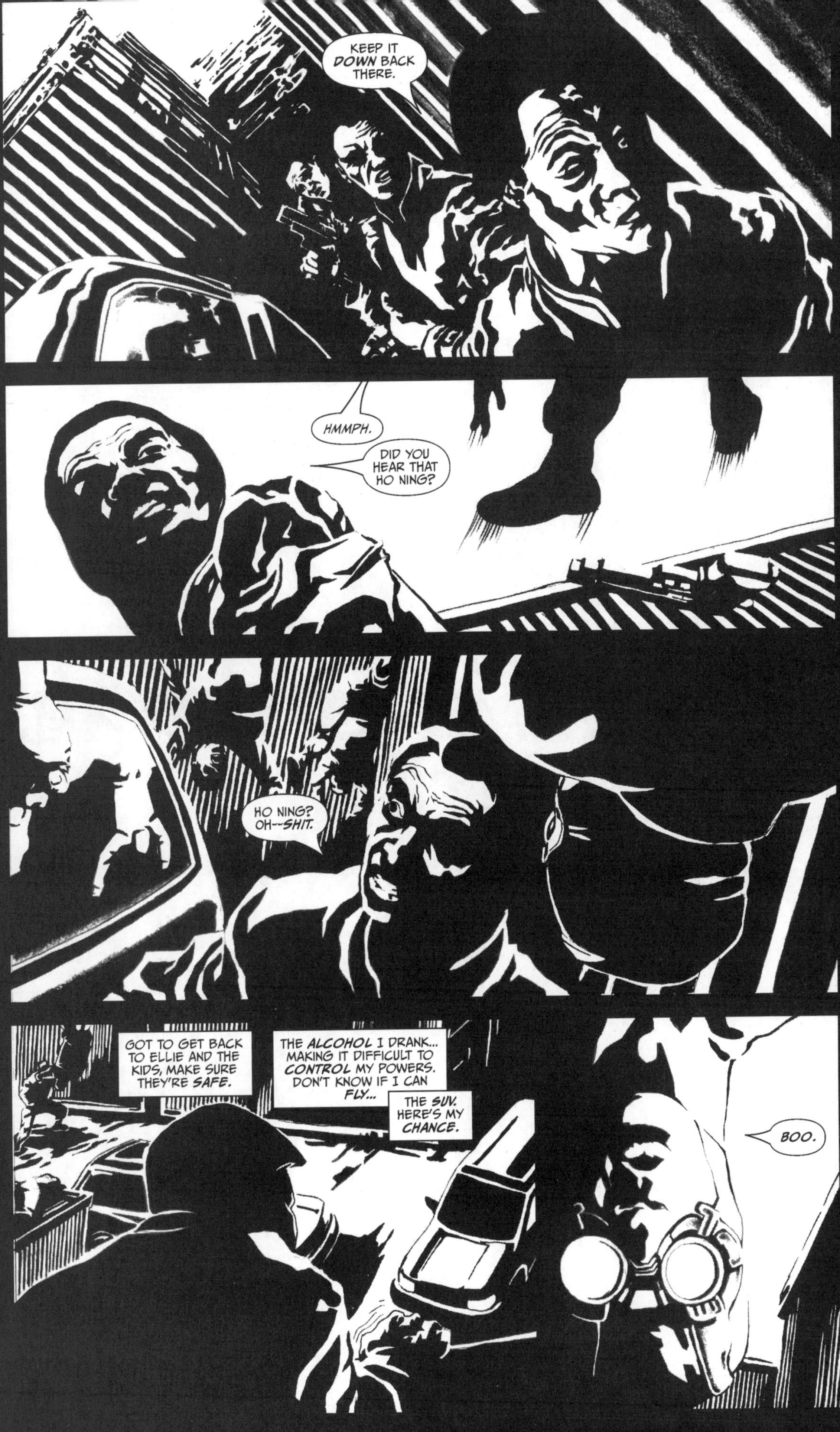
KEEP IT DOWN BACK THERE.
HMMPH.
DID YOU HEAR THAT HO NING?
HO NING? OH--SHIT.
GOT TO GET BACK TO ELLIE AND THE KIDS, MAKE SURE THEY'RE SAFE.
THE ALCOHOL I DRANK... MAKING IT DIFFICULT TO CONTROL MY POWERS. DON'T KNOW IF I CAN FLY...
THE SUV. HERE'S MY CHANCE.
BOO.

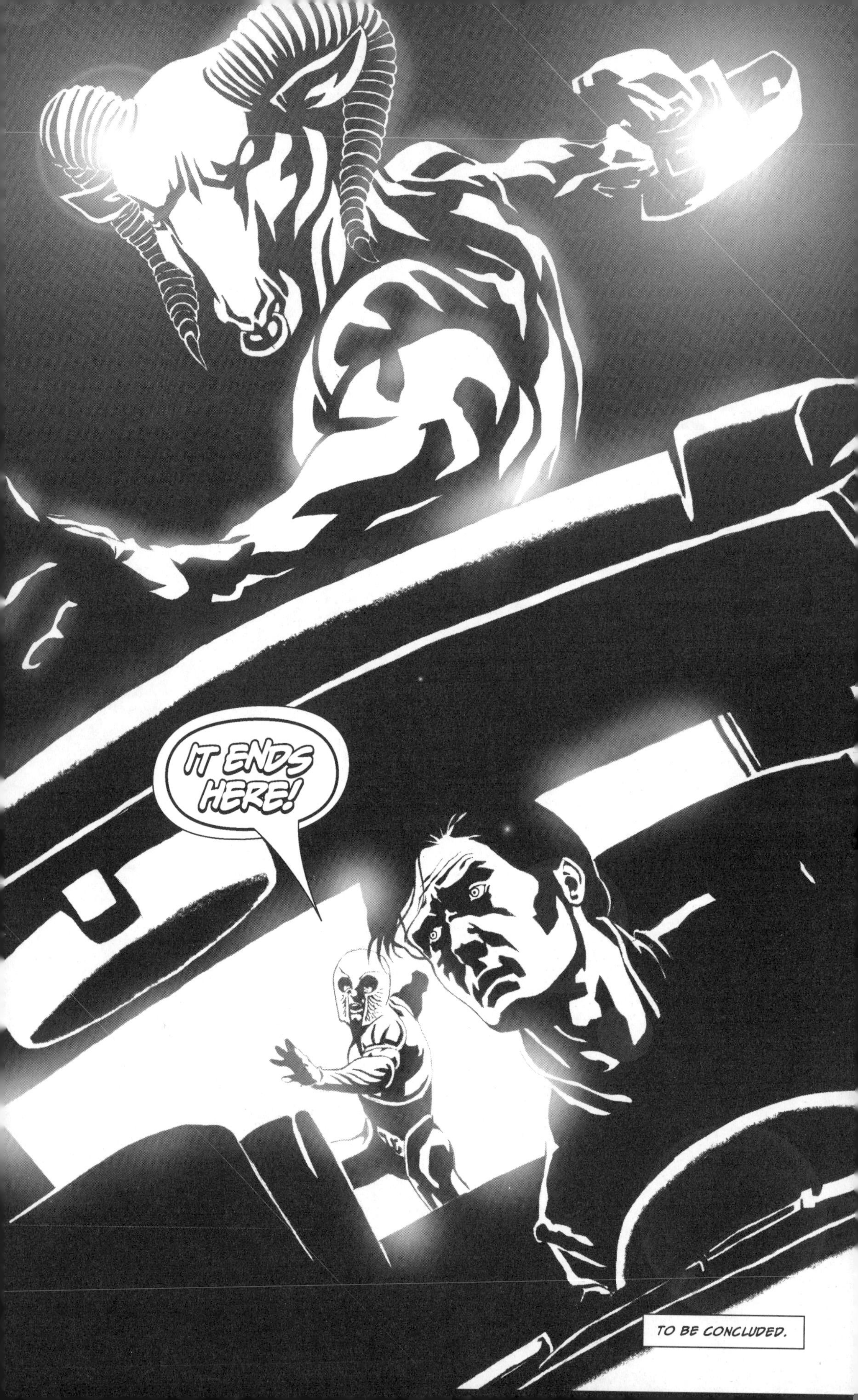
IT ENDS HERE!
TO BE CONCLUDED.

CHAPTER THREE: POINT OF NO RETURN

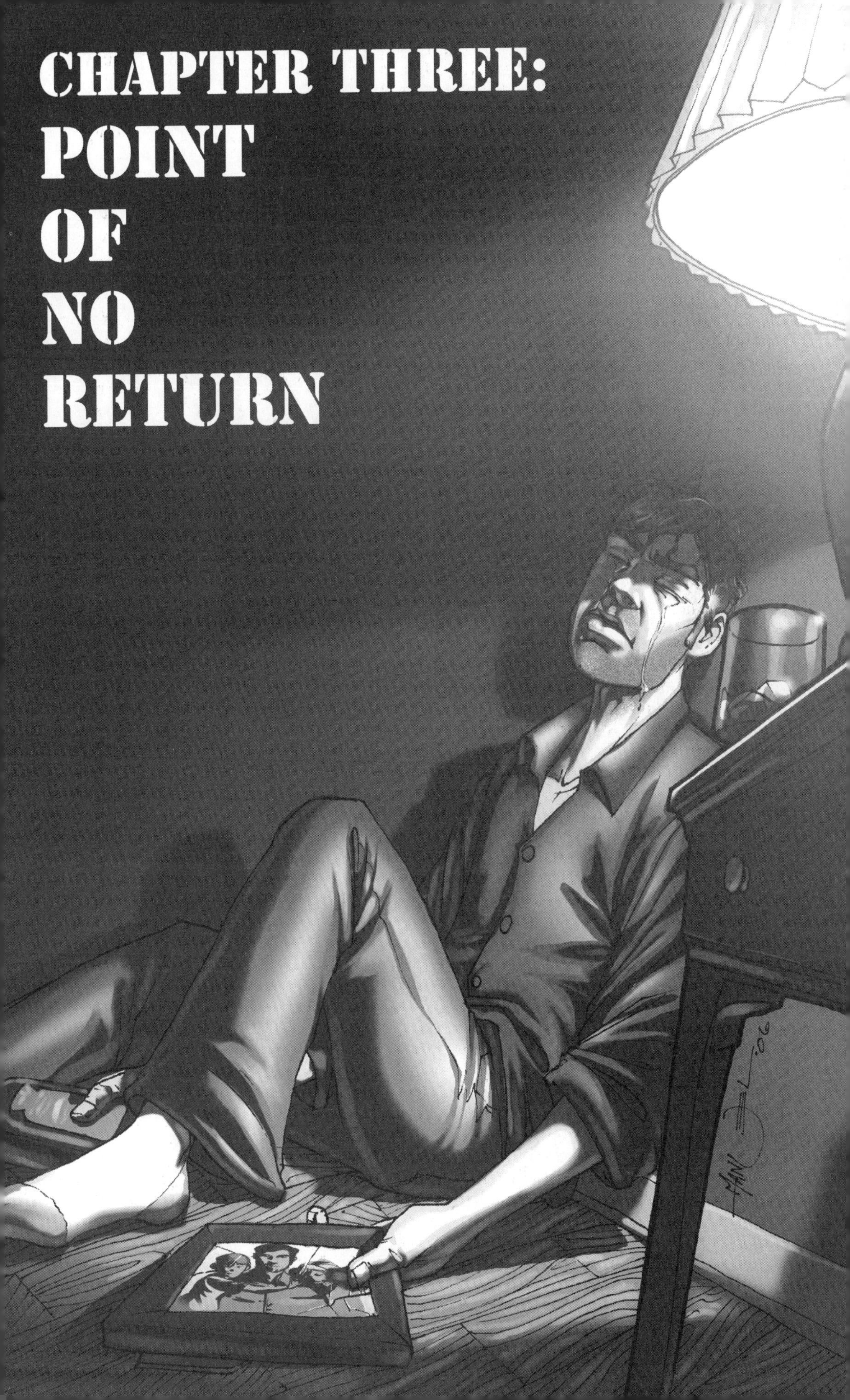

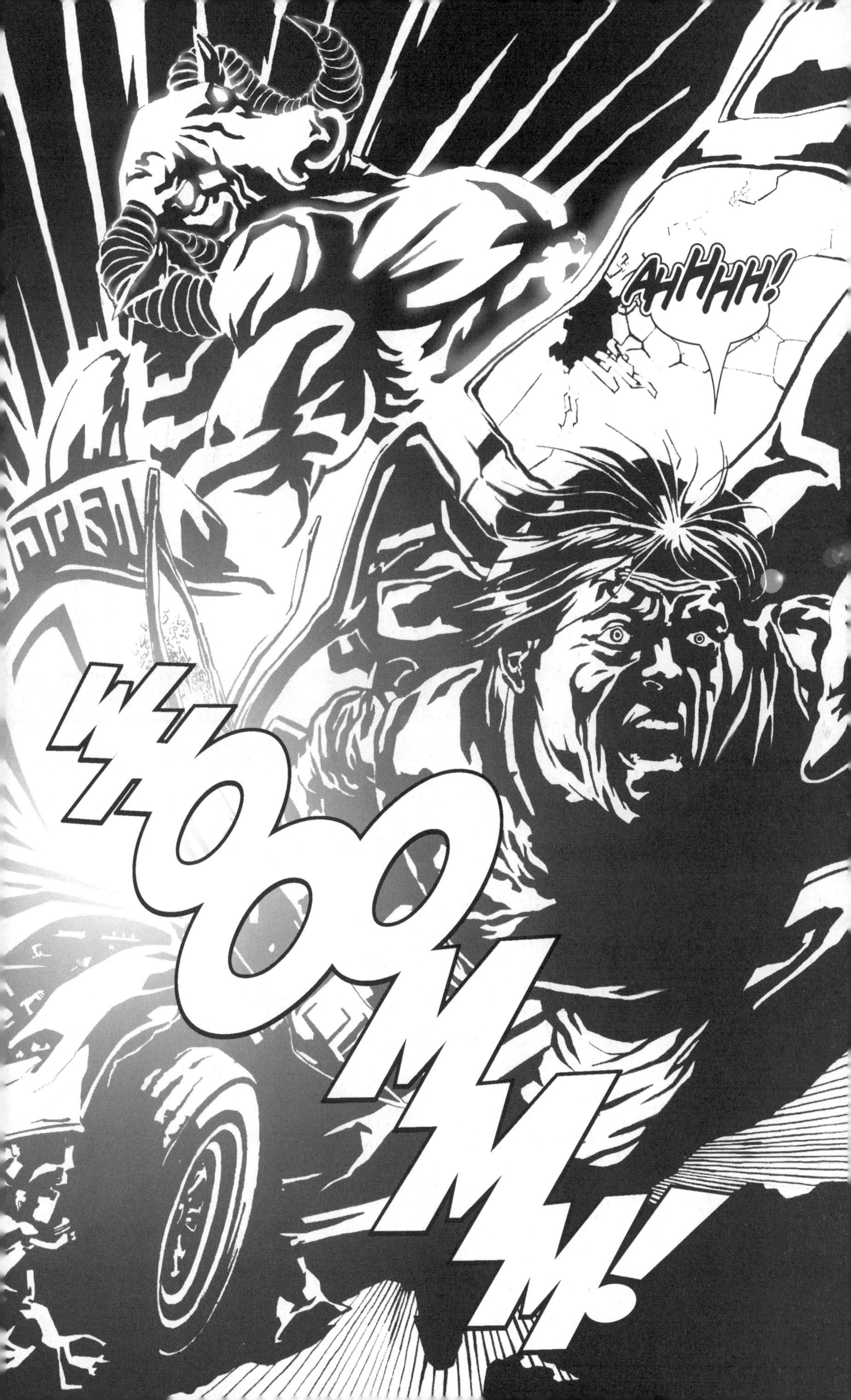
AHHHH!
WHOOMM!

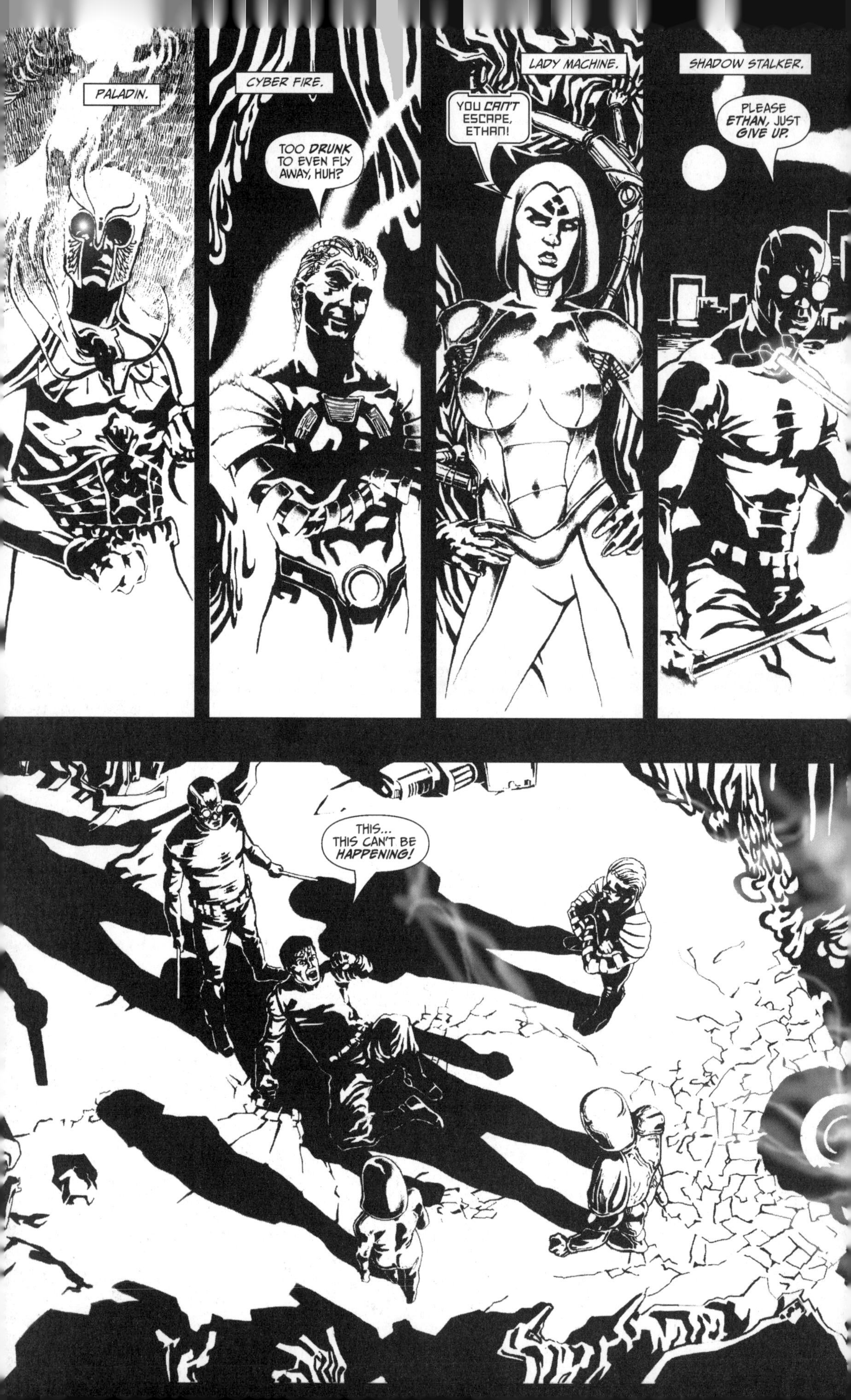
PALADIN.
CYBER FIRE.
TOO DRUNK TO EVEN FLY AWAY, HUH?
LADY MACHINE.
YOU CAN'T ESCAPE, ETHAN!
SHADOW STALKER.
PLEASE ETHAN, JUST GIVE UP.
THIS... THIS CAN'T BE HAPPENING!

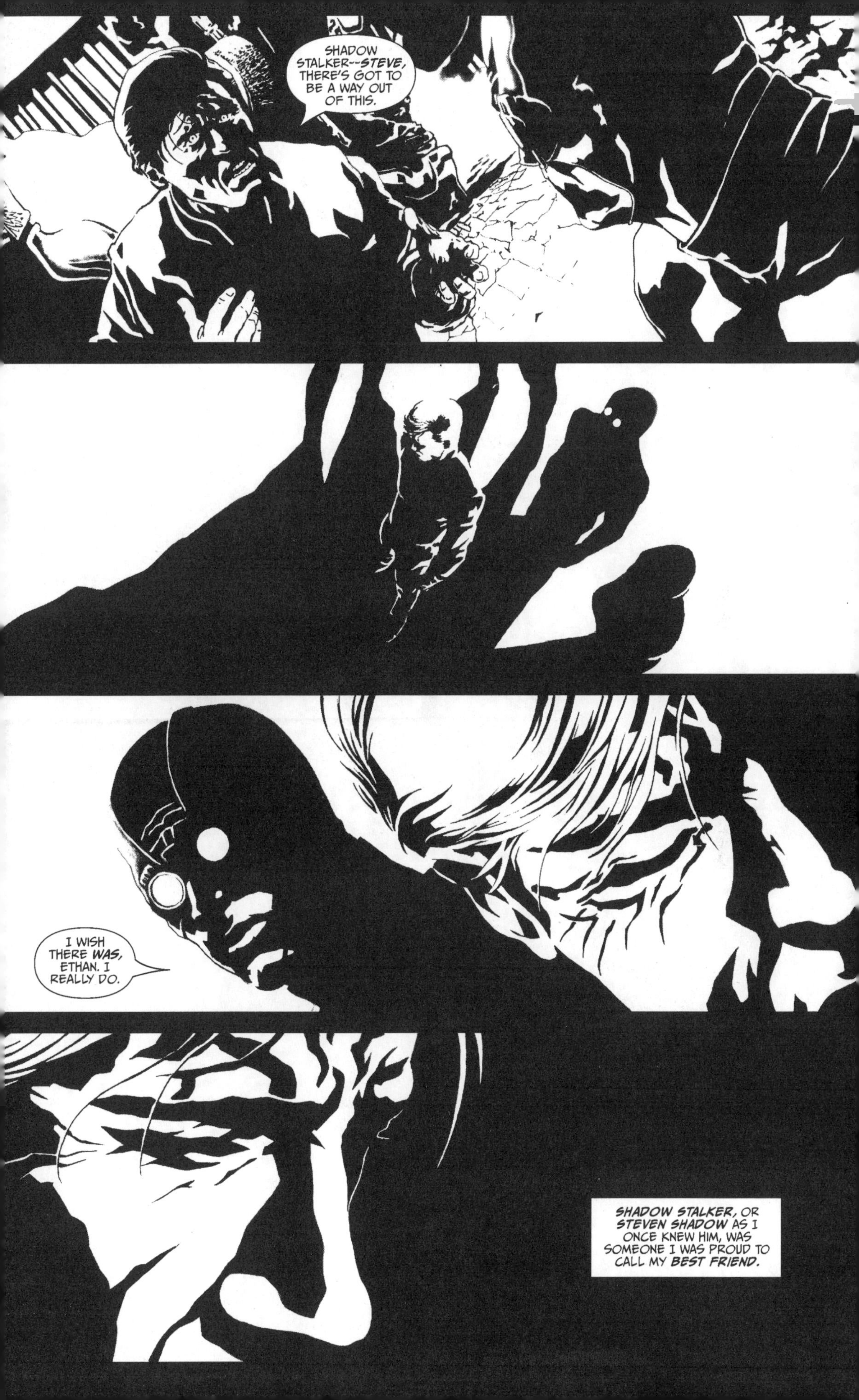
SHADOW STALKER--STEVE, THERE'S GOT TO BE A WAY OUT OF THIS.
I WISH THERE WAS, ETHAN. I REALLY DO.
SHADOW STALKER, OR STEVEN SHADOW AS I ONCE KNEW HIM, WAS SOMEONE I WAS PROUD TO CALL MY BEST FRIEND.

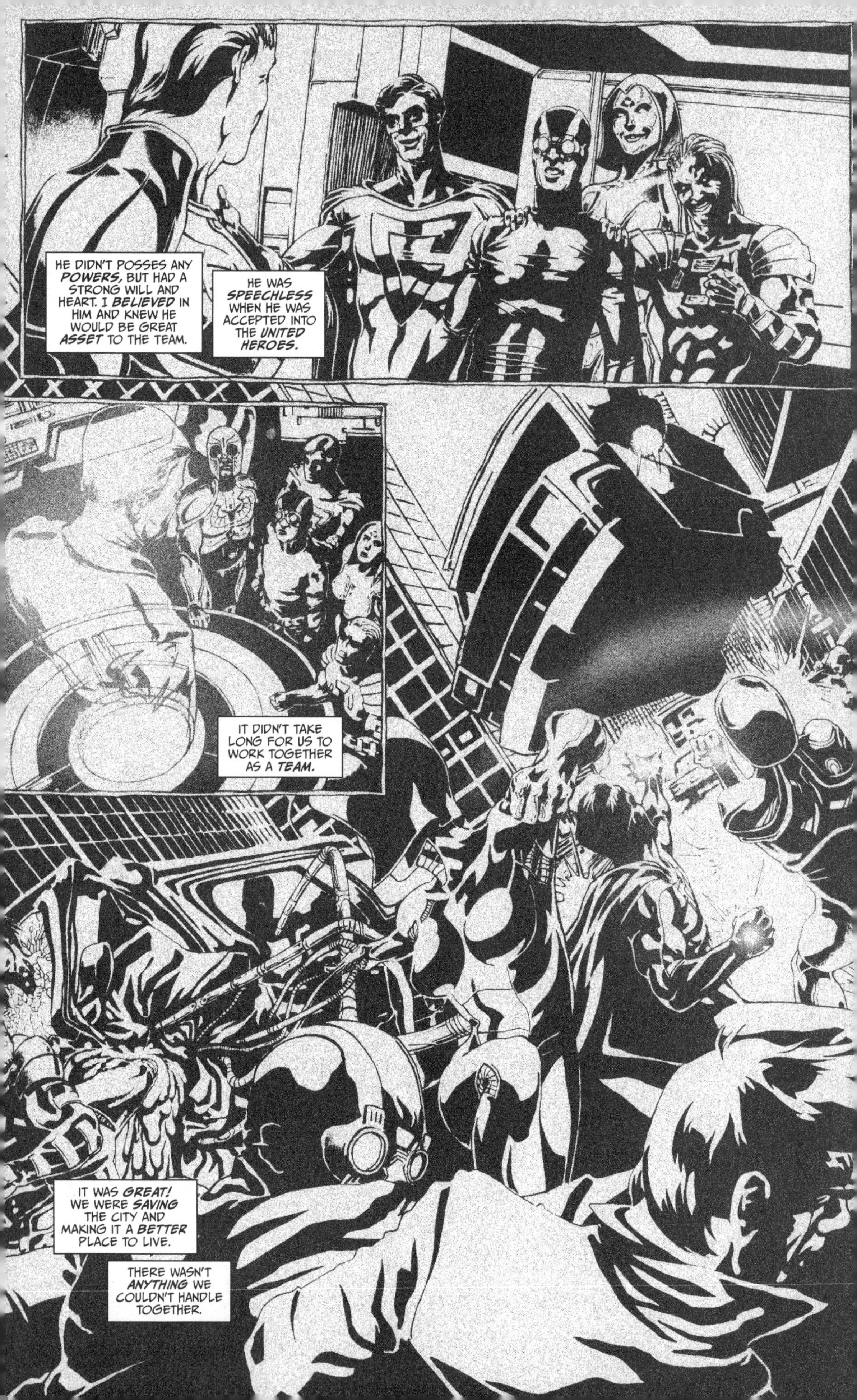
HE DIDN'T POSSES ANY POWERS, BUT HAD A STRONG WILL AND HEART. I BELIEVED IN HIM AND KNEW HE WOULD BE GREAT ASSET TO THE TEAM.
HE WAS SPEECHLESS WHEN HE WAS ACCEPTED INTO THE UNITED HEROES.
IT DIDN'T TAKE LONG FOR US TO WORK TOGETHER AS A TEAM.
IT WAS GREAT! WE WERE SAVING THE CITY AND MAKING IT A BETTER PLACE TO LIVE.
THERE WASN'T ANYTHING WE COULDN'T HANDLE TOGETHER.

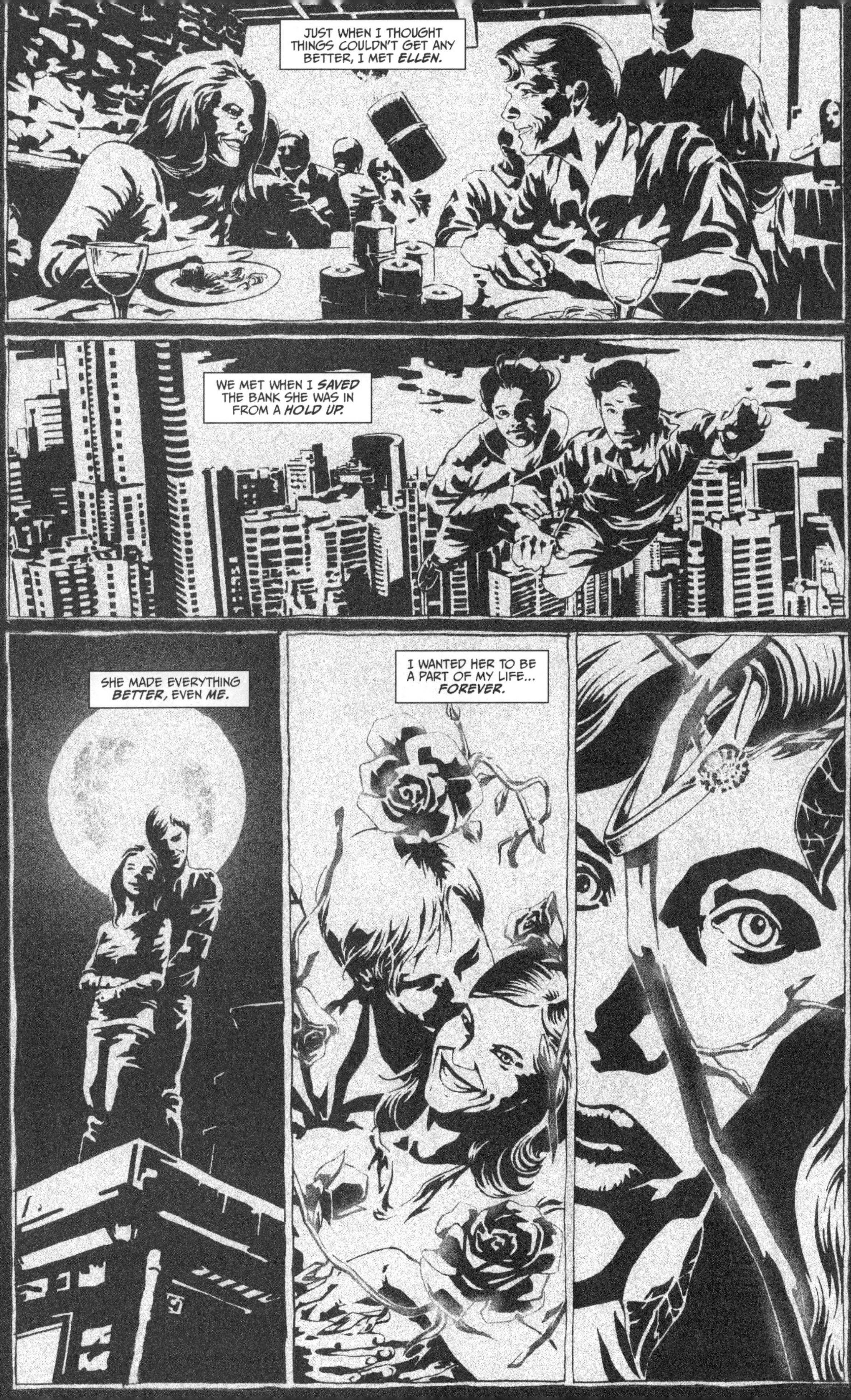
JUST WHEN I THOUGHT THINGS COULDN'T GET ANY BETTER, I MET ELLEN.
WE MET WHEN I SAVED THE BANK SHE WAS IN FROM A HOLD UP.
SHE MADE EVERYTHING BETTER, EVEN ME.
I WANTED HER TO BE A PART OF MY LIFE... FOREVER.

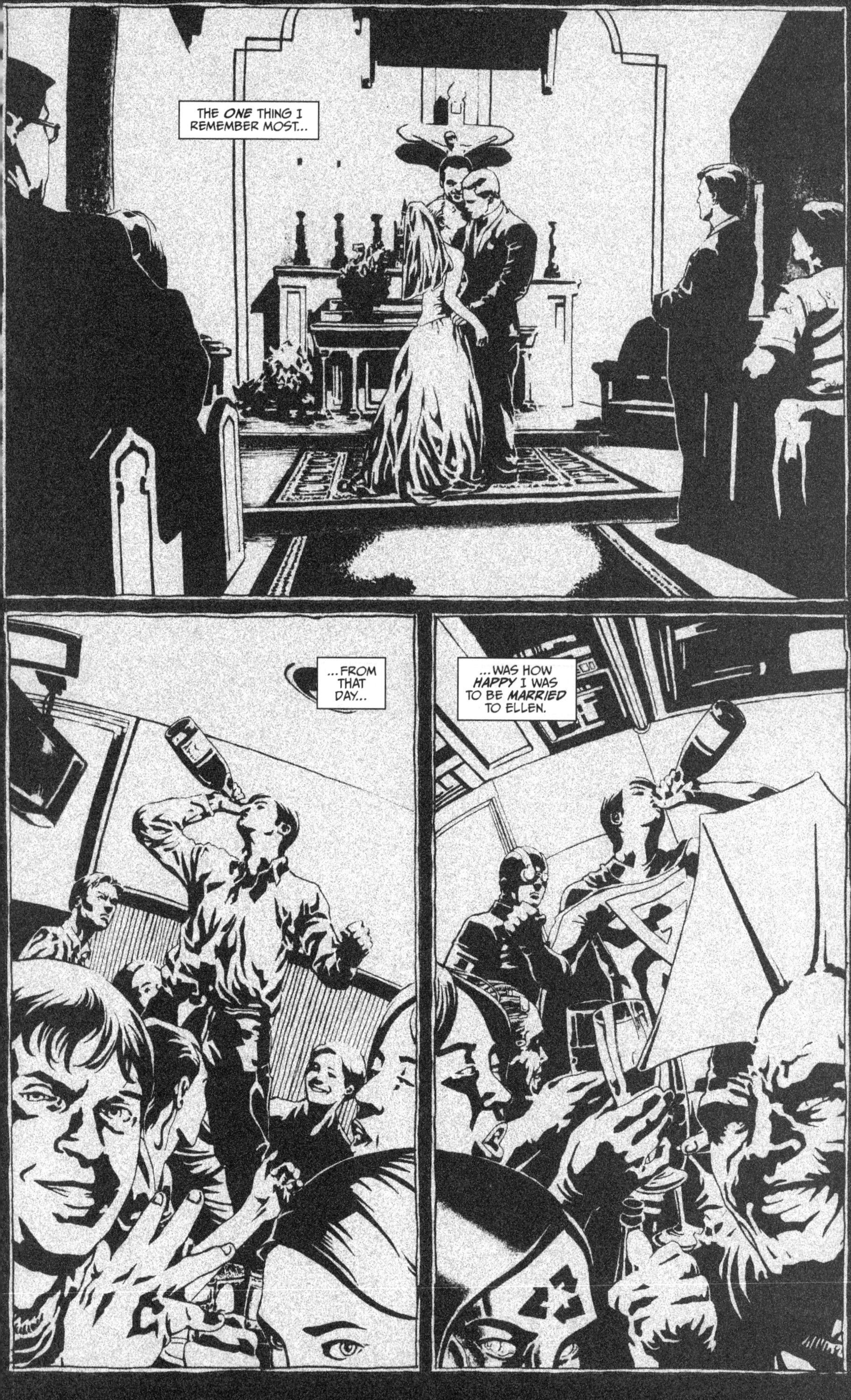
THE ONE THING I REMEMBER MOST...
...FROM THAT DAY...
...WAS HOW HAPPY I WAS TO BE MARRIED TO ELLEN.

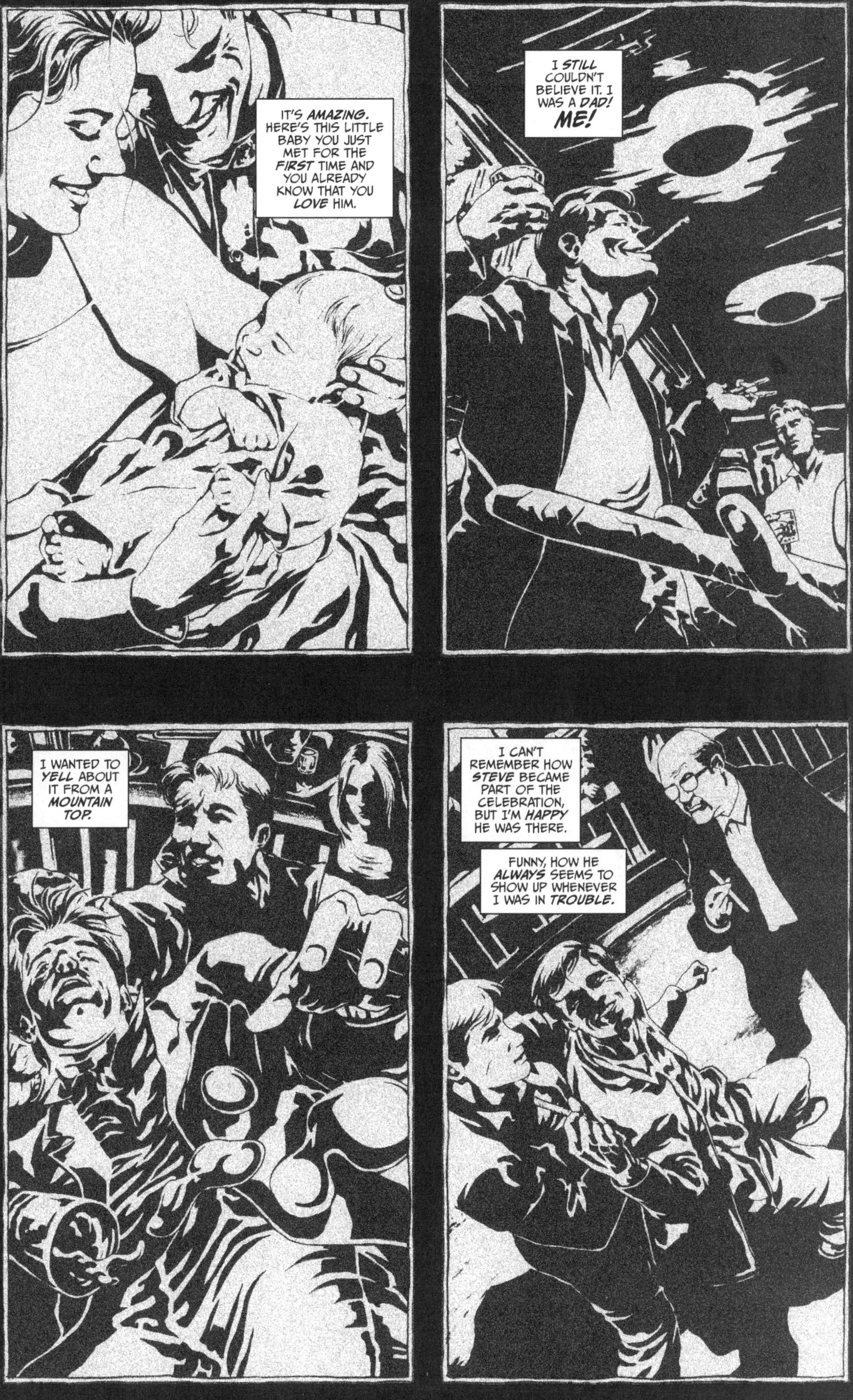
IT'S AMAZING. HERE'S THIS LITTLE BABY YOU JUST MET FOR THE FIRST TIME AND YOU ALREADY KNOW THAT YOU LOVE HIM.
I STILL COULDN'T BELIEVE IT. I WAS A DAD! ME!
I WANTED TO YELL ABOUT IT FROM A MOUNTAIN TOP.
I CAN'T REMEMBER HOW STEVE BECAME PART OF THE CELEBRATION, BUT I'M HAPPY HE WAS THERE.
FUNNY, HOW HE ALWAYS SEEMS TO SHOW UP WHENEVER I WAS IN TROUBLE.

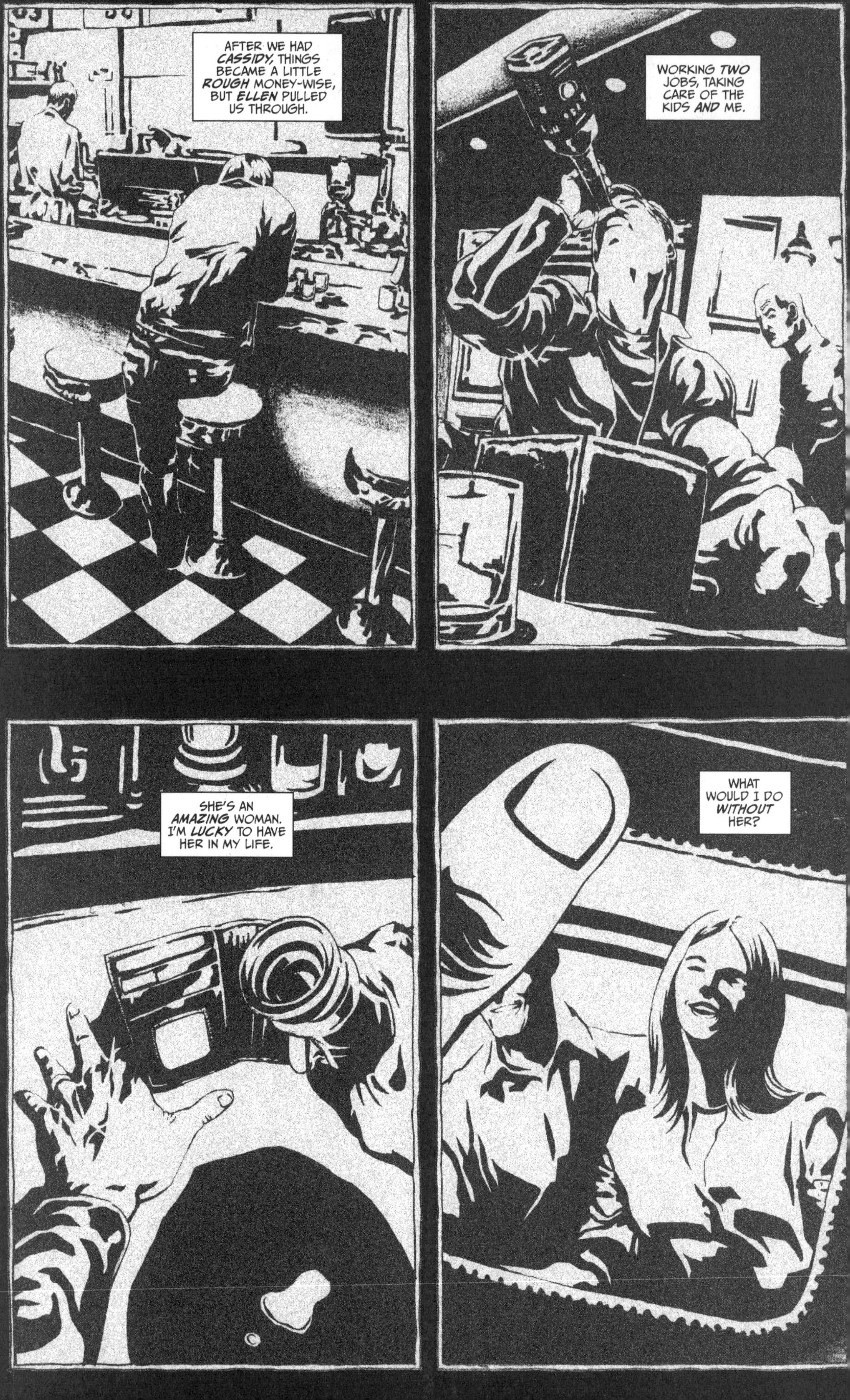
AFTER WE HAD CASSIDY, THINGS BECAME A LITTLE ROUGH MONEY-WISE, BUT ELLEN PULLED US THROUGH.
WORKING TWO JOBS, TAKING CARE OF THE KIDS AND ME.
SHE'S AN AMAZING WOMAN. I'M LUCKY TO HAVE HER IN MY LIFE.
WHAT WOULD I DO WITHOUT HER?

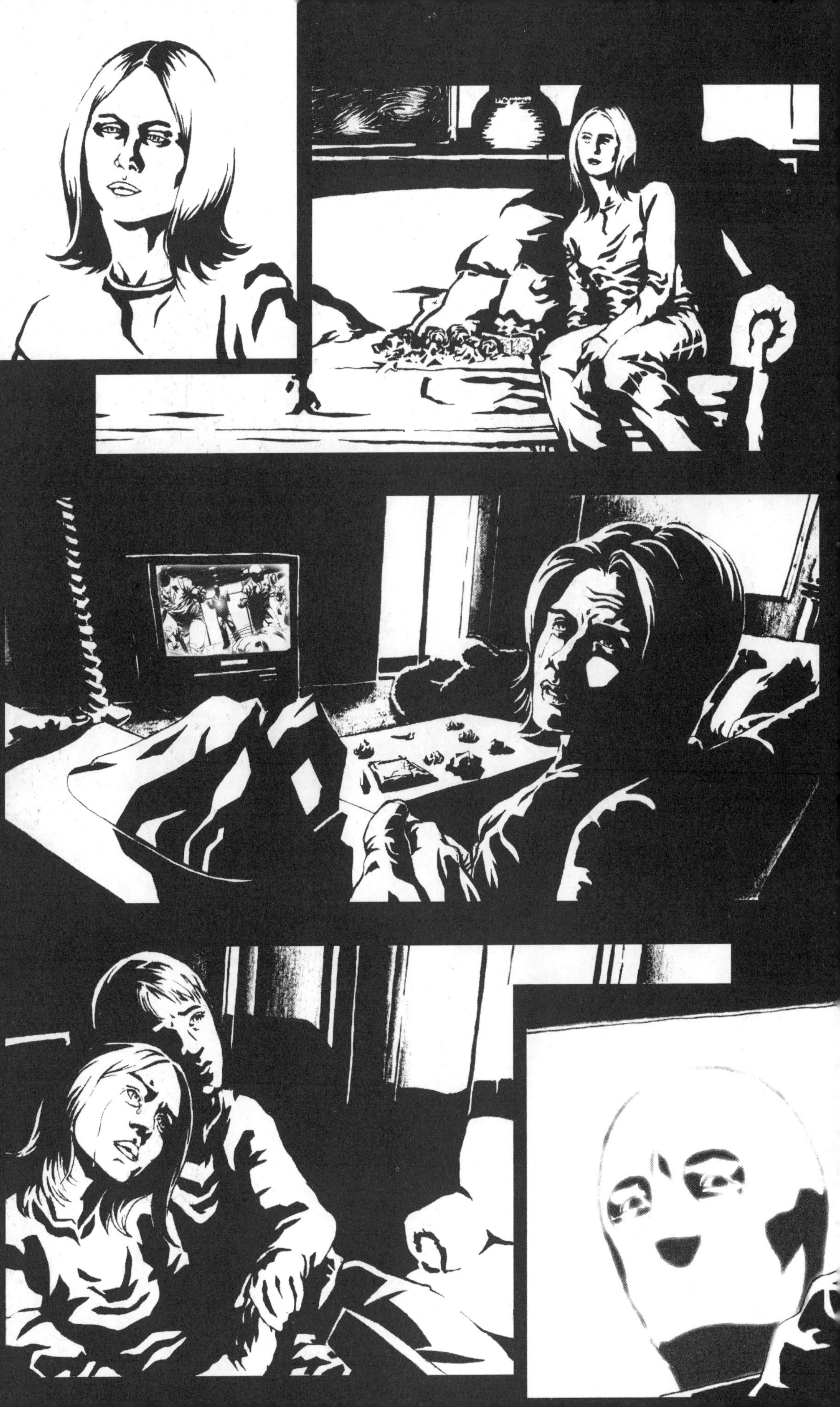

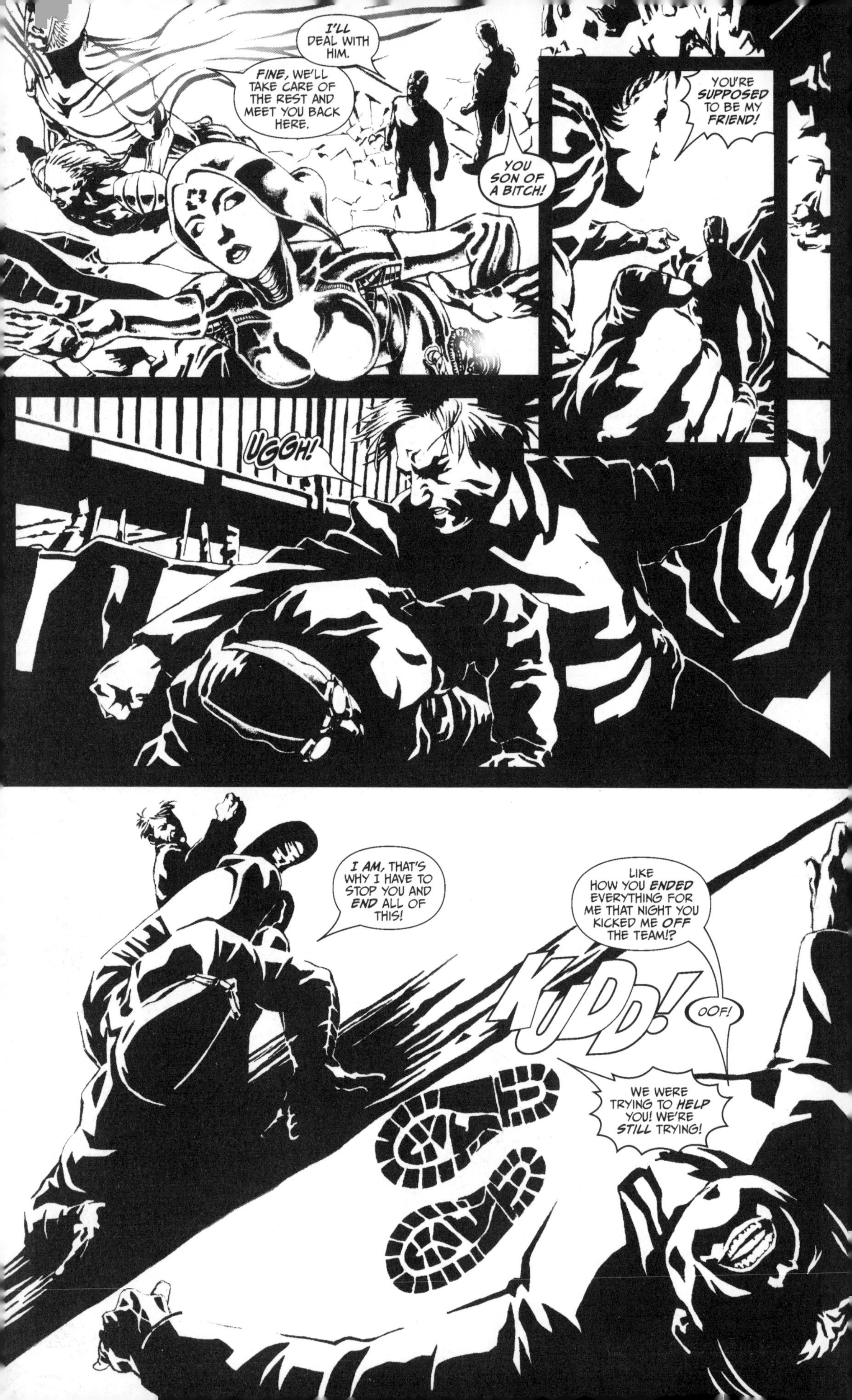
I'LL DEAL WITH HIM.
FINE, WE'LL TAKE CARE OF THE REST AND MEET YOU BACK HERE.
YOU SON OF A BITCH!
YOU'RE SUPPOSED TO BE MY FRIEND!
UGGH!
I AM, THAT'S WHY I HAVE TO STOP YOU AND END ALL OF THIS!
LIKE HOW YOU ENDED EVERYTHING FOR ME THAT NIGHT YOU KICKED ME OFF THE TEAM!?
KUDD!
OOF!
WE WERE TRYING TO HELP YOU! WE'RE STILL TRYING!

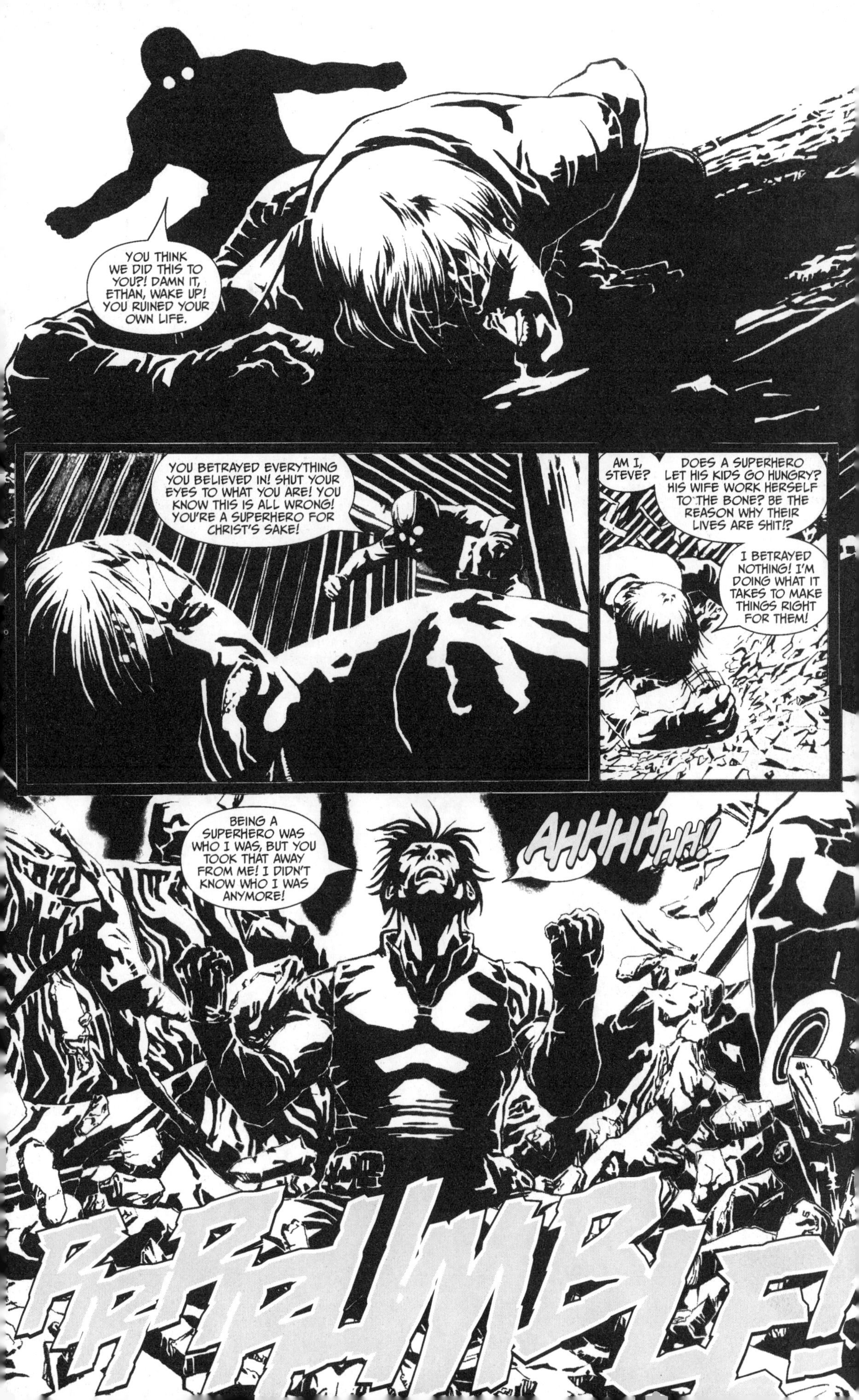
YOU THINK WE DID THIS TO YOU?! DAMN IT, ETHAN, WAKE UP! YOU RUINED YOUR OWN LIFE.
YOU BETRAYED EVERYTHING YOU BELIEVED IN! SHUT YOUR EYES TO WHAT YOU ARE! YOU KNOW THIS IS ALL WRONG! YOU'RE A SUPERHERO FOR CHRIST'S SAKE!
AM I, STEVE?
DOES A SUPERHERO LET HIS KIDS GO HUNGRY? HIS WIFE WORK HERSELF TO THE BONE? BE THE REASON WHY THEIR LIVES ARE SHIT!?
I BETRAYED NOTHING! I'M DOING WHAT IT TAKES TO MAKE THINGS RIGHT FOR THEM!
BEING A SUPERHERO WAS WHO I WAS, BUT YOU TOOK THAT AWAY FROM ME! I DIDN'T KNOW WHO I WAS ANYMORE!
AHHHHHH!
RRRUMBLE!

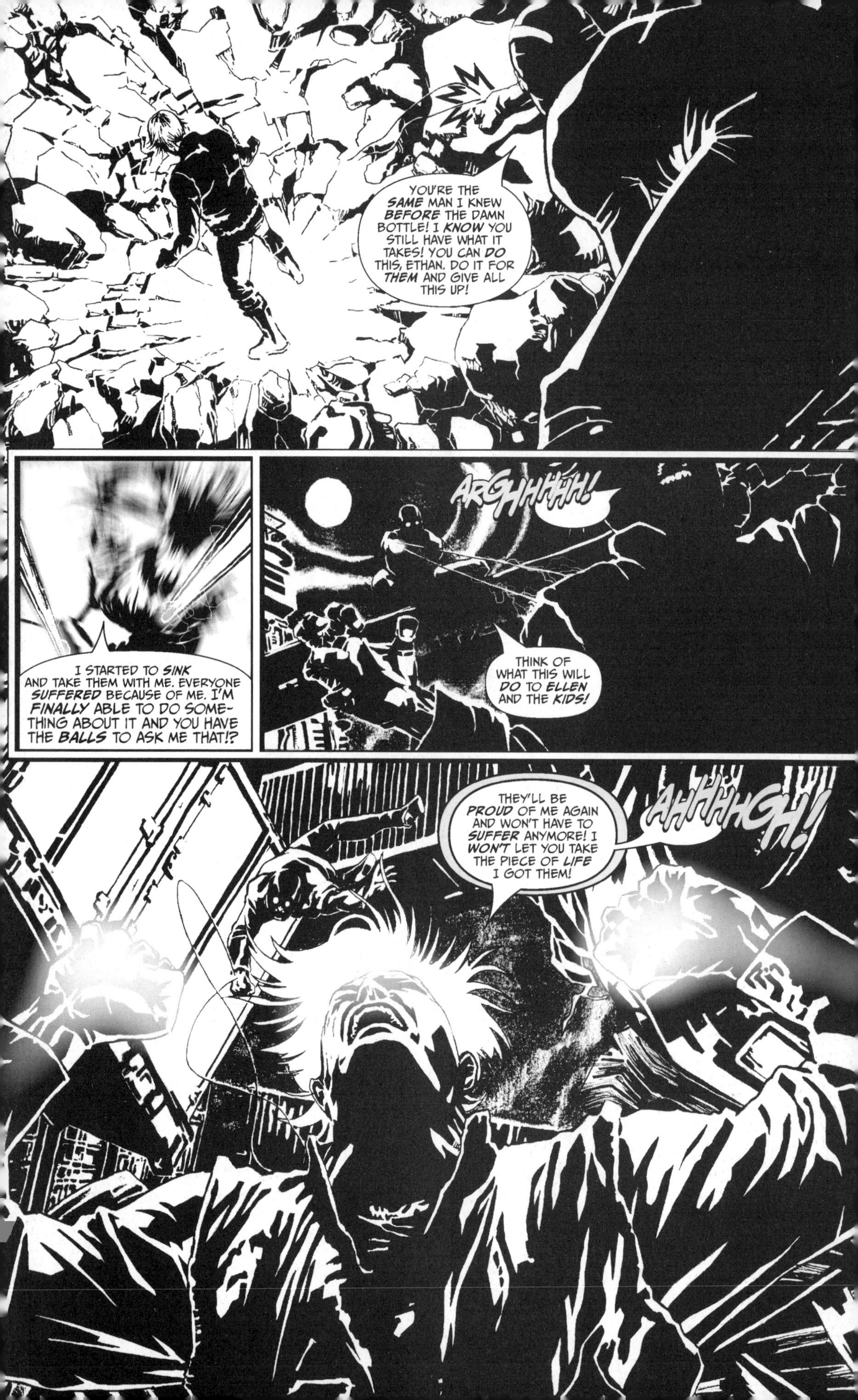
YOU'RE THE SAME MAN I KNEW BEFORE THE DAMN BOTTLE! I KNOW YOU STILL HAVE WHAT IT TAKES! YOU CAN DO THIS, ETHAN. DO IT FOR THEM AND GIVE ALL THIS UP!
I STARTED TO SINK AND TAKE THEM WITH ME. EVERYONE SUFFERED BECAUSE OF ME. I'M FINALLY ABLE TO DO SOMETHING ABOUT IT AND YOU HAVE THE BALLS TO ASK ME THAT!?
ARGHHHHH!
THINK OF WHAT THIS WILL DO TO ELLEN AND THE KIDS!
THEY'LL BE PROUD OF ME AGAIN AND WON'T HAVE TO SUFFER ANYMORE! I WON'T LET YOU TAKE THE PIECE OF LIFE I GOT THEM!
AHHHHGH!

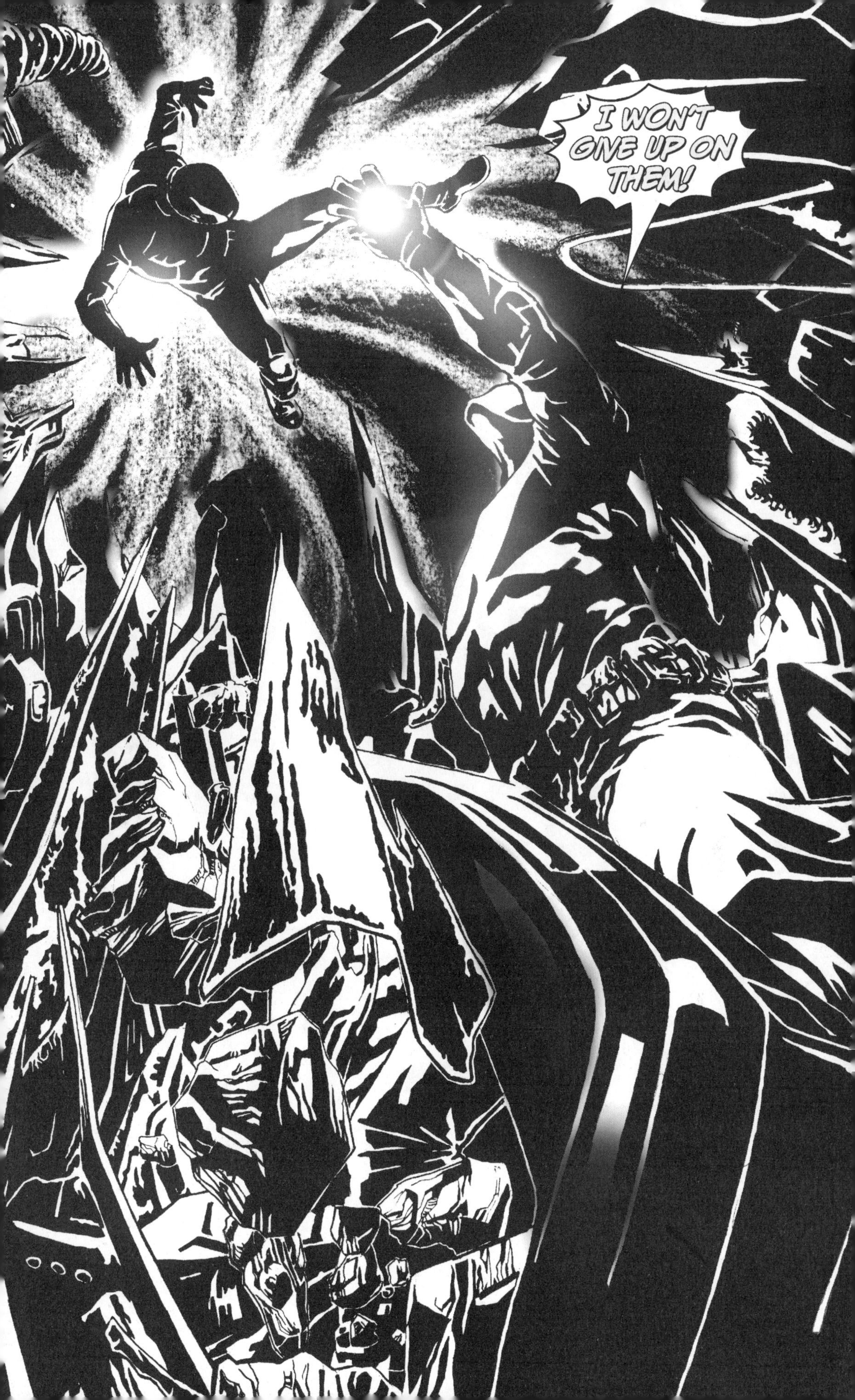
I WON'T GIVE UP ON THEM!

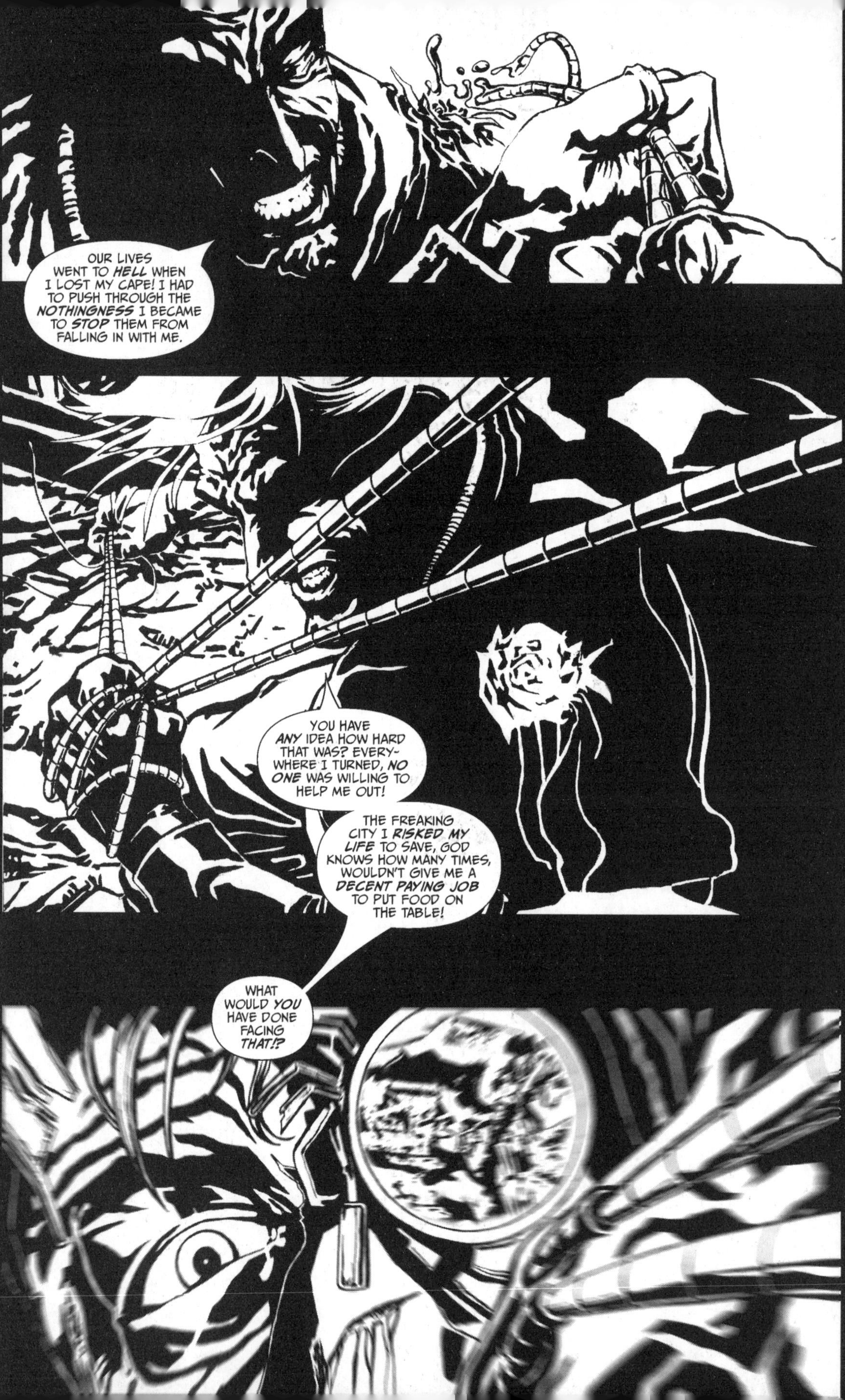
OUR LIVES WENT TO HELL WHEN I LOST MY CAPE! I HAD TO PUSH THROUGH THE NOTHINGNESS I BECAME TO STOP THEM FROM FALLING IN WITH ME.
YOU HAVE ANY IDEA HOW HARD THAT WAS? EVERY-WHERE I TURNED, NO ONE WAS WILLING TO HELP ME OUT!
THE FREAKING CITY I RISKED MY LIFE TO SAVE, GOD KNOWS HOW MANY TIMES, WOULDN'T GIVE ME A DECENT PAYING JOB TO PUT FOOD ON THE TABLE!
WHAT WOULD YOU HAVE DONE FACING THAT!?

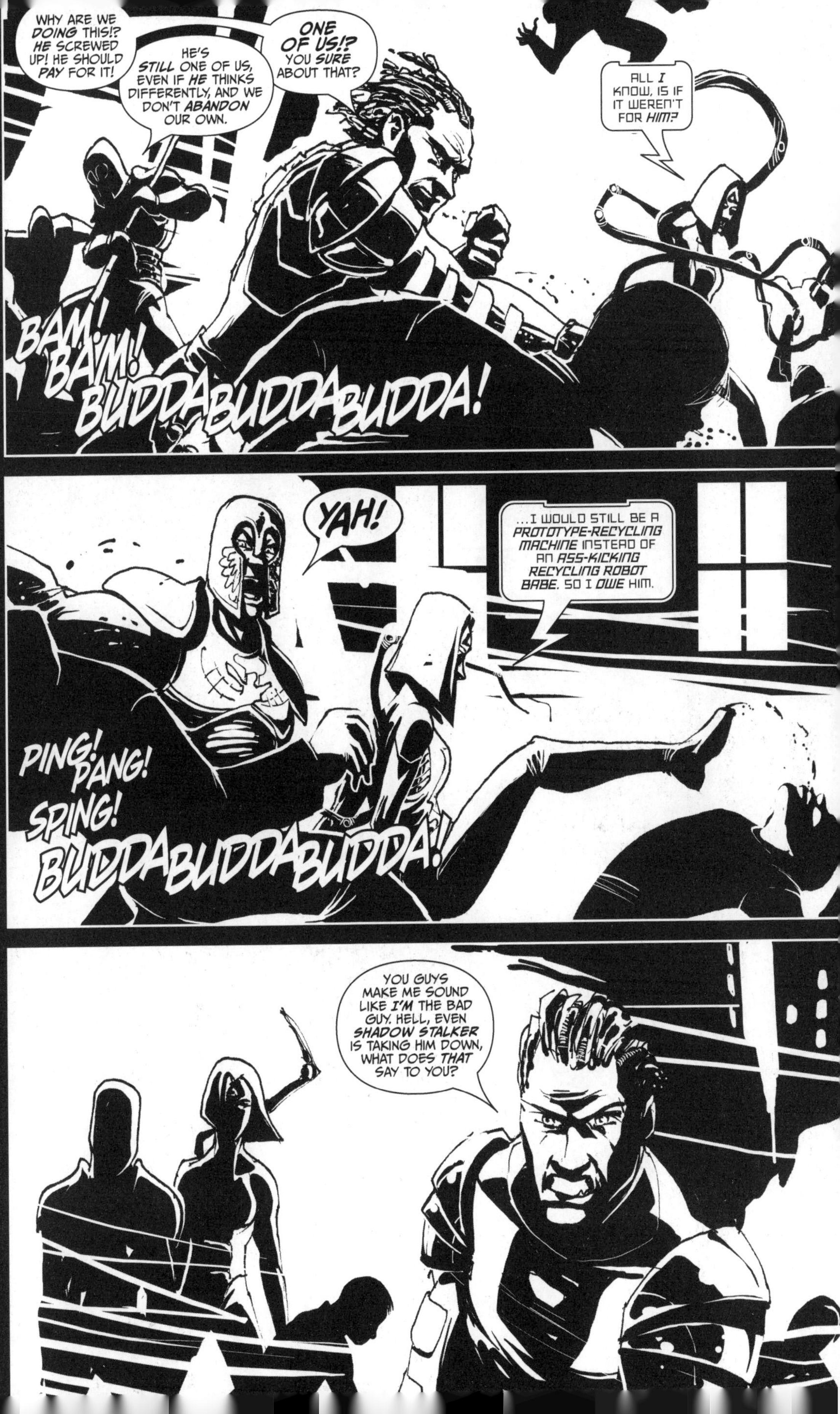
WHY ARE WE DOING THIS!? HE SCREWED UP! HE SHOULD PAY FOR IT!
HE'S STILL ONE OF US, EVEN IF HE THINKS DIFFERENTLY, AND WE DON'T ABANDON OUR OWN.
ONE OF US!? YOU SURE ABOUT THAT?
ALL I KNOW, IS IF IT WEREN'T FOR HIM?
BAM! BAM! BUDDABUDDABUDDA!
YAH!
...I WOULD STILL BE A PROTOTYPE-RECYCLING MACHINE INSTEAD OF AN ASS-KICKING RECYCLING ROBOT BABE. SO I OWE HIM.
PING! PANG! SPING! BUDDABUDDABUDDA!
YOU GUYS MAKE ME SOUND LIKE I'M THE BAD GUY. HELL, EVEN SHADOW STALKER IS TAKING HIM DOWN, WHAT DOES THAT SAY TO YOU?

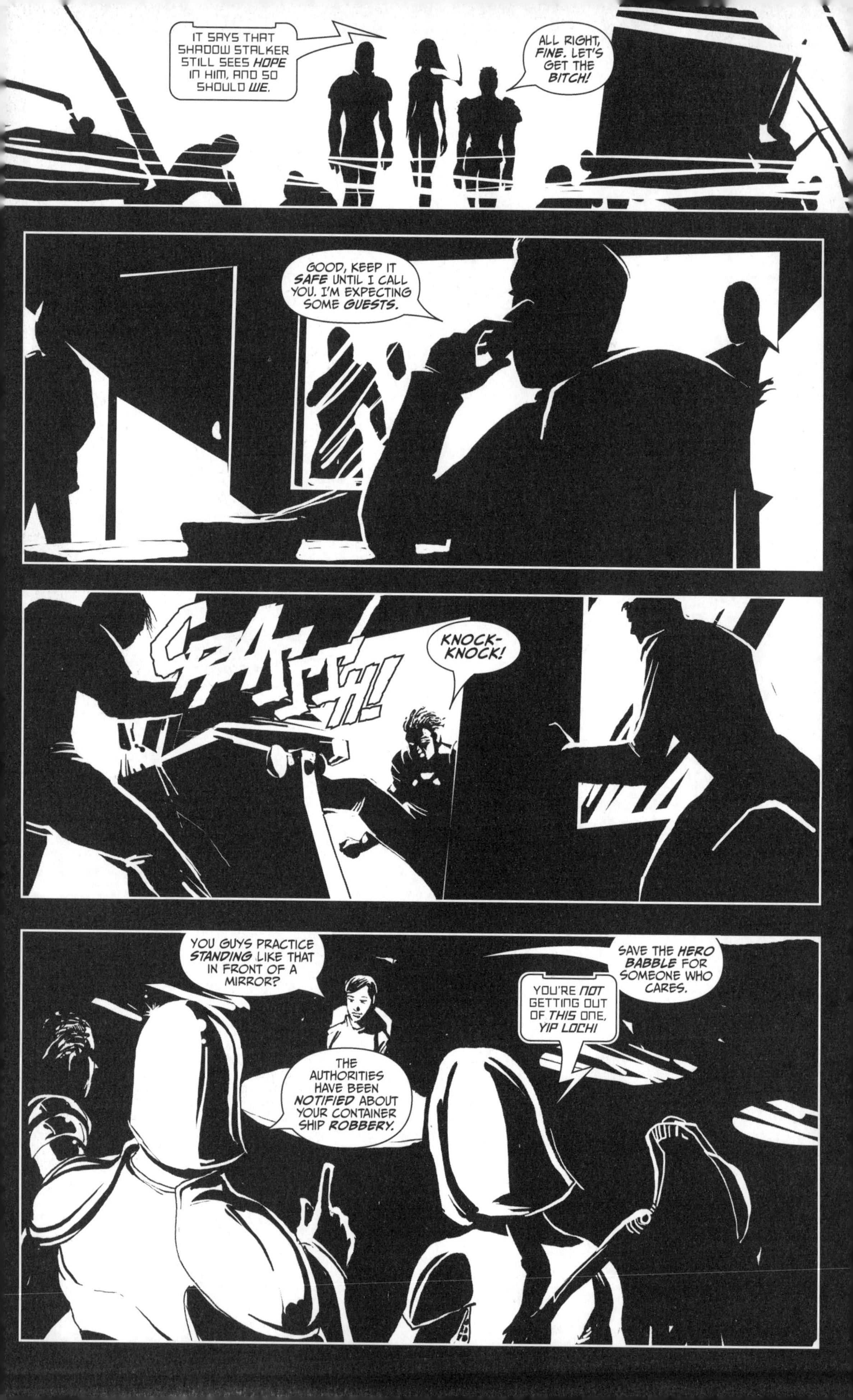
IT SAYS THAT SHADOW STALKER STILL SEES HOPE IN HIM, AND SO SHOULD WE.
ALL RIGHT, FINE. LET'S GET THE BITCH!
GOOD, KEEP IT SAFE UNTIL I CALL YOU. I'M EXPECTING SOME GUESTS.
CRASSH!
KNOCK-KNOCK!
YOU GUYS PRACTICE STANDING LIKE THAT IN FRONT OF A MIRROR?
SAVE THE HERO BABBLE FOR SOMEONE WHO CARES.
YOU'RE NOT GETTING OUT OF THIS ONE, YIP LOCH!
THE AUTHORITIES HAVE BEEN NOTIFIED ABOUT YOUR CONTAINER SHIP ROBBERY.

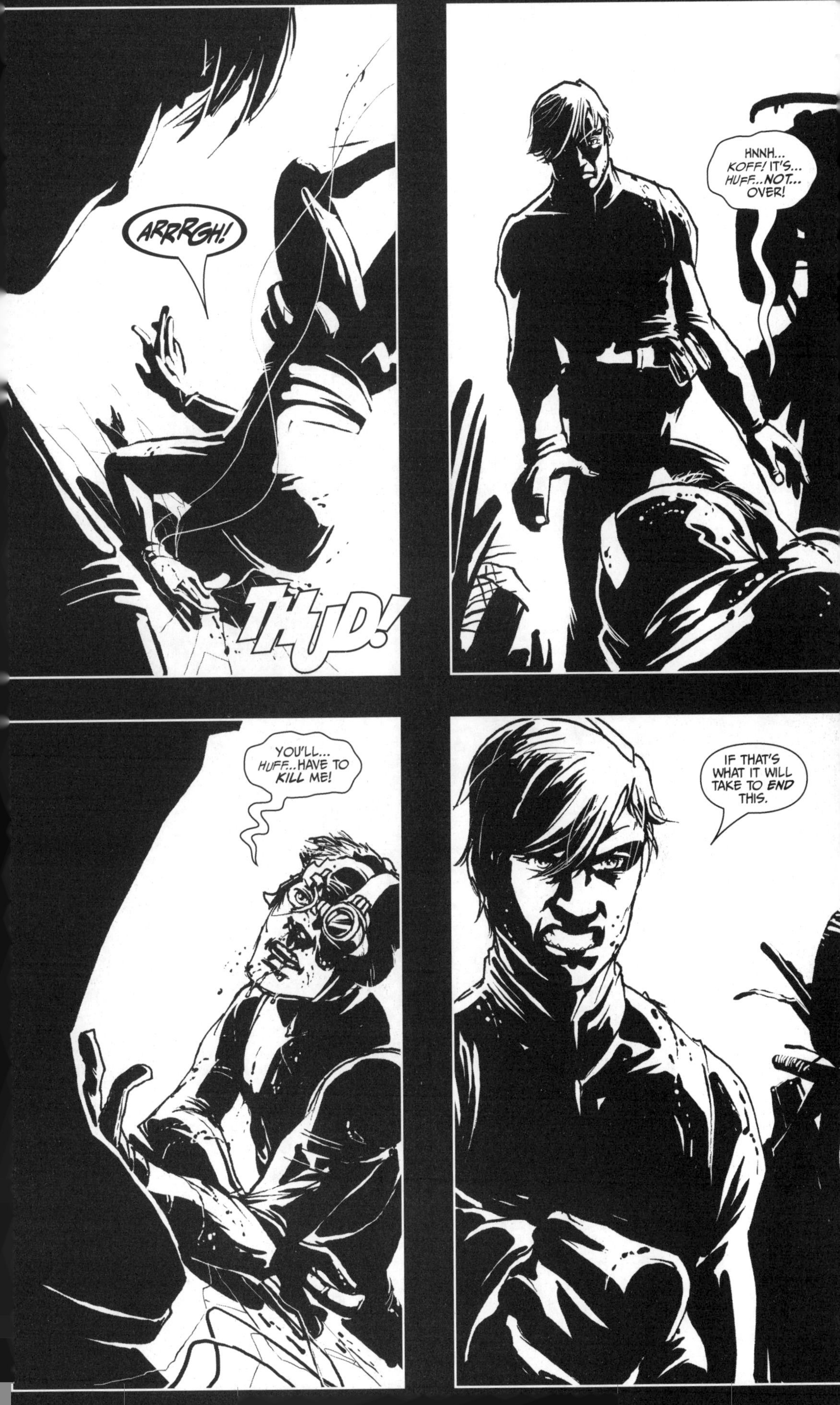
ARRRGH!
THUD!
HNNH... KOFF! IT'S... HUFF...NOT... OVER!
YOU'LL... HUFF...HAVE TO KILL ME!
IF THAT'S WHAT IT WILL TAKE TO END THIS.

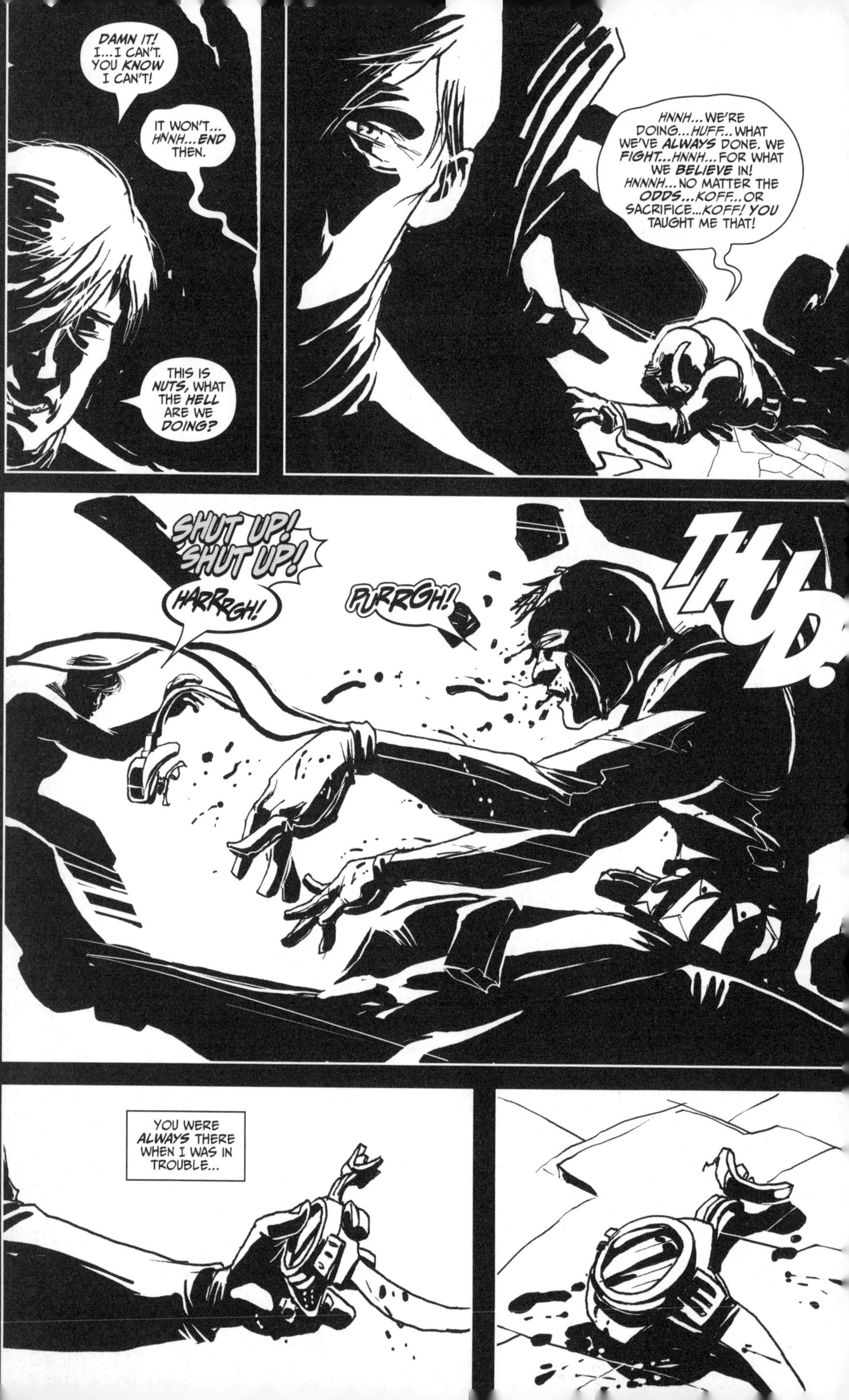
DAMN IT! I...I CAN'T. YOU KNOW I CAN'T!
IT WON'T... HNNH...END THEN.
THIS IS NUTS, WHAT THE HELL ARE WE DOING?
HNNH...WE'RE DOING...HUFF...WHAT WE'VE ALWAYS DONE. WE FIGHT...HNNH...FOR WHAT WE BELIEVE IN! HNNNH...NO MATTER THE ODDS...KOFF...OR SACRIFICE...KOFF! YOU TAUGHT ME THAT!
SHUT UP! SHUT UP!
HARRRGH!
PURRGH!
THUD!
YOU WERE ALWAYS THERE WHEN I WAS IN TROUBLE...

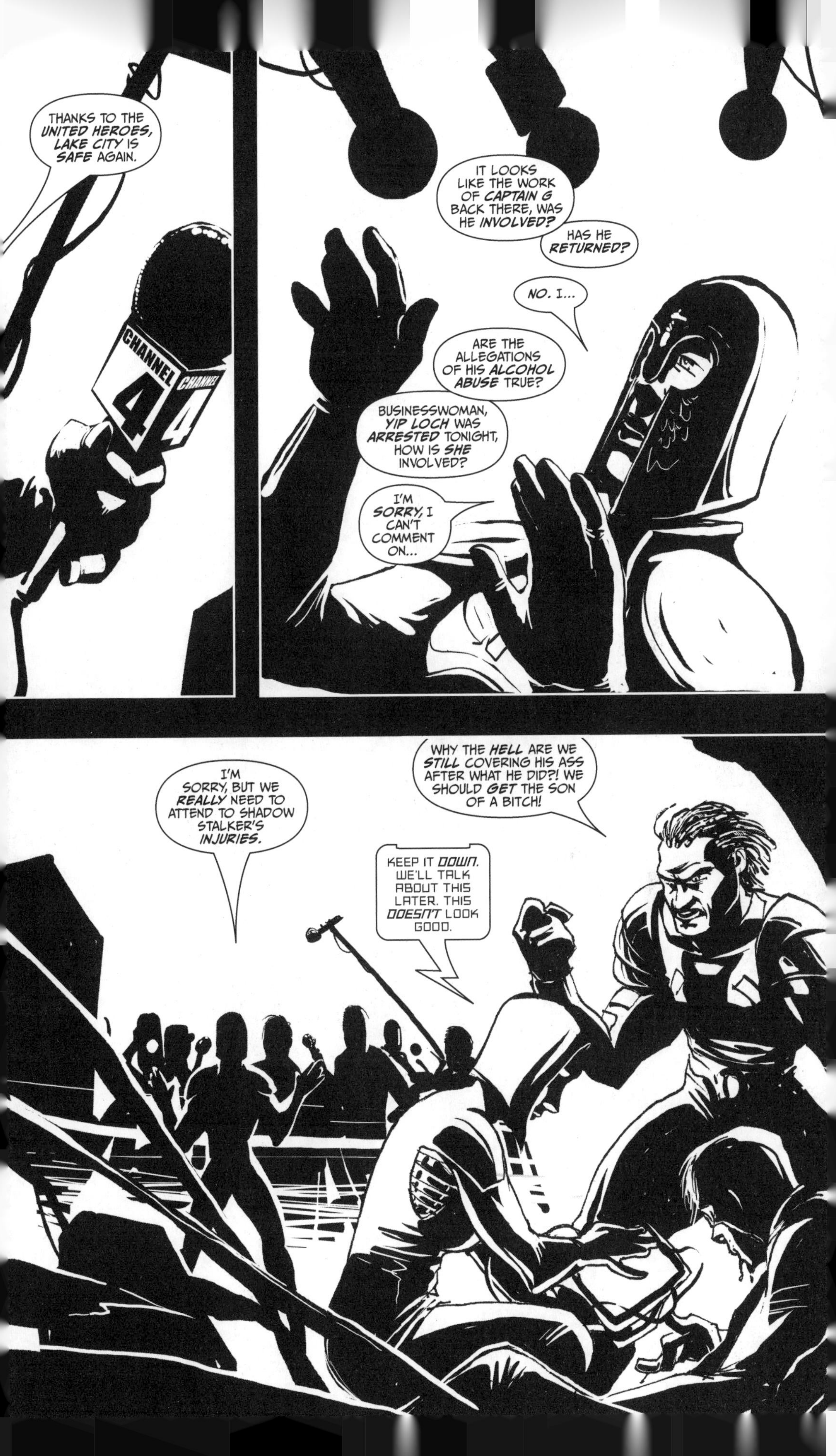
THANKS TO THE *UNITED HEROES*, *LAKE CITY* IS *SAFE* AGAIN.
CHANNEL 4
CHANNEL 4
IT LOOKS LIKE THE WORK OF *CAPTAIN G* BACK THERE, WAS HE *INVOLVED?*
HAS HE *RETURNED?*
NO. I...
ARE THE ALLEGATIONS OF HIS *ALCOHOL ABUSE* TRUE?
BUSINESSWOMAN, *YIP LOCH* WAS *ARRESTED* TONIGHT, HOW IS *SHE* INVOLVED?
I'M *SORRY*, I CAN'T COMMENT ON...
I'M SORRY, BUT WE *REALLY* NEED TO ATTEND TO SHADOW STALKER'S *INJURIES*.
WHY THE *HELL* ARE WE *STILL* COVERING HIS ASS AFTER WHAT HE DID?! WE SHOULD *GET* THE SON OF A BITCH!
KEEP IT *DOWN*. WE'LL TALK ABOUT THIS LATER. THIS *DOESN'T* LOOK GOOD.

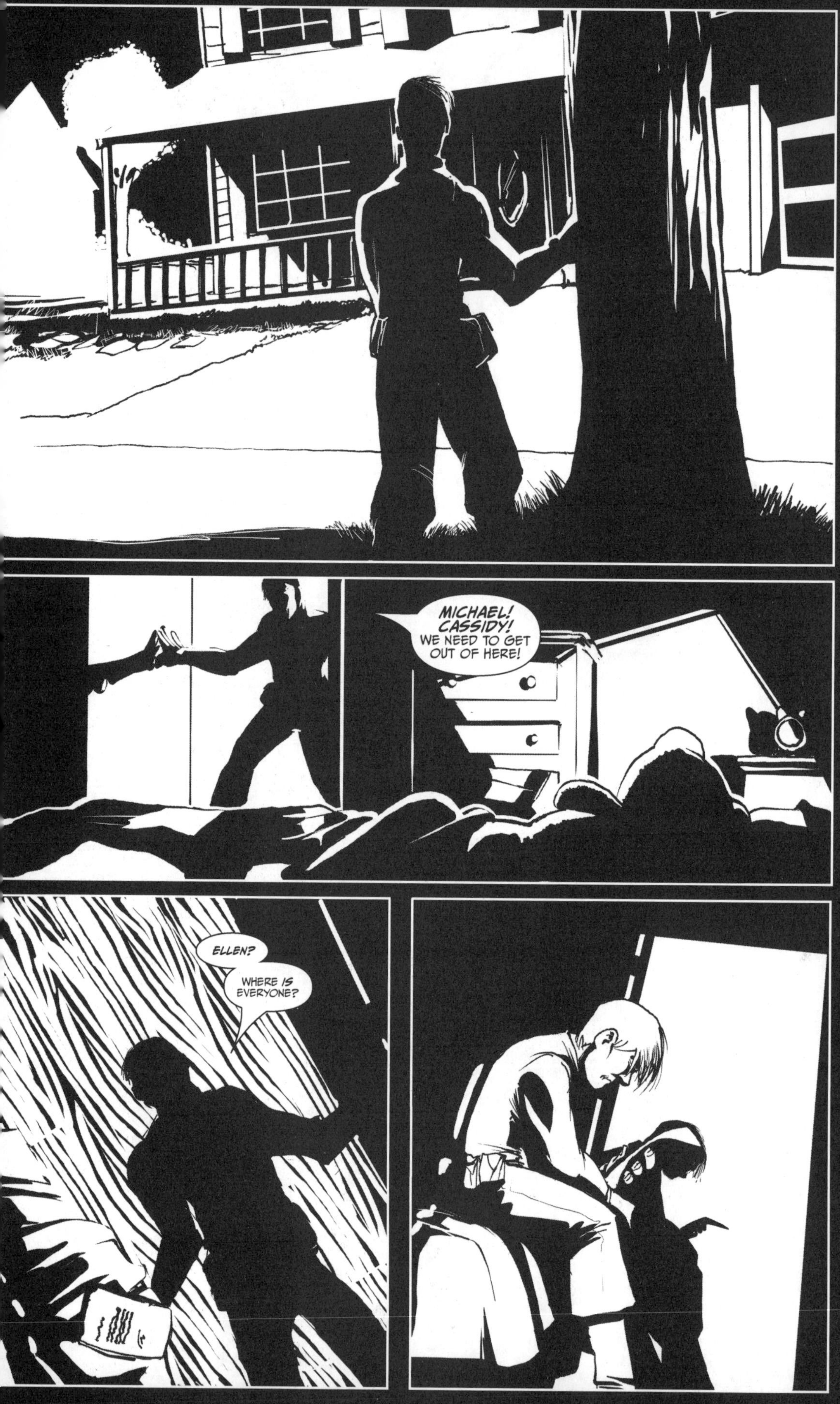
MICHAEL! CASSIDY! WE NEED TO GET OUT OF HERE!
ELLEN?
WHERE IS EVERYONE?

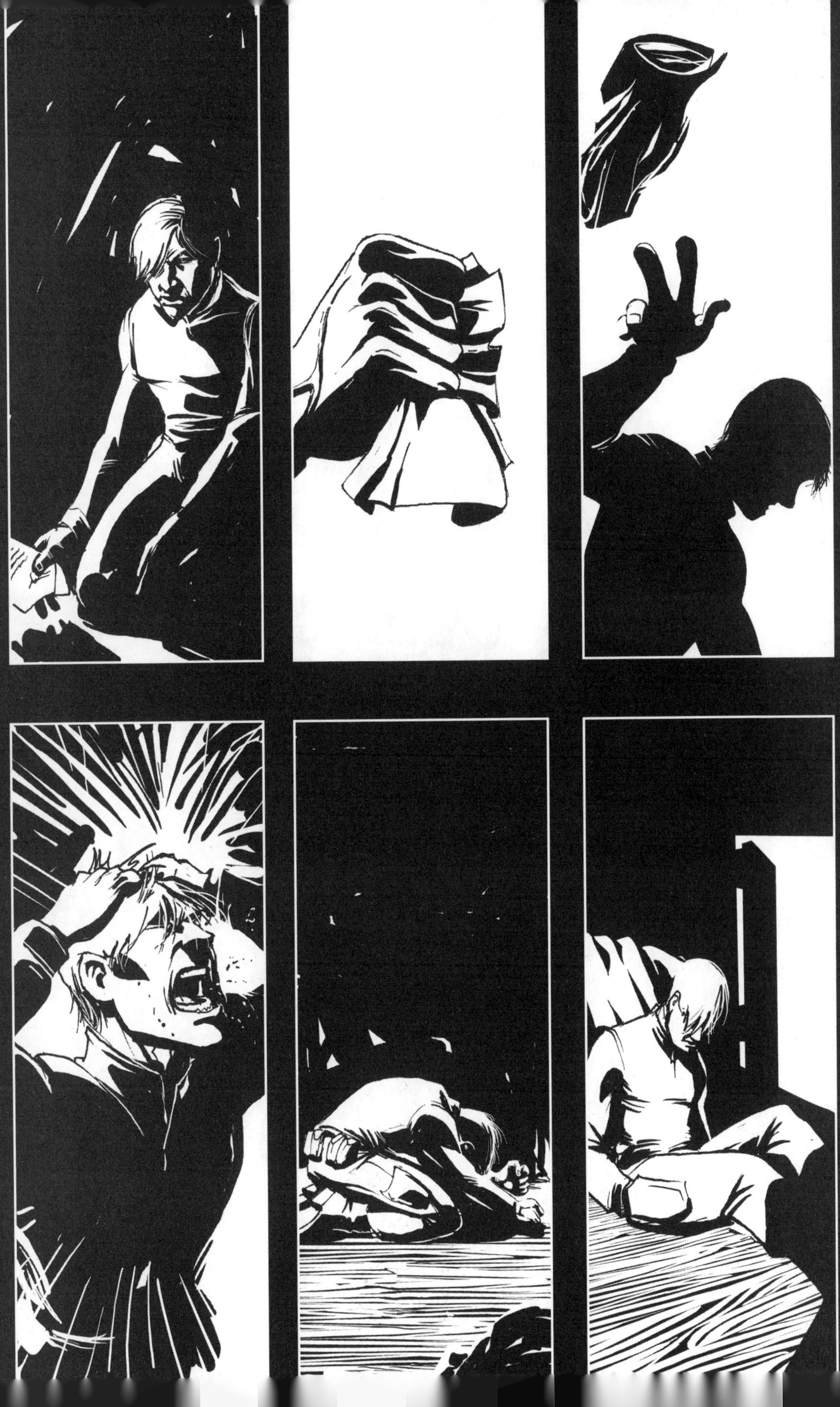

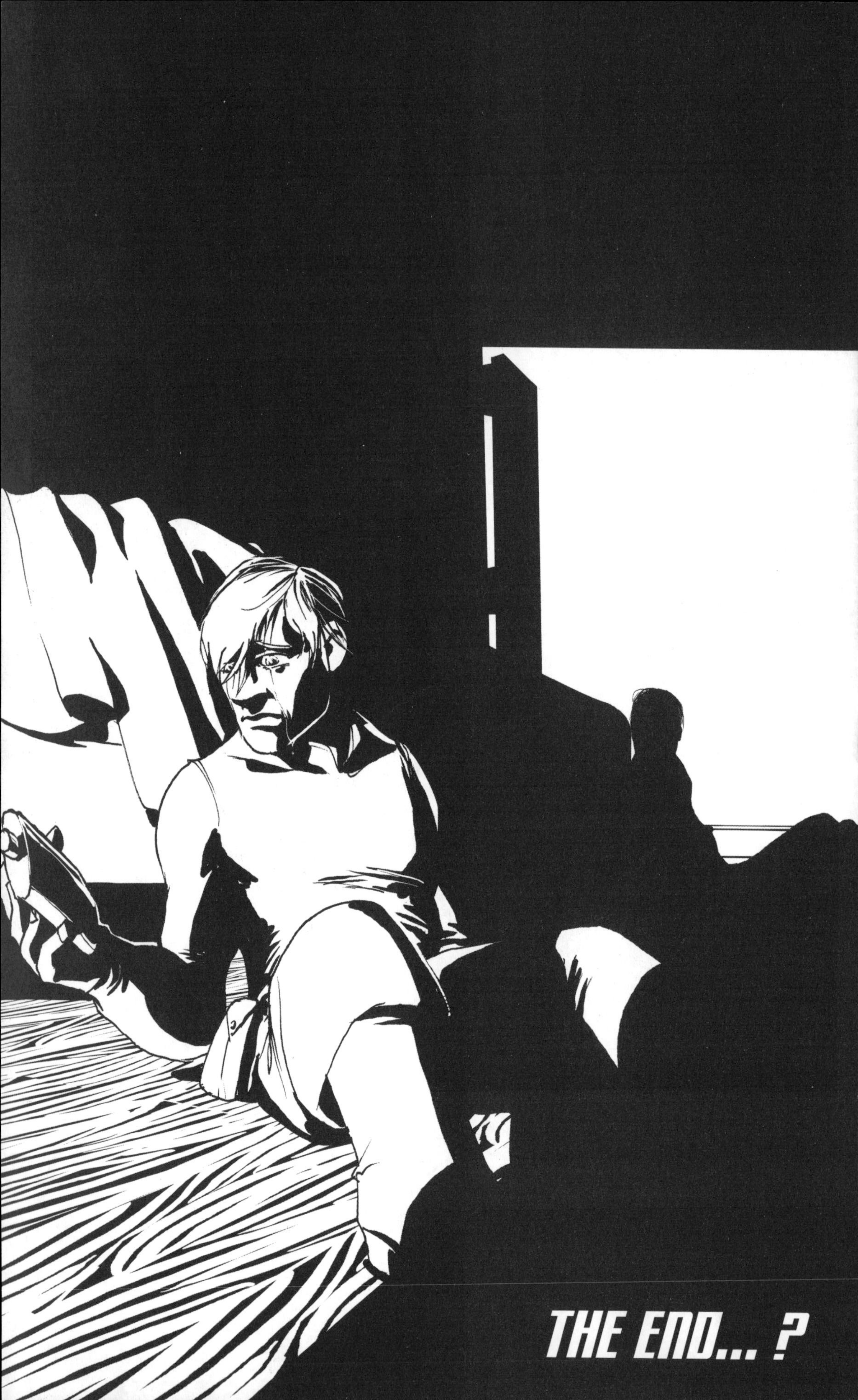
THE END... ?

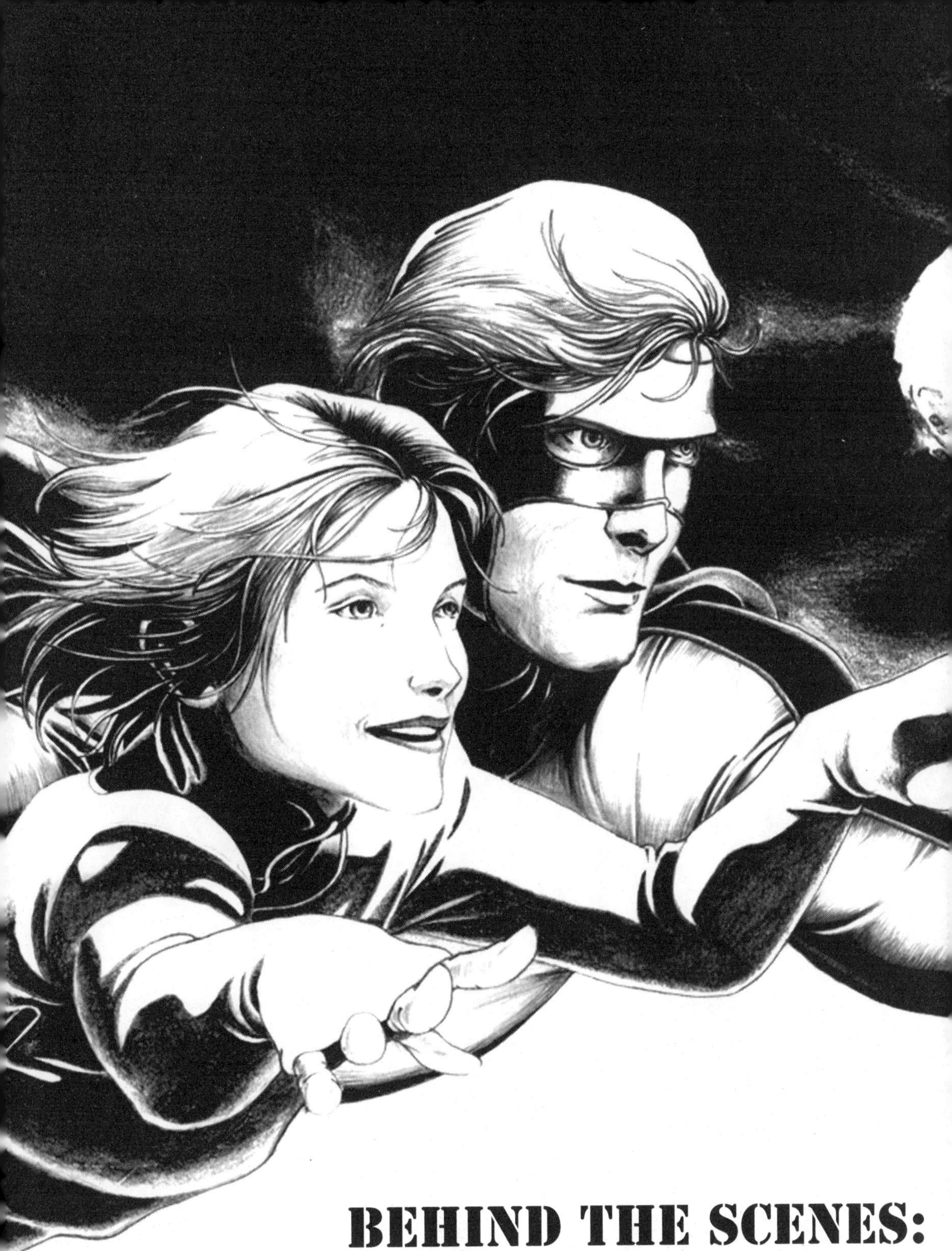

BEHIND THE SCENES: THE MAKING OF AFTER THE CAPE

JIM: What you're about to read on the next several pages is a chronology of the long road AFTER THE CAPE took to get to press.

In all fairness, this was both Howard's and Marco's first series, and the mistakes they made were not all that uncommon for the novice. Our hope is that the following will prove instructive as well as entertaining.

Below is the first pitch I received:

Marco's first costume attempt. The idea was to make Ethan's super-persona generic-looking, since it wasn't germane to the actual story.

Sent: Wednesday, November 09, 2005 2:38 PM

Hi Kris,

Here's the first two issues of AFTER THE CAPE (Working title). Let me know if the attachments get to you all right.

You suggested that I change the names of the hero's super-persona and that of the villains he fights in a flashback. I haven't done this yet, since I'm still looking for suitable names for them.

The Working Pitch

The story centers on a retired superhero whose life at present is nothing like he ever imagined.

How many superheroes have retirement plans?
He's not rich.
He's not educated.
He was a hero.

We will watch how far he has fallen and how much further he can still go.

Ethan is a retired superhero who made sacrifices in his life that are affecting his current life with his wife and kids. He hasn't finished high school, since he chose to 'save the day.' He's married to an ex-rogue that had to come out of retirement and steal for the family's well-being. He can't find any jobs that allow him to face himself in the mirror, and ends up doing work that is less than legal, but helps the constant battle with the bills.

Ethan never expected his life to turn out this way, but that's the reality of life. He was the city's greatest hero and now he's just another statistic. Ethan lost his identity and doesn't realize he's the one burying it day in and day out. Eventually he cracks to reveal his dark side. The city becomes the target of his pent up frustration. A hero's worst nightmare comes true. Ethan becomes a villain of the likes that no one has ever seen. He will leave a legacy not as a hero remembered, but as a villain to be feared.

KRIS: I felt the pitch needed some refining, but I knew at its core that it had a great deal of potential. I had already received the 5 pages of script (originally pages 18-22), and had made some suggestions to Howard.
I didn't want to induce any jitters or add additional pressure, but before we went forward I sent the pitch to Jim to get his thoughts, without telling Howard. Jim agreed the concept had legs, but of course would need to see actual finished pages with artwork. At this point I encouraged Howard to start looking for an artist.

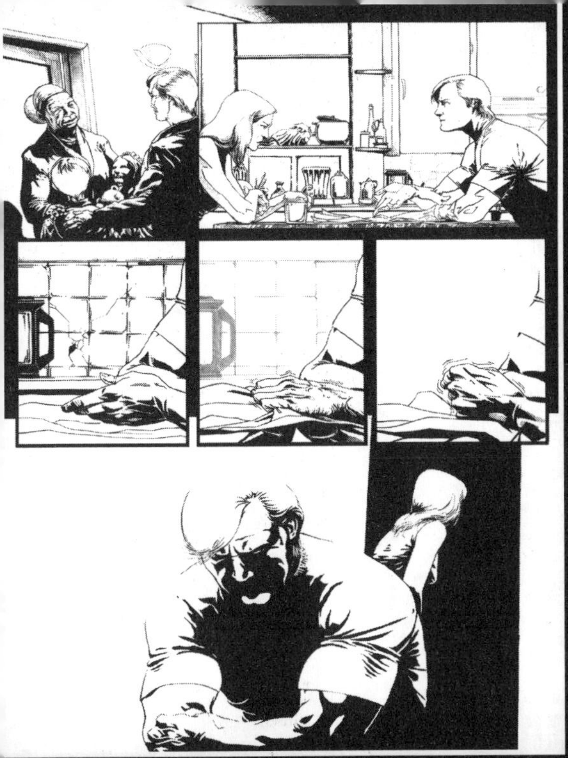

Page 18 (6 panels)

Panel 1
Ethan is with the kids who have their jammies on. They are both have backpacks in which are their overnight stuff. Penny is holding a very used teddy bear in her arms. The three are standing in the hallway with Jenny in her doorway with curlers in her hair, while wearing a mooshu nightgown and bunny slippers.

Show this in an angle where the reader is seeing this in a NE direction. In other words, slightly off a side profile shot.

ETHAN:
Thanks Jenny, sorry it's so last second.

JENNY:
Ethan, it's my pleasure, they're such angels. You and Ellen need some time together.

JENNY (linked):
I know how it is, or at least I did till the SOB left me. There I go rambling again!

Panel 2
Ethan's apartment where we find Ethan and Ellen sitting in the kitchen with the newspaper Ethan was reading at work on the kitchen table between them. They are sitting across from each other. Make sure that the newspaper is a little crumpled.

Ellen watches Ethan as a cup of coffee in front of her steams away. Ethan has a worried and concerned expression as he looks at Ellen while pointing at the picture of The Avenger.

ETHAN:
Ellen, this new guy, he's serious.

ELLEN:
Like he's the first one that wanted to replace you, and stop me. For heaven's sake, if I were going to be caught it would have been at the hands of Captain Gravity and no one else.

Panel 3
Close up of Ellen listening to Ethan. She's sick and tired of him being worried about each wannabe that comes along, which should be seen in her expression that she's fed up with it.

ETHAN (OP):

Page 19 (5 panels)

Panel 1
Ethan is in the kitchen by himself. Ellen's coffee is still on the table, but it ain't steaming no more. Ethan is crushing the newspaper with one of his hands on the table. Keep the newspaper in the same spot as he crumbles it, so his arm is stretched out towards it. While his eyes are open and staring at the empty seat in front of him and grinding his teeth with his mouth closed, transfers his inner frustration to crushing the paper.

THOUGHT (ETHAN):
The silence.

Panel 2
Side profile of Ethan grabing his jacket from a coat hook near the front door. There are also other jackets for Ellen and the kids. If possible try to show the crushed newspaper on the kitchen table where he left it as well as the cold cup of coffee.

THOUGHT (ETHAN):
Every time we argue, I end up feeling like the bad guy...

THOUGHT (ETHAN):
...and worse, I feel guilty too.

Panel 3
Ethan has his hands in his jacket pockets as he walks along the street at night. His head is tilted downwards with a tired, sad expression on his face. He walks by the usual freaks and weirdoes, hookers and drug dealers that are out during this time. He's walking to a diner to clear his head.

HOOKER:
Hey handsome, wanna party?

DRUG DEALER:
I gots what you needs and can gets you what I don't's.

HOOKER:
Hey baby...

Panel 4
Ethan still walking on the streets towards the reader as he passes a dim streetlight. He feels the weight of the world on his shoulders as he walks.

THOUGHT (ETHAN):
What a mess.

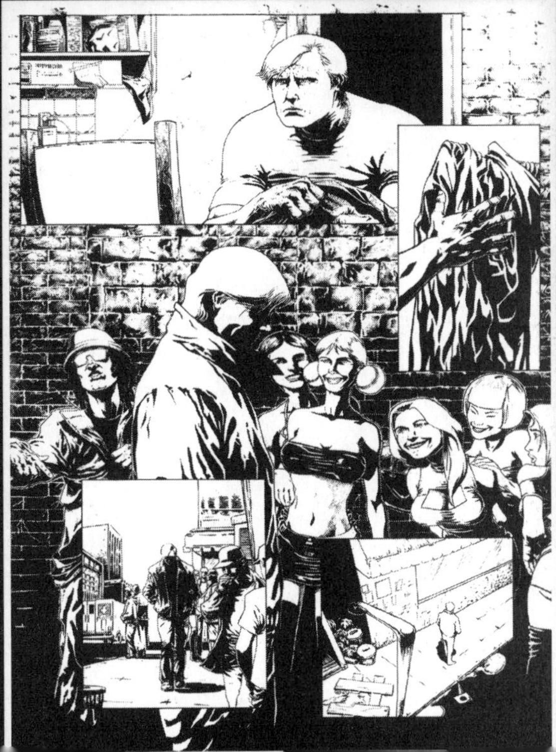

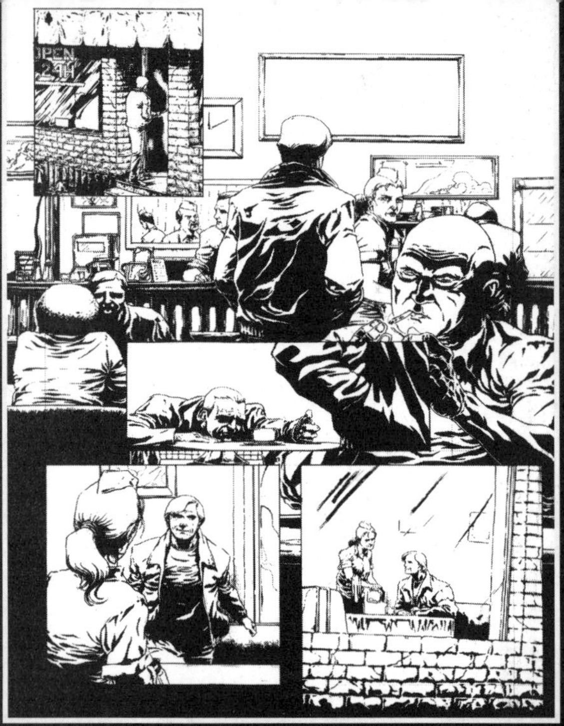

Page 20 (5 panels)

Panel 1
We see the door to the diner with Ethan's hand about to open it. On the door it should have a sign saying opened 24 hours, all day breakfast and fresh coffee.

Panel 2
We see Ethan inside the diner walking by the cash register and three pies that are on pie stands with a plastic cover, where they all sit on the counter where there is a fat man eating pie. We can't see the cook in the kitchen, but there's an ancient waitress with her back turned to us as she talks to the cook. She talks to him though the hole where the cook can pass off dishes to the waitress.

The waitress is dressed in the same uniform from opening day, but of course has let it out, multiple times.

The diner is old and long past it's glory days. There are old black and white pictures of old famous people who have eaten there. Pies and cakes on display, coffee maker, old art deco clock, and of course a milkshake machine.

WAITRESS:
Grab a seat anywhere honey, I'll be with you in a minute.

Panel 3
Ethan walks past an old man who is pretty much sleeping in front of his cold coffee. He's dressed in a brown suit and a bow tie that matches. He's seen better days. He's holding a pocket watch in his right hand that is closed and his left hand is palm down on the table beside the coffee that sits in front of him. He stares blankly forward. Show this with a side profile shot, where Ethan has walked past the old man who is on the left side of the panel, which leaves Ethan on the right or close to it.

Panel 4
Through the old dead diner's window, we see Ethan sitting at booth by the window, which makes up the entire front of the diner. If it's possible to see, there should be the usual condiments on the table as well. Ketchup, mustard, sugar, as well as the menu in a plastic sleeve.

ETHAN:
I'll just have a cup of coffee.

WAITRESS:
Cream?

ETHAN (Linked):
No thanks.

Page 21 (6 panels)

Panel 1
Close up of Ethan's reflection in his coffee as he looks at himself. He's looking for answers to why he's in this mess that's his life. He's tired, very tired of it all.

Panel 2
Use the same shot as page 19, panel 5. Ethan is pouring sugar into his coffee, which distorts the image of himself.

Panel 3
From within the diner, we see a wide shot of the side profile of Ethan with his hand still pouring the sugar and the other mixing it with a spoon. Outside through the window, we can see a mugger, who's wearing a coat, walking along side the diner towards Ethan's direction. Ethan sits facing to the right of the panel.

Panel 4
Same as panel 1. We see a young couple clearly in love and oblivious to the world walking on the street in front of the diner in the opposite direction of the mugger, that is, towards him. They are a few booths back from where Ethan is sitting.

Panel 5
Show them with diner's window splitting the scene between Ethan and the young couple. Ethan looks at the young couple as they walk by him. His head is turned and looking out the window, so we're looking at the back of his head. He has the cup of coffee to his lips.

Panel 6
We see Ethan's face superimposed on the reflection off the diner's window on top of the young couple in love as they pass by in front of him. He has a slight smile while he puts his cup of coffee down to watch and reflect off the couple.

CAP:
Love.

Panel 7
Same superimposed reflection of Ethan, but his eyes are looking at the mugger who's walking towards the oblivious young couple. He ain't smiling anymore. Make it so we can see the mugger preparing to pull a knife on the couple from inside his coat pocket.

The mugger's attention is on the couple, the couple is on each other and Ethan's is on the mugger.

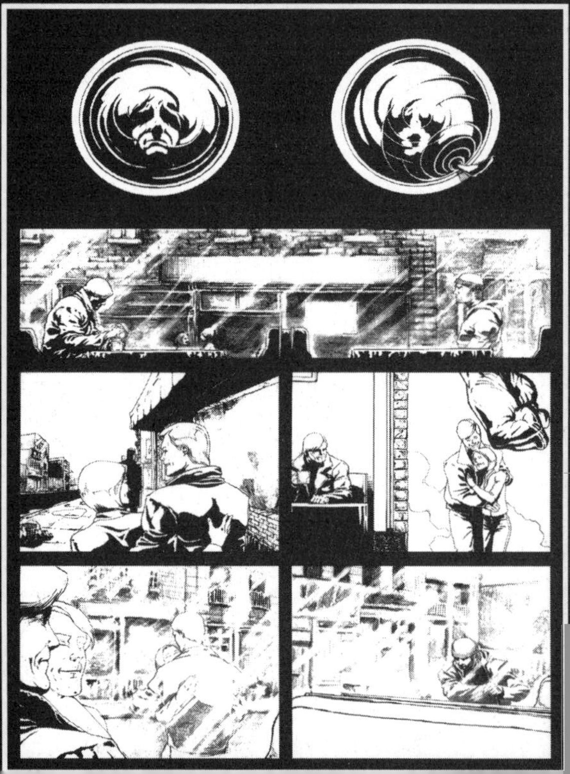

Page 22 (6 panels)

Panel 1
From outside the diner we see the mugger trying to pull his knife out, but Ethan is using his powers to make that impossible. The young couple now notice the mugger with a surprised, "where did he come from," look. Ethan remains fixed on the mugger with a disapproving look on his face.

CAP:
Then life comes in and makes a mess of things.

Panel 2
We see this from outside of the diner. Ethan continues to manipulate the mugger's knife as we see the young couple running away with each other hand in hand.

The mugger has both his hands on his knife trying to keep it leveled. Think of it as though he's holding a barbell in his hands. The mugger's is pissed and bewildered as to what is happening with the knife.

Panel 3
Overhead shot where we can see both the inside and outside of the diner. The waitress is in front of Ethan's table while holding a pot of coffee. Ethan is still looking at the mugger who's struggling with the knife.

WAITRESS:
Hey mister, you want a refill?

Panel 4
Inside the diner Ethan looks up at and turns away from the mugger to the waitress with a, "what?" look expression.

We can see the mugger launching the knife into the air since Ethan got distracted. The mugger has a shocked expression as he looks upward.

WAITRESS (OP):
Sorry, didn't mean to spook ya.

ETHAN:
That's alright. I haven't finished it yet.

Panel 5
From inside the diner we see the mugger ducking as he runs away from the knife he threw into the air. Ethan has a smile as he speaks with the waitress.

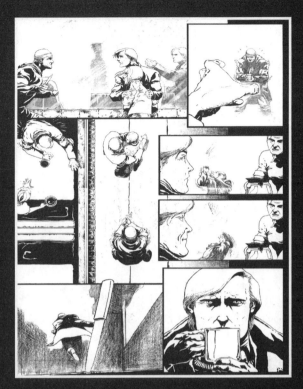

JIM: These were the first pages I saw, sans script. I liked them and the concept well enough to want to continue the project. But, there were several areas that bothered me.

Marco's high-contrast art style reminded me more of Brian Bendis' early work than Frank Miller's (although many would compare him to Frank). I felt he had some trouble with faces, particularly Ethan's, which was too round and expressionless. I also felt he had a bit of trouble with storytelling, so I offered to help whenever we got to a tricky scene.

The part that needed more work was the script. In Howard's first drafts he had Ellen as an unsympathetic retired super-villainess, who returned to crime as a way to help the family out of their financial troubles. My feeling was that this took away from the tragedy of Ethan's fall from grace and how it affected those he loved.

I sent copious notes to Howard on where I felt the story was losing focus, but first I sent my idea for the book's logo.

JIM: Howard, bless his pointed little head, had made several attempts to come up with a logo for the book. Now, he'll be the first to admit that he's no letterer as his attempt to the right will attest.

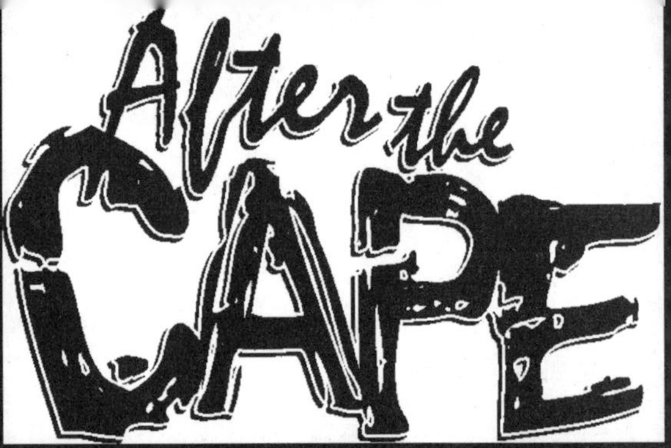
After the
CAPE

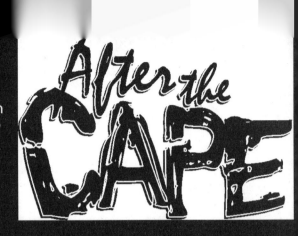

So, Kris handed the assignment over to Jason Hanley, one of Shadowline's letterers. Jason gave us the piece below. Now, I'm a firm believer that logos should be interesting, yet easily read from across a room. And while this logo met that criteria, it was merely functional, but not (by all of our accounts, including Jason's) inspired.

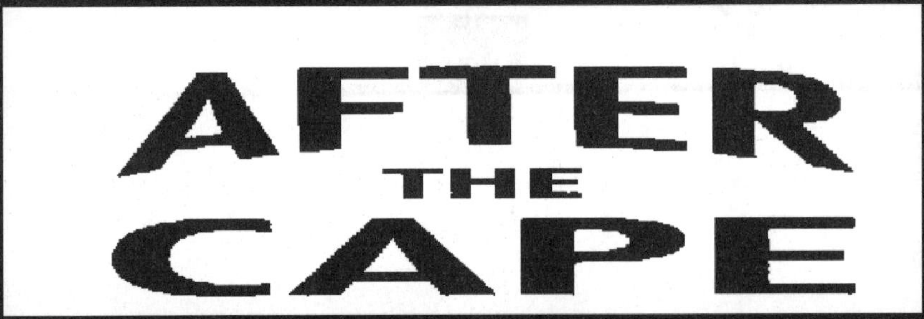
AFTER
THE
CAPE

The fact was, I had a vision as to what I wanted this book's logo to look like. To that end I traced the logo to ACTION COMICS, substituting the appropriate letters. Then, I took my original scribble (below) and re-traced it in Illustrator. While I had drawn many logos in the past for mine and others books, I'd drawn them all by hand. This was the first time I did one in Illustrator. Luckily, I had ace letterers Jason Hanley and Ed Dukeshire to tweak it for me. I believe it's one of the most striking logos on the stands today…even if it's an obvious nick on a classic…or perhaps, especially because of it!

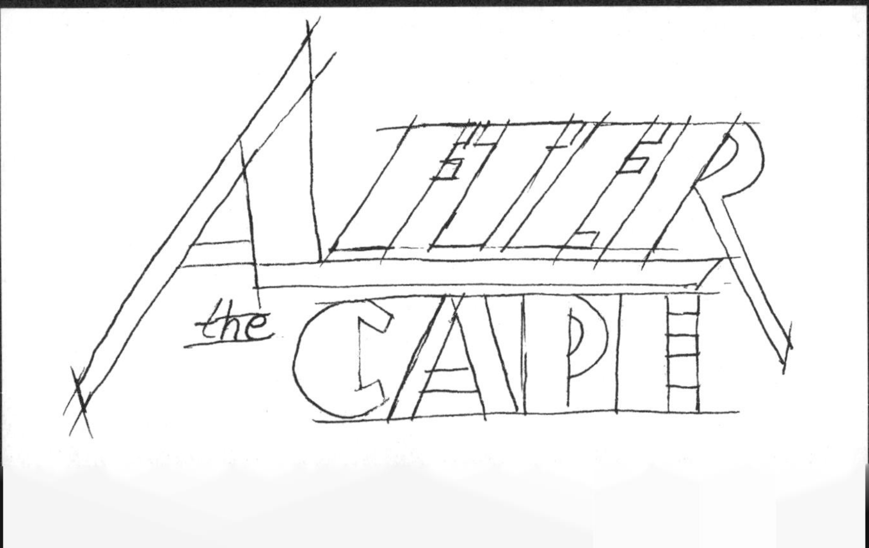
the
CAPE

Issue #1 breakdown

Page 1 (3) Ethan wakes up to start his day. He rather stay in bed, but he needs to get the kids up and ready for school. Ellen is still at work. *This should be a struggle for him. We should get a sense he's NOT a very happy camper.*

Page 2 (5)Ethan gets the kids up, makes breakfast for them and then takes them to Jenny their neighbor who takes them to school. **Give a hint as to how he feels about his wife working two jobs (this should be introduced EARLY)**

Page 3 (6) Ethan is watching television and notices a robbery that he knows he could have stopped, if was still in the superhero business. **KEEP THIS PAGE.** *These robbers should be the same guys who come into the diner at story's end.*

Page 4 (5) He makes breakfast for Ellen, who comes in from her night job as a waitress. She's in a decent mood and gives encouragement to Ethan as he heads out to his job at the sub place he works at. *See later notes, but bear in mind that we want to LIKE her—we want to show her as a sympathetic character.*

Page 5 (5) Ethan walks towards the subway station to go to work. There are other people around that seem to be moving at a quicker pace and look more positive than him. Ethan is in a subway train with people all crowded around him, but all ignoring him. There will be transition into flashbacks. Most likely through Ethan's captions, *Introduce the flashback via the subway window, ala "Heart of the Storm" by Eisner (see attached)*

Page 6-7 (12) Flashbacks begin. I'm thinking of making this into a montage of the following images of Ethan in his superhero persona: in the middle of stopping a bank robbery, saving people from a burning building, flying away as he waves to officers putting a handcuffed super villain into a paddy wagon, gravitating a broken bridge so that the cars that are on it can drive to safety, and helping to untie hostages which Ellen is one of them. This is how they first met. Ethan is courting Ellen. Each panel will show how their relationship grew.

Page 8-9 (12) Still in superhero flashbacks. Ethan reveals his identity to Ellen and proposes to her. Show both of them looking different, to show that time has passed. They were dating for a while, etc. etc. We will end the flashbacks here. *Here's a problem I have—when we START the flashbacks, he's on the subway. When we END he's home. We don't see him in between at all. It's a bit of a jump.* Ethan is taking a drink from a flask (that he will use throughout the story), he's in the bathroom and trying to keep his hands from shaking. He tries to gravitate a bar of soap, but the soap will not remain stable and shakes. Ellen calls from behind the bathroom door to see if he's all right.

Page 10 (5) Ethan's flashbacks are interrupted by a customer at his work. A young pimpled punk is bugging Ethan about putting the wrong kind of cheese on his sub. Ethan will be wearing a dumb uniform and looking less that enthusiastic about being there.

Page 11 (3) *The young pimpled punk complains to Ethan's manager/boss about Ethan screwing up his order.* **You should be setting up STORY B—the bad guys—somewhere in here (you don't need 6 panels for a punk to complain to the boss, this is simply a set-up). Introduce the elements that will propel your story forward.**

Page 12 (4) Ethan gets fired, begs to keep job, but it's no good. Ethan becomes angry and tells his ex-boss to stuff it and walks out.

Rearrange this   clear up the incident with the kid and Ethan's firing on page 10   THEN on pages 11-12 segue to the robbers we'd seen earlier. Establish WHO they are (remember to CLEARLY INTRODUCE all characters on first appearance. This is as easy as having someone say their NAME. Give us their motivations, tell us about them as they'll play an important role in issue's 2 and 3.

Page 13 (6) *Back to Ethan (This suggests that some time has passed between his firing and going to the park)* is sitting on a park bench thinking of what just happened and what he's going to do, while he drinks from his flask. Ethan looks up and sees a statue of himself in his superhero persona. It's covered in pigeon shit. He gets up and walks through the park where he walks by happy families, couples in love, and so forth.

Page 14 (4) Ethan buys a newspaper and then walks into his apartment from the street. This is in the afternoon. Show this as a run-down neighborhood, with old, shoddy buildings.

Page 15 (5) Ethan at home serving dinner to the kids, they eat as Ellen comes home from her night job as a waitress. This is where we get to know HER a little better. *She should be TIRED, nearly despondent. We should get that she loves her family, loves her husband still. We need to make HER sympathetic, not a bitch. The POINT of the story is Ethan's anguish, his bad choices for the right reasons. Make Ellen THE REASON, not the cause.*

Page 16 (6) Dinner ends, kids go off to watch TV/play **(we don't want to make these two unsympathetic to the readers by having them punish their kids for no reason).** The newspaper that he bought has circled jobs that he was looking into while at home before she came home, which is on the counter. Ellen sees it and gets upset. We start to see her frustration or, better, her anguish—we should get the sense that this isn't the first time he's blown a job. And they can barely make ends meet NOW.

Page 17 (5) Ethan and Ellen continue to fight, Ellen is fed up and goes to their bedroom. Ethan is left alone. *Again, see notes for page 15—they can FIGHT—but make sure that Ellen remains sympathetic.*

Page 18 (5) Ethan leaves to cool off and heads for a diner. He walks by drug dealers and hookers. This is the kind of place Ethan and his family live. *AND HE KNOWS, DEEP DOWN IT'S ALL HIS FAULT!!!! This is incredibly important to understanding his character and establishing his motivation.*

Page 19 (5) Ethan walks through diner to find a seat to be alone. There are other people in there who want to escape what happening outside as well there. Ethan spikes his coffee with his flask, contemplating his sorry life, and what it has become.

Page 20 (6) Ethan watches a couple walk by that makes him think of how it used to be with Ellen. Story B—the bad guys—come into the diner to rob it while Ethan is lost in thought.

Page 21 (6 panels) Go back and forth between the robbers and Ethan, he HAS to make a decision here whether or not he's going to get involved. SOMEONE needs to be placed in mortal jeopardy (perhaps a gun gets cocked to a waitress' head?) THAT makes the decision FOR him

Page 22 (5 panels) Ethan disarms them (making the guns too heavy would probably work best)—the triggerman grabs the waitress, throws her at Ethan, knocking him off-balance. Close in on the trigger man—he KNOW who Ethan is—this AINT over by a long shot (he says this as the two are running OUT of the diner)—Last panel is Ethan righting the waitress, all eyes in the diner on him. "NEXT: Consequences."

ISSUE #1 SCRIPT FIRST DRAFT

This was Howard's first stab at a script. Kris and I discussed the script, her notes to Howard are in Italics. Then, I came in after and made a few notes of my own (bold).

Howard had originally written this as a 23 page story, rather than the 22 pages we require. You'll note that Kris re-wrote pages 21 and 22.

THREE ISSUE BREAKDOWN

JIM: Not satisfied with Howard's ability to pace the story after reading his first draft (He seemed to be going in all directions at once, thus losing the focus of the story and all story beats) I requested a single paragraph breakdown of all three issues (right). I wanted to know what happened in each of the issues.

Issue one

We are introduced to Ethan Falls, formerly Captain G, his family and the criminals, Mint and Pez. We learn a lot about the family's financial problems and how it affects their lives. His wife, Ellen, works two jobs to keep the family stable and Cassidy and Michael are in school. Mint and Pez are planning an armed robbery. We learn about Ethan's past as a superhero and his increasing health issues related to his powers, resulting in his retirement. We learn how Ethan and Ellen meet and fall in love. We learn of Ellen's frustration and the constant arguing as Ethan loses job after job. We learn about Ethan's drinking problem at the diner where he goes to cool off. Mint and Pez recognize Ethan when he stops them from robbing the diner with his gravity powers. They leave with everyone staring at Ethan.

Issue Two

Continuing from the diner in issue one, the cook scares off Mint and Pez when he comes out with his shotgun. The cook blames Mint and Pez's botched up robbery attempt, as well as their accusations of Ethan being Captain G on their drug use. Freeing Ethan to keep his secret. We learn more about the family's financial problems and how their lives are affected. After failing to find a job, Ethan increasingly drinks at home. The kids try to cover for him when Ellen comes home from work. Ellen leaves for her night job and tells her husband that the kids know about his drinking. The mean landlord reminds Ethan of the rent due at the end of the week but the children protect Ethan, and the landlord leaves. Ethan goes to bathroom to hide his shame. He learns of Ellen collapsing at work and rushes to her side using his powers in the open. Mint and Pez see this and follow him. Ethan recognizes Mint and Pez's car. He threatens them and demands that they leave him alone. A conversation ensues where Ethan's guilt for his family's dire situation wins out over his morals. Ethan gets Mint and Pez to help steal rent money. Ethan lies to Ellen about where he got the rent money and agrees to attempt to continue working, while it really involves more stealing. Mint comes up with a plan to get rich by killing Ethan and his family, and then selling the story. Mint and Pez prepare to record footage of Ethan.

Issue Three

Ethan continues to lie to Ellen about having a new job, while getting involved in bigger crimes. Mint and Pez secretly record Ethan's criminal acts. With their financial issues under control, Ethan becomes happier and stops drinking, which improves his family's life. Mint and Pez set their trap for Ethan, which he unknowingly walks into, setting in motion their plan. Mint leaks Ethan's secret to the media after leaving him unconscious at their latest job. Ethan finds himself pursued by the authorities. He runs home to tell Ellen everything so they can run away together. Meanwhile, Ellen discovers Ethan's dark secret on the news and runs away with the kids. Ethan finds a "Dear John? letter when he gets home. Mint and Pez are on route to kill Ethan and his family. Ethan drowns his sorrows with the bottle, regretting all the choices he's made that led to him losing everything.

Ok, Jim and I have gone over the breakdown together and bounced it back and forth between us. We've stamped down the pacing and re-focused the story to the important parts.

Howard, you've made some rookie mistakes here, which isn't unusual...since you're a rookie. :P You have to remember that this series is more about the emotions and turmoil rather than the actual characters themselves. They are parts of a much larger story, which is what happens "After the Cape"

You have to make the characters likeable if you want the readers to care. They can be flawed, they just need to be understood. In this case, you were making Ellen out to be a real bitch. She doesn't need to be. Ellen loves her family. She works hard to make ends meet. She didn't expect this kind of life. She just wants Ethan to accept his lot and work with her to have a better life. He's not. He's living in the past, bitter and sorrowful over what's become of him. He loves Ellen, he loves his kids, but this is ALL HIS FAULT. Where they live, their financial sitch, etc. You really need to KNOW who your characters are. And you need to show the readers who they are as well. Would they really punish the kids like that? Yell in front of them and upset them, then send them off to their rooms like THEY were at fault? The readers won't like your main characters if you do this. And when Ellen leaves at the end, you want the readers to FEEL Ethan's pain. You don't want them thinking "the bitch is better off gone"! You want them to root for the couple to stay together and fix things so when they DON'T, and Ethan screws up, the emotional impact is all the greater at the end.

You need to work on your set-up, and your introduction of characters, and you need to focus on the scenes that matter. The ones that show the emotion of what your characters are going through. Ethan getting fired from a menial job isn't the main focus of this issue, so there doesn't need to be 2 whole pages devoted to it. The focus of this issue is Ethan and Ellen's relationship. Where it was, who they were, and what they've become. Jim and I have re-focused the outline to reflect that.

Ok, and your ending. The way your issue ends needs to yank the readers into the next issue. They have to WANT to pick up the next one. You need to end with a tease or a cliffhanger of some sort. Something that demands an answer to the question 'what happens next?'. This issue didn't have that. So while we were shifting the focus, we threaded a "Story B" into it, and not only set up the series better, but we gave you an ending that will entice readers to pick up issue 2.

Unfortunately, I don't think the pages that Marco already drew survived. Not sure, you'll have to check. They may work, I didn't look.

Lastly, we really want to see the outlines for issues 2 and 3 before we move forward with this. Seeing how we had to re-work this, we're thinking it might have had an effect on those two issues, PLUS when we see the contents of those, we may have to adjust even more on the first one, to accomodate events that should be set up from the get-go. So please get those two breakdowns up in their own threads as soon as you can.

JIM: Kris' response to the breakdown. She underscores all of the problems we've been having with the plots thus far and what we see as workable solutions to bring the story of Ethan's fall from grace into focus.

Hi Jim,

I went over your points and questions. The story can be told in black and white within three issues. I have made the changes as per your suggestions and guidance that I greatly appreciate. Below you can find the answers to the questions you had.

I also wanted to thank you for hand drawing a logo for After the Cape. It was a great surprise and very appreciated.

After your comments I see what you mean about spotlighting Ethan. Originally I had Ethan's wife, Ellen come out of retirement to do petty thievery to help pay the bills, rent and so forth. I made her into an ex-rogue so that she would represent Ethan's failure in saving the woman he loves (because she had to return to a life of crime). Ellen will now be a normal person who will have two jobs, one during the day as a secretary and the other at night as a waitress. She barely sees their two kids and is trying to keep things stable for the family. She fell in love with Ethan when he was a superhero, since he was secure, caring and an exciting person. She's very frustrated with Ethan now. He's not the same man she fell in love with and married. She wants him to be content, wants to feel secure being with him and simply be happy.

Ethan is in his late thirties. From his teens to late twenties, he made many enemies when he was a superhero. Enemies that he feared would hurt his family to get to him. This is one of the reasons for his retirement. The other is his superpower. He can control gravity, but at the cost of great physical strain. When he was younger he had a stronger threshold to use his gift, but it wore him down every time he used it and became more difficult to control as he aged. So for the sake of his family's safety and his own health, he retired.

During his superhero days he fought crime from the common criminal to super villains. He wanted the city he lived in to be safe for the common person. He became the beacon of hope for the people, until he left. **What he learned during his crime fighting days was that much of the crime originated from the three crime families that controlled city. He helped to put two of the three heads, better know as the three kings, behind bars before his retirement, but one remains active. It's well known in the criminal underworld that they want to know Ethan's real identity so they can give him payback.**

Now Ethan has trouble keeping a job. Ethan lacks the emotional satisfaction that he used to have during his superhero days. **Thus, his constant itch to do the right thing. Such as when he was working as a store clerk at a corner store, he would tell customers that they could get their milk cheaper at their competitors. He kept losing jobs over these kinds of deeds, which affected his family's well-being and is one of the things that he and Ellen argue a lot about.** *He needs to work low-profile jobs that don't draw attention to who he used to be. His motivation is severely lacking, which hinders getting promotions or raises, which further sinks him into depression. He's caught in a cycle*

that he can't get out of, making too little money, which causes arguments at home, which only makes his work suffer more.

Ethan begins stealing after accidentally shoplifting while getting the groceries. The excitement and thrill of getting away with it, and being able to help out his family from it, *further entices him to continue to steal, and he starts to branch out and steal more than just groceries.* Ethan steals in secret from his family, because it's something that he's ashamed of, but at the same time gets a guilty pleasure from it as well. He continues to steal, because of all the things he has tried, it provides best for his family. *He lies and tells his family he got a raise/promotion.* It allows Ellen to quit her night job as a waitress, so she can spend time with their kids. Eventually Ethan is caught—*he is in the wrong place at the wrong time, caught by criminals with the same intention.* They recognize him and blackmail him to do bigger crimes for them. Ethan wishes to expose them, but by doing so, he will also expose his shameful secret to his family, *and his identity will be out in the open* as well. *The more he steals to keep his secret, the more he find he is enjoying himself.*

During one of the jobs he's forced to do, Ethan accidentally uses his powers to save an innocent bystander. His superhero secret is revealed to the criminals he works for, who use it as more leverage, forcing him to use his powers on bigger jobs. Ethan is hurting both emotionally and physically at this point. If he stops stealing, his criminal partners will sell him out to three kings, which would mean the worse thing for him and his family.

Howard—How does the series END? How does he get out of this? What happens?? Jim is not your audience, he is your publisher and this information is necessary. Give me a summary of the ending and we'll tack on here and clean it up, and it'll be good to go.

Thanks,

Howard

JIM: Howard's response to all of the notations and edits we've sent thus far. He explains how he saw things intially, including the characters' ages and motivations.

Considering the power of Marco's high-contrast art style and the dark nature of the story, I felt the book would work best in black and white.

This is with Kris' edits. The stuff she wanted to omit is bolded, the comments she added are in Italics.

JIM: On the next two pages are my notes to Howard after reading his breakdown for issue #2.

I was trying not to be merely constructive, but instructive without being condescending.

Most of this is off the top of my head from notes I made while reading. I had a sense of where I thought he wanted to go and what I thought he wanted to do and tried to light the path for him to get there.

In response to these notes Howard wrote long dossiers on all of the principal characters, parts of which can be seen in the Sketchbook section of this book.

Howard,

I hope the below proves helpful...

1. I want you to think about what your story is. Who are you characters? Where do you want them to be at story's end? How will you get them there?

2. I want you to think about each issue as a three act play. What happens in each act to move the story forward?

3. I want you to think of each individual (in totem) as an act--moving your characters from point a through z throughout the arc.

4. I want you to start thinking about your supporting cast as more than just "blocks" to move your main character forward--Ethan, Ellen, the kids, the bad guys. Each of them needs motivation, personality and an arc.

Here are a few tips:

I find it very helpful to write an outline--write one for each character, write one for the issue at hand, write one for the larger story. Blend and integrate them, weave them in and out of one another.

Then, once you know where everyone is going do a pag guide--page by page, start with your ups, your strong emotional or action marks--the things that will propel the story forward, then fill in the gaps with characterization (right now everyone except Ethan is a cipher). Remember--action/conflict to start, slow down, action, characterzation, cliffhanger/resolution. "Action" can be emotional, not fisticuffs.

Bigger clue--there should be arcs for Ellen as well as the bad guys, not just Ethan.

Switch scenes at opportune moments (the most dramatic) to build tension. Right now your plot is a series of flashbacks and repeated scenes (grocery stores, the family photo, etc).

You need to build characters--you need to leave us wanting/needing more. You need to propel the story forward so we want to know what happens next ("it was the best of times, it was the worst of times"--the greatest line ever written. Why? Because you understand it instantly and you want to know how we got there immediately).

Figure out your story--figure out your characters (do not make them cardboard cut-outs) then, come back to us.

You have a great idea here--do it proud and reach a bit higher, try a bit harder.

Jim again:

I've been thinking a lot about your story I hope that the following helps a bit.

It seems to me that you have three basic storylines here:

Your lead story is Ethan, obviously. His battle with depression, with the bottle, his feelings of uselessness, and his bad choices.

Story B is Ellen. We need to see more of her, get to know her. She's tired; emotionally and physically drained. She can't do any more than what she's doing and it's wearing her out. Her love for Ethan, her love for their kids, all of these things need to be played up so the ending (her leaving him) has an emotional impact on us.

Story C is Pez and Mint—who are these guys? It seems to me that they're small-timers, petty crooks that see Ethan as a way to a big score.

As I noted, Ellen and the bad guys are ciphers right now. One way to flesh them out is to write a dossier on them. This will help you in understanding who they are—how old are they? How much schooling have they had? Write down a character profile—their religion, politics, and favorite movies, whatever. Model each on people you know, this way you can hear their voices.

Next you need to plan your story out in linear time. Right now you're leaning on a combination of way too many flashbacks and fast-forwards. You need to maintain an inner consistency. You can't have Ethan not have enough money for groceries in one scene, and then buying a van in the next. That just doesn't work. By creating a timeline, you create a logical progression for Ethan's fall from grace.

There are also some problems with motivation:

When Pez and Mint confront Ethan why doesn't he use his powers against them? One possible answer is that he's sick of doing things the "right? way, what has it gotten him? Here's where your original themes that he has no pension, no skills, etc. come into play.

What is the job they want him to pull? It has to be big enough that they NEED him for it, yet not so big that it winds him in jail.

At this point, the two thugs seem perfunctory and I'm wondering if the story wouldn't be a LOT stronger if you removed them. They really don't seem to serve much of a function. Ethan starts stealing because he can think of no other way to take the burden off of Ellen. As he steals more and more, he drinks more and more and lies more and more—to himself, to his wife. If Ellen is going to leave him over this, then she has to build to a point where that makes sense. This isn't the first time he's blown it; it's the last time. We should see Ellen at work (talking with a co-worker?) We should get a sense of her

frustration early on—not anger, necessarily—just that slumped shoulder SIGH of being simply overwhelmed by life. This makes her a more sympathetic character and provides logical justification for her actions at the end of the arc. Her feelings of betrayal would be increased if she somehow discovered this. If he tells her, she's more likely to want to work through it with him. Maybe his actions have placed her and the kids in some danger I'm not sure. Just don't lean on flashbacks and repeating scenes over-and-over again.

I'm going to urge you to take some time, think about what's written above, make those dossiers and create a definitive timeline for the story.

One of the secrets to creating a comic series is to end each issue on a powerful note. Make the reader want to come back for the next issue. This is usually done with a cliffhanger. It's far more difficult to do this when your story is an emotional, rather than an action-oriented one. Ask yourself where those moments are. Most stories (and this is true for comics, television, books—start off with "action" then slow down for characterization, then more "action" in the middle, characterization and ending with a cliffhanger or (at story's end) resolution. Think of it as a roller coaster, if you will.

Kris is pretty darn good at arranging and re-arranging scenes. We can help.

ISSUE #2 PLOT

JIM: Over the next three pages is the unedited plot that Howard sent over to us for issue #2.

ATC #2 breakdown

Well, I blathered a bit on this one. I needed to throw in what he was thinking/feeling cause I find that there are things Ethan will do that would not corresponds to what he's thinking/feeling. It's like when you're feeling depressed, you move through life in slow motion, you do things out of habit/necessity, but your thoughts are elsewhere. I hope that makes sense.

Page 1 (3) Ethan is at home looking out the window through the broken blinds at the street below. It's been a week since the incident at the diner, but he's playing is cautious. We'll use captions with Ethan recapping what happened at the diner and right when we last left him. From there we'll go into a small flashback to the diner.

Page 2 (5) Flashback to the diner from issue one. The criminal's guns are on the ground. The criminal guarding the door (Pez) is puzzled to what just happened as he holds his arm that was holding the gun. The other criminal (Mint) has experienced this before (During the flashback of Ethan's superhero glory days in issue one, he was one of the criminals he stopped). He figures that it's Ethan that's doing it. Mint stares right at us and repeats the same line from issue one that he knows who Ethan is. Mint pushes the waitress at Ethan knocking them both down. Then Mint goes down to the ground and glares at Ethan again with an an evil smile. This happens as Pez pulls Mint off the ground and out the door. The cook has just come out with a sawed off shotgun.

Page 3 (4) Flashback to diner continued. The cook startles everyone back from the shock of being robbed. The Cook cries out something like, "Crazy druggies think we're actually making money in this shit hole. Idiots even dropped their guns? Everyone basically goes back to normal. Ethan is helping the waitress up, as the cook picks up the guns that the criminals left behind. Ethan comments about the cops needing them for prints, which makes the cook laugh and replies about how there haven't been any cops crazy enough to come to this part of this town for years. The waitress thanks Ethan. He leaves the diner with a worried expression. End of flashback.

Page 4 (5) Back to Ethan looking out the window as he was on page one. Pull back from page one to show more of the apartment so that we can see that his kids are at home. They ask him what he's doing. He's tells them he's doing nothing. Flashback to a close up of Mint repeating the line that he knows who Ethan really is. Back to present with Ethan rubbing his eyes with his thumb and index finger. He turns to his kids with a smile and plays with them. He's keeping what happened at the diner a secret from his family.

Ethan through captions tells us that he has not told Ellen about what happened at the diner. He promised her that he would never use his gravity controlling powers, since it's strains him physically and he has difficulty in controlling it now, not to mention it would expose who he was and that there are people who want to give him payback for the things he's done to them. He's worried and afraid, but knows that he can't hide forever.

Page 5 (6) Ethan walking outside trying to look inconspicuous. He's wearing a zipper sweat top with the hood pull over the baseball cap he's also wearing. Ethan is looking around and seeing if Mint and Pez are lurking around the neighbourhood. We'll show him walking around the neighbourhood in different outfits, much like the one described above, but with each outfit he's covering up less, to show that he's becoming more confident that he's safe. Ethan will mention in captions how he feels stupid about the whole situation and how he couldn't live with himself if anything happened to Ellen and the kids. He also mentions that it's been two weeks with no sign of Mint and Pez, which makes him feel safe to go out without worry. He doesn't really, but he's trying to convince himself it is. "They must have given up looking for me. It's been a while. Yeah, they must have gone to look for me elsewhere. Yeah, that has to be it. Ethan is about to go into a grocery store as he thinks about Ellen.

Page 6 (7) Flashback to Ellen leaving for her day job in the apartment. She looks tired, but keeps smiling. Ellen kisses Ethan, to give him reassurance and her support at getting a new job and just to stay positive, as she has always done. Ethan smiles back. There's a framed photo of the family with them all smiling that we will see on a wall by the door. Ethan in captions comments on how great Ellen is to him. How she keeps everything together, even when he feels like falling a part. He wants to make it up to her. We're back to the present with Ethan holding a basket partially filled, and with the other hand he's holding a can/jar with a picture of a woman smiling in the same manner as Ellen in the flashback. Ethan feels useless and a burden to Ellen.

Page 7 (6) Ethan still in the grocery store. Ethan holding the basket with one hand, picks up a small bottle of booze (anything but Zima, heh.). He contemplates about getting it. He's feeling low about not contributing and keeping the secret of the diner from Ellen. He puts it in his jacket pocket unconsciously, as he pulls out his money from the other jacket pocket, to see how much he has, which is very little. Show a few crumpled up dollars and change. He's doesn't even have enough to get what's on the list, so he returns some items from his basket back to the shelf. As he does this, he feels worse. Make him feel guilty and ashamed, with each item he puts back. When he cashes out, make sure that the storeowner is a very happy and a nice old man. This will reflect back on to Ethan when he discovers that he just lifted the bottle of booze he was thinking of getting, but couldn't afford.

Page 8 (5) Ethan is back in the apartment alone. There's a framed photo of the family with them all smiling that we will see on a wall by the door. In the last issue the framed photo will be taken away when Ellen and the kids leave. Ethan goes and puts the bag of groceries on the countertop and then goes to hang up his jacket. He discovers the small bottle of booze he's lifted by accident when the bottle in his jacket taps the wall when he goes to hang it. He's wonders for a second how it ended up in his jacket and then realizes how it did. With how he's been feeling, this is just a kick in the gut. He can't believe himself. He feels stupid, bad and guilty all at the same time.

Page 9 (5) He thinks for a second about keeping the bottle with a grin. He paces by the kitchen table. His heart races and his palms begin to sweat. He clams and tells himself that he'll just go back and return it, but then he thinks about taking a sip. His drinking

problem kicking in again. What harm can come from that? So he does, but a sip turns to two and so forth, until he realizes he finishes it all. He sits at the kitchen table staring at the empty bottle. The little guilt that he had gives way to him feeling alive again. He's happier than we have seen him so far in the present.

Page 10 (5) Ethan convinces himself that it's all right since he took it by accident, and it didn't hurt anyone. He hides the empty bottle, like it's a trophy, and tells himself that he'll never do it again. He's goes and finishes putting away the things that he's bought. As he does this, his mind races through the thought of getting the rest of the things on the list. Things they need. It's not like he's going out to rob a bank or something.

Page 11 (5) He goes out and walks into an other grocery store. He's picking up the rest of the things from the shopping list, but the canned items are heavy and people would notice. He uses his powers to lighten the load. With the excitement of stealing, he doesn't feel the strain he used to. His mind is racing with thoughts of how to get away with this, keeping his cool, etc. Ethan back in the apartment with the door closed. He can't stop smiling. He stops using his powers and we can see the weight of the things he took pull down on his jacket. It was easy and it made him feel good, proud even.

Page 12 (7) Ethan continuing to steal from grocery stores. Ethan walking from a grocery store smiling, back at the apartment wearing different clothes putting groceries away and then where he's keeping the money he's not spending on them. This is to show that he's been doing it for a while. Using captions we'll overlay Ethan talking about how he's saving the money from buying groceries and will surprise Ellen with being able to pay the rent on time and some of the bills too. He's happy as he does this. it's putting food on the table, but then he thinks about Ellen working two jobs. How she's pushing herself so hard for them. He wants to help her out of it. He does as he's walking past different shops, the displays will make him think and reflect about Ellen, about having a happy family and so forth. Things that he promised her. He wants her to quit her night job. She's been working hard for too long and he wants her to be able to spend more time with the kids, not to mention with each other. He eventually walks by a pawnshop on his way home, which gives him an idea. He looks at the items in the pawnshop and he thinks about stealing things beyond food. Ethan stops himself thinking about it cause it's wrong, what was he thinking?

Page 13 (5) In their apartment, the kids are watching a cop show on television, while Ellen is about to leave to go to her night job. They say their good-byes, the kids giving her a big hug and her kissing Ethan. He knows he has to do it for her. He will steal so she doesn't have to work so hard anymore. He makes the decision to do it. He ponders what and how to do it, while he sits with the kids watching television.

Page 14 (6) The cop show the kids are watching gives Ethan the answers. He figures that he could follow up on the crimes that he stopped during his superhero days. He knows what places were good to hit and pretty much how to get in and out of them. The more he thinks about it, as the cop show progresses in the background, the more he likes the idea.

Page 15 (6) Ethan buying a stolen beat up old van from a guy off the street. Show Ethan at other location loading his last stolen item into the van, dressed in black and has his face covered. He closes the door to the beat up old van as he's inside it. Inside he takes off the hat and whatever he's using to cover his face up, so we can see him, as well as the things he's stolen from a T.V. and stereo store. He's looking at what he took and is smiling. Ethan is proud of his accomplishment. He actually pulled it off and is proud of himself. With each theft, he makes it that much closer to making Ellen's life easier. Ethan drives away and doesn't notice Mint and Pez who are parked in a dark alley across the street.

Ethan through captions tell us: how he told Ellen that he got a job at a warehouse where he works at night. How he decided to get a van with money that he made with the last few jobs he's pulled, to help to make better hauls and how he gets money from different pawnshops so they don't get too suspicious, and how he plans to encourage Ellen to quit her night job. He also talks about how things are becoming normal for them. How he can finally help with rent and bills, about being happy for a change and spending more time with the kids. He talks about making more money so they can eventually move out of the shit hole they live in. He wants to give Ellen the life she deserves.

Page 16-17 (12) Mint and Pez, the criminals that were going to rob the diner are in their car across the street from where Ethan is pulling off his latest heist. They are at first pissed that someone got there before they did, but as they watch, Mint recognizes that it's Ethan when he uses his powers to gravitate the stolen goods safely to the ground. Mint and Pez grin at each other. Mint talks about payback, since Ethan got him arrested one too many times in the past. We flashback to the flashback of Ethan's superhero days, but this time from Mint's point of view. Mint also flashbacks to other times Ethan stopped him in the past.

Page 18 (5) End of flashbacks. Mint tells Pez about Ethan ruining a big job that would have set him on easy street, but Ethan messed it all up and got him thrown in prison. Pez pulls out his gun and wants to help Mint rub Ethan out, but Mint stops him he has a better idea. Mint starts the car and they follow Ethan.

Page 19 (6) Ethan drives the van into an alley and uses his powers to hide it under boxes, garbage cans, etc. etc. Ethan take a breather after he does this, which Mint notices. We see this from Mint and Pez's point of view. Ethan changes his clothing and puts his thieving clothing into a backpack that he carries with him as he walks down the street towards his apartment.

Page 20 (4) Ethan walks into his apartment past the drug dealers and hookers. We see this from Mint and Pez's point of view. Mint and Pez drive up in front of Ethan's apartment and stop. Mint has a nasty grin as he looks up at it. Pez is looking from the passenger seat as well. Mint tells Pez that they'll let Ethan get a little more practice before they get him.

Page 21 (5) Ethan is at home and is happily greeting his kids and Ellen who is still in her waitress uniform (night job). Ethan gets them to sit down at the kitchen table. He has something that he wants to talk to them about. Ellen is a little sacred, since this usually

means he's lost a job. Ethan asks the kids if they would like mom to only work in the day, and they agree of course. Ellen is a little confused, and Ethan tells her that he got a promotion and a raise, so she doesn't have to work her night job anymore. She's tells him that she's happy as long as he's happy. She doesn't agree just yet, since she's a little afraid that he might repeat his cycle of becoming depressed, but she feels that he's back to his old self.

Page 22 (4) The entire family is happy. They're all on the sofa watching television. Ethan turns to look at Ellen. She smiles back at him in a loving way. We see Mint and Pez driving away in mid conversation, where Pez says something like, "...and after that we kill him right? Mint replies, "no man, I kill him."

S: At this point, Jim and I realized after reading the [f]inal outline that Howard's [out]line needed more work [than] we thought. We didn't [wan]t to give up on the story, [nor] did we want to take over. [We f]elt that he could take the [char]acters and the situation [and] rearrange them into a [stro]nger plotline for Howard. [Of c]ourse, only if Howard was [ame]nable to the idea.

Howard,

I'm posting this just to give you some of my general thoughts going in and an idea of what I intend to do.

As I've said all along, I think there's a really GOOD story here, but I also think you're having a hard time finding it.

To that end, my plan is to sit down with your basic story points and attempt to re-plot it for you.

I agree with Kris' earlier comment that "Pez" and "Mint" are just too cute. As I see their names over-and-over I like them less and less. They will be changed.

Now, I don't usually do this with someone else's creation (it's a LOT more work than I want to put to into something that I don't have a stake in) and if you would prefer I didn't--speak NOW or forever hold your pee.

Once I start, I promise this is going to be QUITE different (for one thing, Ethan is too damn YOUNG--he should be approaching middle age).

So, I leave it up to you. If you don't want your story messed with, that's cool. And, again, I'm not 100% sure I'll be successful--I'm just going to give it a whack here and see what, if anything, I can do (with your permission).

Howard,

Before you get into this please note that while trying to stay true to your basic story, I've changed virtually everything. Your first reaction will most likely be to reject it all, but please re-read it and think about it. I've left a lot up to you.

I wrote out all three issues just like this, but longhand (old fuddy duddy me)--before I go through all of the trouble typing out the other two issues I thought I'd gauge your reaction to THIS.

You can place this in the "Shadowline Universe" if you like, or not—your choice. You can simply reject it out right if you so choose. My hope is that you take it and embellish it.

My thought throughout was that this was a story of a man's fall from grace. The story is left open at the end for a sequel concerning itself with redemption.

One thing, it WILL have to say "plotted by Jim Valentino" regardless. Believe it or not, I put a lot of time and energy into this, and it wasn't easy. I believe that this is a bit closer to what you were shooting for, but your mileage may vary on that.

The script is up to YOU, Howard—don't freak out and don't get nervous. Pull every emotion you can draw on into it, and it should ring true. Put yourself in Ethan's shoes; consider Ellen's emotions and the emotions of his friends. Remember that every story is about PEOPLE…even if they are wearing panties and capes.

There is no deadline, no timeline, so don't freak. Think, feel and let those emotions guide you and you can't go far wrong, and remember that Kris and I are here to help.

KRIS: After Howard gave Jim permission to re-vamp the outline, Jim took some time and re-worked all 3 issues. The idea was to give Howard a general idea of how to pace the story. A guideline that he could follow to make sure his beats were on target.

While we wanted the story to remain Howard's, we also wanted it to be as strong as it could be.

On the next five pages are Jim's reworking of the plot. Note how he has maintained most of the fundamental story elements while changing the beats to emphasize Ethan's fall and Ellen's plight, the true thrust of the story.

Issue #1--plot--Jim

1-2--Domestic scene, pretty much as you wrote it—Ethan gets the kids up and off to school, Ellen comes home from her night job...DIFFERENCE IS that Ethan tells her NOT to worry he's just got a bog promotion and she'll be able to quit her second job in no time...she's ecstatic!

4--Follow as he leaves the house. He's thinking that this last job will be the big one and then he can stop. He takes a drink from his flask, notes that he has an hour before he meets "the boys", sees a bar across the street and thinks that "One won't hurt"

5-7--Flashback (segue with "One too many or something along those lines, picking up on the one won't hurt line). Ethan, in his Captain G costume surrounded by several other supers (you can make them generic or whatever) they're doing a crisis intervention. His drinking IS a problem—a BIG one. One of them, a real hard-ass type, has had enough of it, another (who will be his friend throughout) is trying to rationalize/help. At any rate they vote him off of the team until he can get his shit together. He's pissed. Half-sloshed throughout this, he swears he doesn't HAVE a drinking problem and he doesn't need them anyway. He splits and goes into a bar.

8--In a bar and out of costume—Ellen comes in, she's noticeably younger she's heard (the team mate pal called her) what happened. She's there to support him. She loves him and she knows that he's worth it. He promises her that he'll get his drinking under control...it's not really a big deal anyway (remember, the first sign of addiction is denial)...he takes a drink.

9--Use the exact same pic of him taking a drink to segue out of the flashback—he's thinking that he doesn't HAVE a drinking problem. The bad guys (Pez and Mint—change their names—use the first names of your two best friends) come into the bar, pissed. He was supposed to meet them an hour ago (which tells us how long he was in the bar—another symptom of his alcoholism).

10--Ethan, completely sloshed, gets pissed at them, after all HE'S the brains of this outfit! They try to sober him up with coffee...use the coffee (pot or cup, whatever) to segue to Ellen's job at a dingy diner. She's talking to another waitress, excitedly telling her that Ethan is finally getting his shit together and how she believes the bad times are over.

11--Continue in the crappy little diner Ellen goes off to wait on a customer while the other waitress makes a comment to the slob of a cook about how delusional Ellen is. After all, once a bum, always a bum.

12--Use the word "bum" for your segue (as in "get up, ya bum!) Water is thrown in Ethan's face by "the boys" The combination of that plus the coffee has him sober enough to leave the bar with them under his own steam.

Issue #1-plot (Cont.)

13-15--Scene switches to a small bank—the three of them walk in wearing all black (Rather than show them changing, clue the reader in via their dialogue) including black ski masks (mandatory for all bank robbers, ya know). Ethan uses his power to increase everyone in the bank's personal g-force, essentially pinning them to the floor, unable to move against the increased gravity while the boys empty out the tellers' drawers. The whole thing is over quickly and without violence and they split (you MAY want to toss in a scene with an old person, maybe someone with a pacemaker as the increased gravity could, conceivably, cause a heart attack. Thing is that while he may be a thief now, I don't think that Ethan would want to actually HURT anyone and this may present a good opportunity to get that across to the reader—he would probably decrease the old person's gravity back to normal so as not to hurt them).

16--The kids come home from school, both parents are gone (still working) so they turn on the TV (as kids are wont to do). Their show is interrupted by a breaking news bulletin about the bank robbery. The older kid watches and gets a look of recognition on his face—maybe he says (under his breath) "dad??" something to clue the reader into the fact that he knows.

17-18--In the "hideout" (probably one of the boys' apartments Ethan and the boys are going to split up the loot but Ethan, drinking again, gets greedy. He decides that it's HIS powers that are making these jobs work and, therefore, he should be getting half the take while they split the other half. The boys are NOT real happy about this and one of them puts up a fight—Ethan, using his powers, ends the fight pretty quickly. He walks out with half of the money leaving behind a lot of resentment.

19-20--On Ellen as she opens the door to their apartment to Ethan and the kids yelling "Surprise! Ethan got Chinese and a cake to celebrate his new "promotion." He tells her that ALL of their money worries are over—he wants her to quit that lousy job at the diner and tomorrow they'll go looking for a home out in the burbs. She's ecstatic…but the kid (the one who recognized him on TV) isn't. He's just about to confront his father when the phone rings.

21-22--Ethan answers and gets an "Oh, shit!" look on his face. The person (unseen) on the other end of the phone knows who pulled that job today. More, he knows where Ethan's family lives, where the kids go to school, where the wife works. If Ethan wants them to be safe, he's going to have to work for this guy (you may decide to show him in shadow with the two boys there in the room, telling us that THEY sold Ethan out as payback for the shit he just pulled). We end with Ethan sitting on the bed, hanging up the phone after agreeing to meet…and reaching for the flask.

To be continued…

Issue #2—plot —Jim

1--We open on the family pulling up to a nice single story suburban house in a brand new SUV. (Not a Hummer, just a nice middle of the road SUV). They can't believe it! Their own home! Everyone's all smiles, the kids are excited, Ellen is positively glowing and Ethan looks proud.

2—Continue as they go inside—Ellen starts to cry tears of happiness, the place should be nice—hardwood floors, big living room, bedrooms upstairs. She hugs Ethan (who's beaming) he should say something along the lines that he promised he'd do good by her. She should be responding that she never lost faith in him. The kids go tearing up the stairs to claim dibs on a room.

3—While the kids are upstairs Ellen lets Ethan know that he's going to get VERY lucky tonight. He's glad she's happy, the movers will be here tomorrow but in the meantime, he has to get to work. She reminds him there's only one car how will her and the kids get back to the apartment if he takes it   he tells her not to worry, now that he's quit drinking he can fly under his own steam again.
Little scientific aside you probably shouldn't use, but ought to know; since his powers are magnetic it would make sense that he could use the Earth's magnetic poles (Lee Lines) to levitate (fly).

4—Splash, Ethan taking off—he should be close to camera waving down at Ellen who's on the porch. She should be smiling, prouder than she's been in year—all those bad years gone, their lives finally coming together! She can't believe this is happening!

5-6—(Use that as a dialogue segue) Switch scenes to the super-hero team, they can't believe this is happening (except for maybe the Cyber chick whose brought it to their attention). We show, on a big monitor screen (all super-hero team HQs have big monitors, it's the law) the bank scene from issue #1 (can't remember the page—Marco, just c/p it onto the screen here). We then show other robberies we haven't seen yet—an armored car lifted into the air by unseen force, dropped and split open, whatever else you can think of. While we shouldn't see him in any of these scenes there should be little doubt that it's Ethan—the ALL have the signature of his magnetic powers. His friend on the team (Shadow Stalker?) should be really bummed over it (you can set that up by showing his reaction throughout theses pages, interceding it with the robbery scenes). Last panel we focus on him, saying solemnly "Let's talk to him, first."

7-8—Cut to Ethan—he's walking into a real swanky, high class restaurant (NOT an Italian restaurant, please—too clichéd). Everybody knows him, people turn toward him, smiling. He walks confidentially toward a back room, the thugs (both well dressed) step aside to let him pass. We follow him through the great dark wood doors and into a large well-appointed office. This should be impressive, wood molding/paneling—rich textures wall paper, Louis XIV furniture, roaring fireplace. He walks up to a huge redwood desk. We shouldn't be able to see who's sitting behind the desk   in the last panel turn the camera so we're looking at Ethan from the boss's POV—he offers Ethan a cigar. Ethan

---

Issue #2--plot (Cont.)

says no thanks, but he WILL take a drink.

9—Someone should be handing Ethan a drink (Brandy, I'm thinking, so it would be in the appropriate glass—not a shot glass)—we turn the camera around so it's behind Ethan (Marco choose the angle) and at last we see the BIG BOSS, the guy who was behind the phone call last issue. We need to hip the reader to that fact—they need to know that this was the mysterious voice—this should come through in the dialogue. Perhaps he says something to Ethan about he's glad to be working with him, Ethan can say something along the lines that it was an offer he couldn't refuse (but not as clichéd, please). Thing is, leave no doubt in the reader's mind that this was the guy (or gal) who made that call. End on THE BOSS telling Ethan that he's done well and that they're impressed "it's not often a hero turns."

10—On Ethan, he's sitting in a chair, pouring drink after drink—In captions we get inside his head—the BIG BOSS is talking, but he's tuned him out. This bastard threatened his family—he doesn't give a shit about him and as soon as he has the chance he's going to make him pay for that—shove that big old desk where the sun doesn't shine. We need to feel his anger and his resentment toward this guy and this situation.

11—Continue on this scene—there may be a few smaller panels coming out of Ethan's thoughts and melding to the BOSS' speech (whatever it is) But there should be a big panel with the BOSS coming out from behind the desk, shaking Ethan's hand and placing his hand on his shoulder in a fatherly gesture. The Big Boss is telling him that he's part of their family now and, as such, they'll always protect him...and his family. Ethan takes another drink (he should have pretty well emptied the carafe by now).

12-13—Cut to Ellen, she's in the new house orchestrating the movers—she's trying to keep the kids from getting underfoot (it should be early evening, so they may be complaining about dinner—helps to set the time frame) trying to tell the movers where to put things—dealing with all of the usual frustrations of moving. She should be a bit frazzled (but not bitchy—remember we want the readers to like her) when Shadow-Stalker (or whomever Ethan's friend is from the super-team) shows up. He's in civvies—but she knows who he is—she's surprised by his coming—he apologizes for his timing, but he says (very seriously) that they have to talk.

14—Continue on Ellen and this guy—they walk outside to the back yard...a clever way to do this may be to show them from inside the house, looking out a window. He has his head bowed, it's painful for him to tell her this—we can see it in his body language, she puts her hand over her mouth in shock. End the scene on him from her POV—he tells her that he's sorry, but (the team) may have to take him down.

15-17   Cut to Ethan (night), he's in his "work clothes" (This shouldn't be his Capt. G costume but some type of black ensemble)—there's some kind of robbery (your choice but don't repeat yourself and make it a bigger job than before—a train, a plane, a ship on the docks, a big job). He may be using his powers to do some heavy lifting (in lieu of a crane?), but he has a whole crew of thugs to do the dirty work while he kicks back, getting completely sloshed. Write him arrogantly—he's the big man, he's untouchable, all these guys work for HIM. He's getting pretty full of himself.

18—Back to Ellen in the new house (night)—she's shutting the door to the kids' bedroom, telling them goodnight and that daddy will be home soon. We follow her as she walks downstairs—living room, entryway, hallway, whatever is crammed with boxes. Boxes everywhere! She collapses to the floor (or maybe the final stair?) and starts crying. This needs to be extremely powerful—based on what Shadow Stalker told her this evening she knows that all of this is a sham. Ethan has lied to her!

19-21—Back to the scene of the crime Ethan, in his drunken state, is becoming obnoxious, bragging about how he can't be stopped (or some such nonsense)—when, suddenly, the super-team shows up! Howard, make sure that you introduce all of the members here—this can be as simple as a caption with their name in it next to them, but we should get some idea who they are...then we can see what they do when they stop this robbery and take out the aforementioned thugs.
At any rate, cut back and forth between the heroes taking out the thugs and Ethan who is hiding from his erstwhile teammates. He realizes he's too drunk to fight them, he's panicking. The last thing in the world he wants to do is fight these guys, he's gotta get out of here, got to run—get back to Ellen and the kids.
Now, it's going to be a very fine line here because he's not a coward per se, he's just drunk and he's not stupid—you have to get that across deftly.

22—(Splash) Ethan's way is blocked by one of the team members (I don't care who you use, maybe the chick that seems to hate him). Whoever it is make sure it's someone who's more powerful than he is and someone whom he should definitely be afraid of. Whoever it is, they should be exuding power and Ethan should be freaked.

To Be Concluded...

Issue #3—plot--Jim

1-3--Picking up exactly where we left off last issue Ethan is confronted by his pals on the super-team. There's no way out for him—he's too drunk to fight or to even attempt an escape. And even though his pal, Shadow-Stalker is saddened and heartbroken that it's come to this, he knows he HAS to do his duty and take Ethan down. Ethan tries to talk S-S out of it, but the hero can't do it. Ethan bows his head in shame and despair...

4-8--(Flashback)...And remembers (use the bowed head as your segue here). Ethan narrates the flashback, recalling when he invited S-S into the fold. Everything was perfect then, his best buddy was being accepted into the most prestigious team since the Knights of the Round Table, the future looked bright, the possibilities endless.
We see flashes of Ethan happy, in his prime—fighting alongside his teammates, sitting in meetings with them laughing and smiling (NO ALCOHOL!!!) and, in his secret identity, romancing the beautiful young Ellen, the girl of his dreams.
We see them at their wedding—the double reception—one in civvies and one in their HQ, surrounded by the Earth's greatest heroes...and we see Ethan hoisting a champagne bottle as a worried S-S looks on. We see how happy Ethan was at the birth of their first child and how he passed out cigars—drunk in a bar.
We see him huddled over a bottle of whisky in a seedy smoke filled bar—he knew he never belonged. He was never quite good enough, never quite as altruistic as the rest of them. But Ellen was there...and the kids. They were all he wanted, all he ever needed.... (show Ellen's young face)...

9--...Segue to Ellen NOW. She's in the new house, devastated. She's sitting on the couch, watching the tapes of Ethan's crimes, crying—heartbroken. Their eldest child comes up behind her—he knows that the man on the TV is his father. We should see in their faces the hurt and betrayal they feel.

10-14--Back to Ethan and S-S now facing one another, the rest of the team leaves S-S to take care of his pal. Ethan is angry—that flailing arms anger one gets when drunk. He WON'T let then ruin his life again like they did before. He attacks—this whole scene should show them using their powers—There should be lots of pyrotechnics here. S-S tells him that HE ruined his OWN life. Shadow-Stalker asks him WHY—why did he betray everything he believed in? Ethan screams back, hurt, crying, unable to accept responsibility—because THEY betrayed HIM—he was Caesar in the Senate—he had nothing left—what was he SUPPOSED to do? HOW could he make it? The reader needs to feel the ANGUISH that this is causing both of them. S-S for his betrayal—but, Ethan also feels betrayed (don't forget THAT! It's important)

Issue #3--plot (Cont.)

15-16--While this is going on the rest of the group should be closing in on the BIG BOSS and his (her?) hired goons. We should see their powers in action and get a sense of who they are. Some should be sympathetic to Ethan, some not depending on their personalities. They make short work of the thugs and the BIG BOSS seems nonchalant—(s)he knows that this will get thrown out of court and (s)he'll walk.

17-18--End of the battle—Ethan has WON. S-S tells Ethan that he's going to have to kill him. Ethan hesitates, but he CAN'T do it. S-S warns him that this isn't over. Ethan knows. He's sorry...he's so sorry for everything. And, with that, he knocks out his former friend (do this dramatically—this shouldn't just be a punch in the nose—this should be a freight car falling on him or whatever—this has to have a lot of impact).

19--Cut to newscasters reporting on the incident and how the super-team stopped it—once again, the heroes cleaning up our city and making the world safe again. Toss in whatever interviews or character bits that seem appropriate—but MAKE SURE that the heroes keep Ethan OUT of the spotlight—they're STILL protecting him and this could be a sore point for some of the members. (we can pick this up if we do a sequel).

20--Ethan walks up to the new house—it's dark and there are no lights on inside. He KNOWS what he's going to find, but he has just enough courage left to see for himself anyway. He goes in—it's empty. He checks the kids' rooms, empty. He walks into his and Ellen's bedroom. He picks up a note off the foot of the bed. WE should not see what's on the note—we only see his face as he breaks out crying—this isn't just a tear down the cheek, but a heavy sob session.

21--Six panels—three across, two down camera stays still the entire time and, if you can pull it off, this page should be totally silent, no words should be necessary—Ethan falls to his knees at the foot of the bed, he crumples up the note, throws it across the room with a scream, buries his head. Last panel: He reaches into his coat (or whatever) and pulls something out.

22--Splash page: Ethan is on the floor, slumped against the bed, utterly wrecked and broken. A flask is hanging out of his hand, carelessly.

Caption: **The End?**

AFTER THE CAPE #1 was released on March 17, 2007. It sold out within it s first three days of release, as did issue's 2 and 3. Marco Rudy was unable to complete the last nine pages of the story so Manny Trembley stepped in at the 11th hour to finish the series.

A sequel is planned for late 2007 or early 2008.

MARCO RUDY
SKETCHBOOK

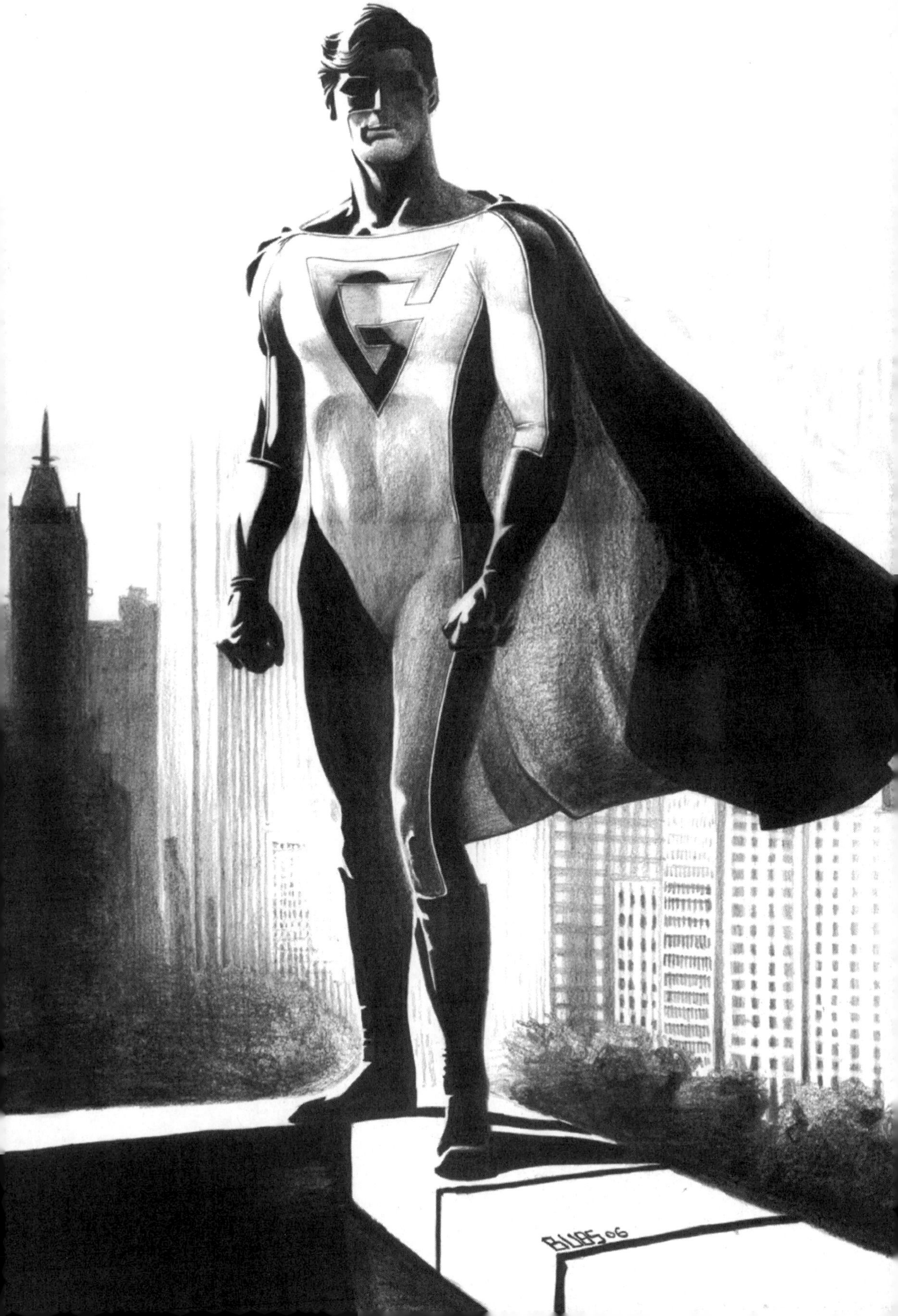

ETHAN

Gender: Male
Age: 33
Ethnicity: American
Hair: Brown
Eyes: Blue
Skin: Pale
Height: 5’7�?
Weight: 140lbs

Mannerisms: Tends to drink fairly heavily when stressed, depressed or when he can’t think of how to solve an issue. He keeps things bottle up so he tends to physically express how he feels. Like when he’s having an argument, he wouldn’t show how he really felt on his face, but would crush a newspaper in hand and bite down hard.

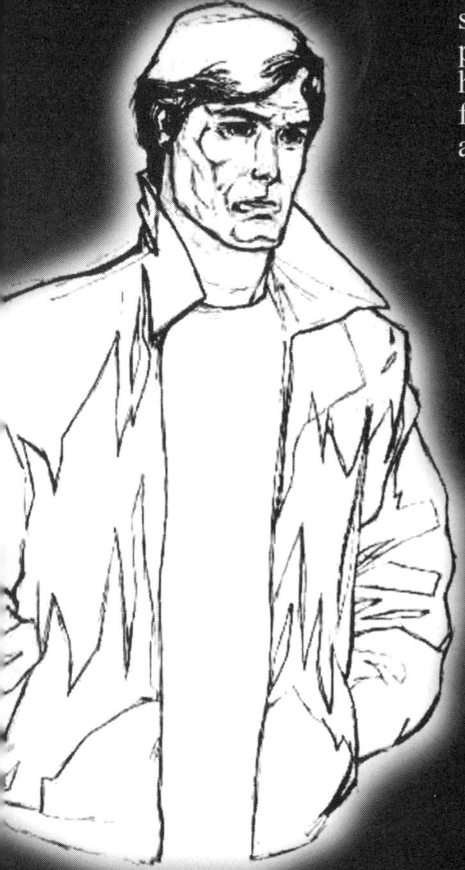

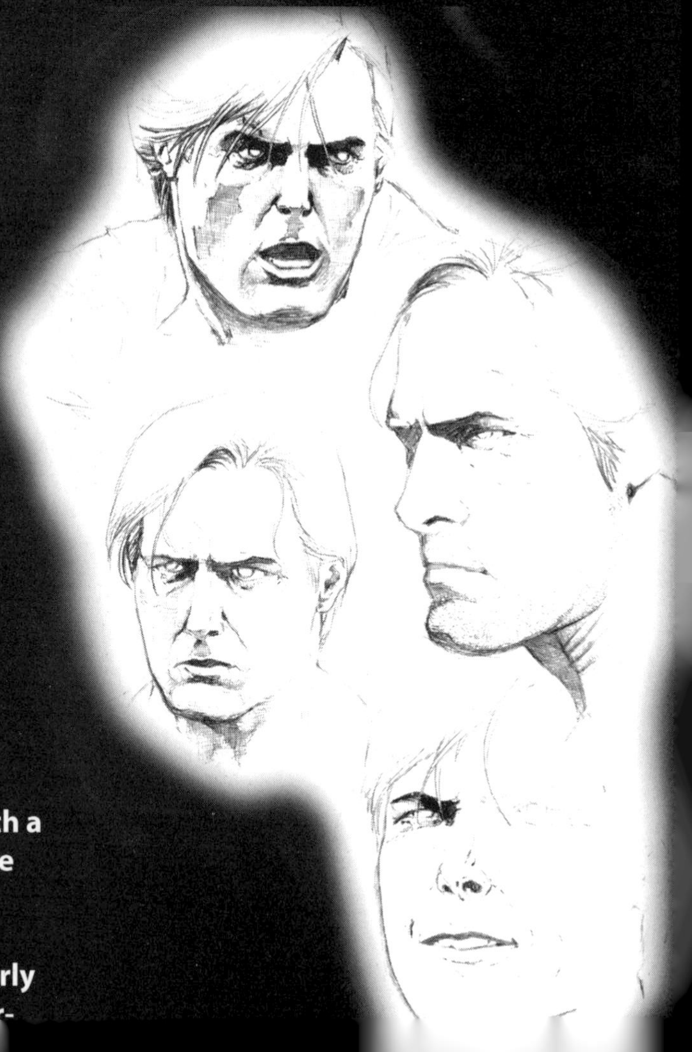

Early studies of Ethan by Marco with a small part of Howard’s exhaustive description of his character.

Opposite page, more of Marco’s early costume designs for Ethan’s super-

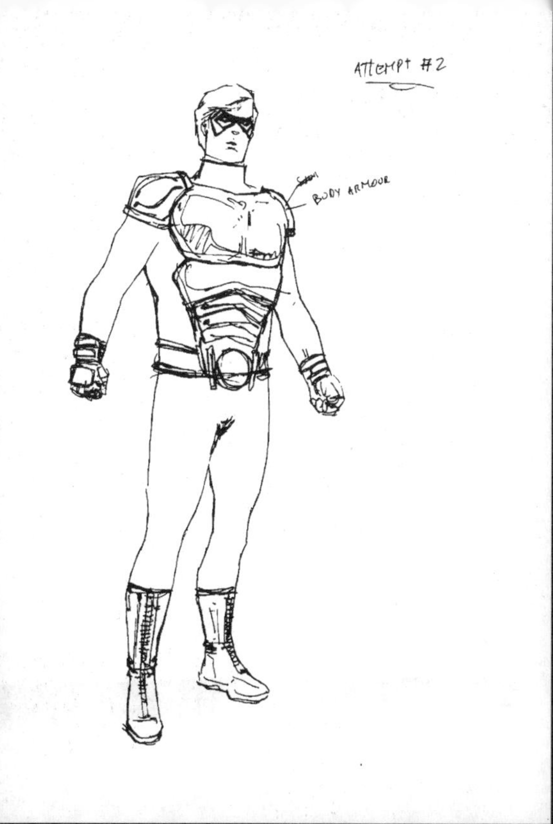
ATTEMPT #2
BODY ARMOUR

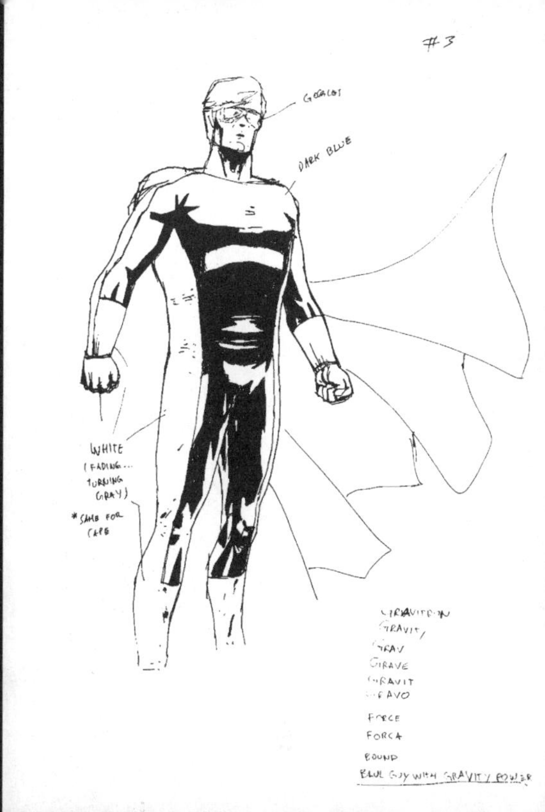
#3
GOGGLES
DARK BLUE
WHITE
(FADING...
TURNING
GRAY)
* SAME FOR
CAPE
GRAVITY
GRAV
GRAVE
GRAVIT
FORCE
FORCA
BOUND
BLUE GUY WITH GRAVITY POWER

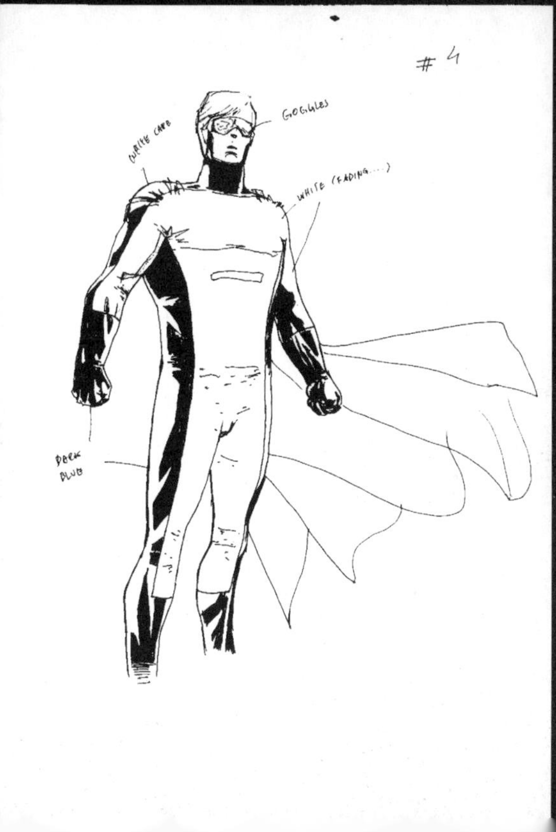
#4
GOGGLES
WHITE CAPE
WHITE (FADING...)
DARK
BLUE

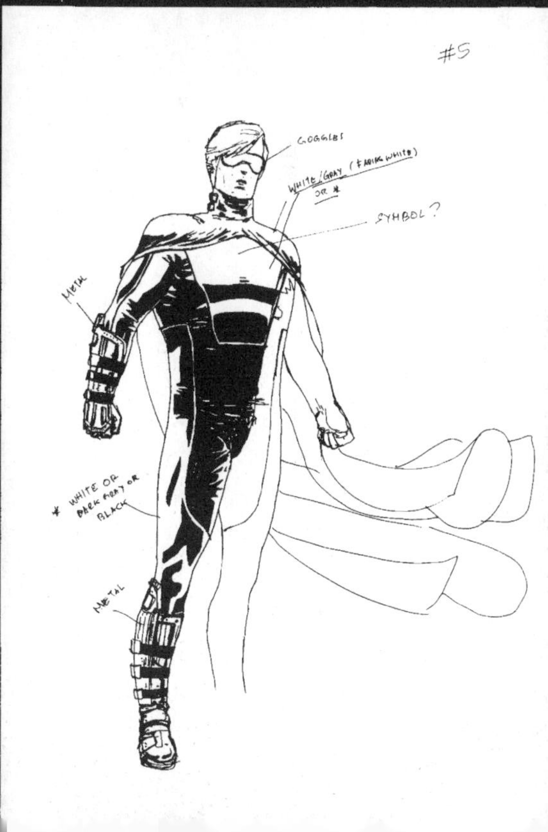
#5
GOGGLES
WHITE/GRAY (FADING WHITE)
OR *
SYMBOL?
METAL
* WHITE OR
DARK GRAY OR
BLACK
METAL

ELLEN

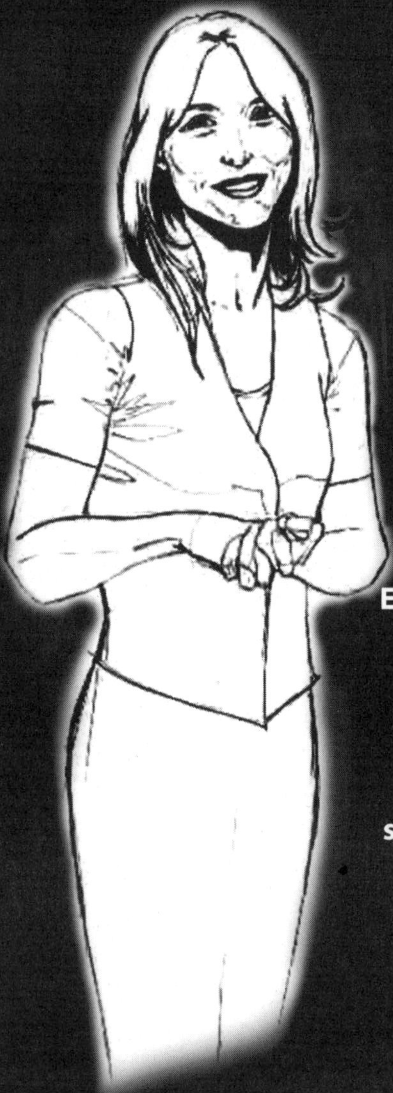

Ellen Falls
Gender: Female
Age: 30
Ethnicity: American
Hair: Dirty blonde
Eyes: Blue
Skin: Pale
Height: 5'6"
Weight: 130 lbs

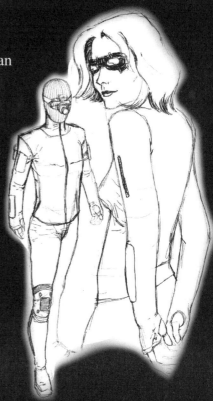

Early studies including some designs for Ellen based on Howard's original notion of having her as a retired super-villain (right). An idea quickly discarded.

Appearance: Even though she is overworked and stressed, she is still beautiful. She has a classic look to her. When she smiles she will light a room, but at the same time when she's angry, you can tell a mile away just by looking at her eyes. Her body type is average for a woman who had two kids. Her hair is shoulder length and straight. She wears two types of work clothes, one to her office job, which is normal office attire in the day and one at night as a waitress, where it's a uniform.

Mannerisms: When mad, she will go silent and stare. Give you the "look" and then she would talk to you. Not yelling, just talking, but what she does it's straight to the point and it hurts people who aren't ready for that kind of truth. She sighs and closes her eyes to compose herself when facing challenges